Advance Praise for *More Than a Motorcycle*

"*More Than a Motorcycle* captures the essence of the paradox at the heart of leading change: you must motivate people to demand what, in their minds, they really don't want. A powerful insight very well delivered."
  —Watts Wacker, Chairman, First Matter Inc., and
  Coauthor of *The Visionary's Handbook*

"This unique book is surely one of the best I have read on leadership and management. It is inspirational and authentic. Only those with a high view of competence and commitment and a genuine respect for people could have written this book. I thoroughly enjoyed it."
  —Max De Pree, Author of *Leadership Jazz* and
  Leading without Power

"Finally, a book that tells the truth about organizational change! This rich saga relays the fears, the mistakes, the partnerships, and the successes that show how change really happens. What glistens through is the true journey and its demands on us: humility, learning, community, love, and inclusion of others. I thank Teerlink and Ozley for writing this book and applaud their courage in doing so. They respected us enough to give us the straight story."
  —Margaret J. Wheatley, Author of *Leadership and the
  New Science*, and Coauthor of *A Simpler Way*

"This honest, detailed, and compelling description of the transformation at Harley-Davidson is a must-read for anyone struggling to accomplish organizational change. Teerlink and Ozley provide valuable lessons on how to work cooperatively with employee representatives, and remind us all of the wisdom of the saying, 'technology makes it possible; people make it happen.' "
  —Jeffrey Pfeffer, Thomas D. Dee Professor of Organizational
  Behavior, Stanford Graduate School of Business, and
  Author of *The Human Equation*

"Teerlink and Ozley take readers through Harley's long and bumpy journey from near extinction to world-class competitiveness. This aged icon of a free-spirit lifestyle achieved its remarkable turnaround through a radical change process that literally freed all of its employees to contribute meaningfully to the company's success. The book's clear, concise, and powerful ideas about effecting organizational change and continuous improvement make it a must-read with broad business applicability. An exhilarating ride."

—Thomas J. Usher, Chairman of the Board and
Chief Executive Officer, USX Corporation

"Full of practical insights for management, union leadership, workers, and theorists, *More Than a Motorcycle* documents how Harley-Davidson recovered from a top-down, confrontational, almost bankrupt company to a more cooperative, people-driven industry leader. Teerlink and Ozley objectively present all the spurts, near disasters, wrinkles, and warts of a real turnaround, all the time linking the company's practical actions to many of the most advanced management theories of the time. This book is a rare gem that will stand the test of time, future practice, and theory."

—James Brian Quinn, Professor of Management, Emeritus,
Amos Tuck School of Business, Dartmouth College, and
Author of *Intelligent Enterprise* and *Innovation Explosion*

"A wonderfully educational and well-told story about the transformation of an American icon. *More Than a Motorcycle* is a must-read for anyone interested in effective organizational change."

—Edward E. Lawler III, Director, Center for Effective Organizations,
University of Southern California

"Anyone involved in leading organizational change should read *More Than a Motorcycle*. Teerlink and Ozley tell the story of resistance to change and explain why the building of trust is so necessary for success. If I had had the opportunity to read this book before my experiences with Saturn, I would have fewer gray hairs today."

—Skip LeFauve, Retired President and CEO, Saturn

"*More Than a Motorcycle* provides an honest look at the complex and courageous transformation of a major American company and its people. Although the setting is Harley-Davidson, any organization hoping to renew itself and succeed in the twenty-first century can learn much from Teerlink and Ozley: that we must learn to act out of mutual respect and collaboration rather than confrontation and self-interest. This book should be required reading for all leaders committed to change in labor and management alike. My thanks to the authors for sharing their experiences with us."

—Boyd Young, International President, PACE International Union

MORE
THAN A
MOTORCYCLE

[signatures: Lee Ozley, Rich Teerlink]

MORE THAN A MOTORCYCLE

The Leadership Journey at Harley-Davidson

Rich Teerlink and Lee Ozley

HARVARD BUSINESS SCHOOL PRESS
Boston, Massachusetts

04   03   02   01   00   5   4   3   2   1

Library of Congress Cataloging-in-Publication Data

Teerlink, Rich, 1936–

    More than a motorcycle : the leadership journey at Harley-Davidson / Rich Teerlink,
Lee Ozley.

      p. cm.

    A post-1981 history occasioned by the 95th anniversary of the company in June 1998.
Includes index.

    ISBN 0-87584-950-4 (alk. paper)

    1. Harley-Davidson Incorporated—Management. 2. Motorcycle industry—United States.
I. Ozley, Lee, 1939– II. Title

HD9710.5.U54 H3778 2000
338.7'6292275'0973--dc21

                       00-025209

*This book is dedicated to all the men
and women with whom it has been our privilege
to work throughout our careers.
It is they who have been the teachers, and we
who have been the students.*

"It wasn't, of course, the beginning,
for who can say when a voyage starts—not the actual passage
but the dream of the journey and its urge to find a way."

—WILLIAM LEAST HEAT-MOON
River-Horse

Contents

Chronology of Events / x

Acknowledgments / xv

Authors' Note / xvii

Introduction / 1

1   The Prelude / 5

2   Getting Under Way / 19

3   Agreeing on a Road Map for Change / 43

4   Awareness Expansion: Testing the Commitment / 69

5   The Business Process / 83

6   Evaluation and Development / 107

7   Upending the Pyramid / 121

8   The Whole Package / 145

9   Lifelong Learning / 167

10   Determined to Communicate / 191

11   Partnering: A Case in Point / 209

12   Signposts of the Journey / 233

13   Reflections on a Journey / 255

Index / 271

About the Authors / 277

	1987	1988	1989
Business Process	Initial SBP to Board of Directors ←→		"Umbrella" to Board ←→
		Executive Committee work on values, issues ←→	
Communications	Communications task force group via Joint Vision Process →		Needs survey focus groups
		Revitalized Town Hall meetings (at least quarterly in all locations)	
Compensation and Benefits	Compensation task force group via Joint Vision Process →		Report focus on behaviors ←→
			STIP change recommendations ←
Labor-Management Relations	Internal management discussion, investigation ←→	One-year contract ←→	Problem-solving negotiations ←→
		Joint Vision Process implementation	
Lifelong Learning		Learning centers ←→	AE I ←→
		Joint Vision training	
Organizational Structure			Research and discussion ←→

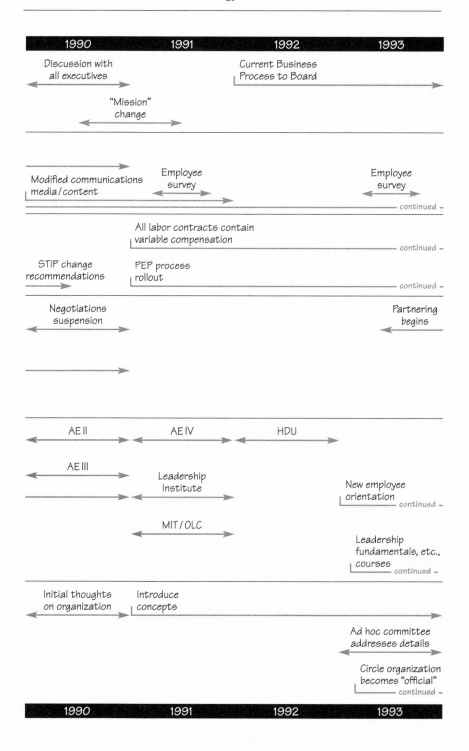

1990	1991	1992	1993

Discussion with
all executives

Current Business
Process to Board

"Mission"
change

Modified communications
media / content

Employee
survey

Employee
survey
— continued —

All labor contracts contain
variable compensation
— continued —

STIP change
recommendations

PEP process
rollout
— continued —

Negotiations
suspension

Partnering
begins

AE II

AE IV

HDU

AE III

Leadership
Institute

New employee
orientation
— continued —

MIT / OLC

Leadership
fundamentals, etc.,
courses
— continued —

Initial thoughts
on organization

Introduce
concepts

Ad hoc committee
addresses details

Circle organization
becomes "official"
— continued —

1990	1991	1992	1993

	1994	1995	1996
Business Process	Learning modules		
	Manufacturing strategy and Plan 2003 to Board		
Communications			Communications Department established
	Modified communications media/content		
Compensation and Benefits	variable compensation	Employment security for all employees	
	PEP process rollout		
Labor-Management Relations	Partnering begins	Joint new plant design/location search	
	JPIC		
	Existing plants want to bid on expansion; long-term agreements (Wisconsin in 1996, York and Kansas City in 1997)		
Lifelong Learning	Learning modules on Business Process		
	New employee orientation	Training "Best Practice" circle	
	Leadership fundamentals, etc., courses	Partnering training	
Organizational Structure		Information Systems, Manufacturing, and Engineering create "subcircles"	
		All labor agreements include commitment to shared leadership using natural work groups	
	Circle organization becomes "official"		
	1994	1995	1996

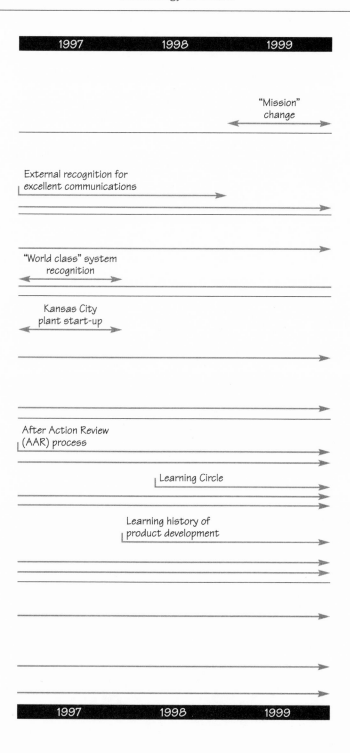

Acknowledgments

SO MANY PEOPLE HAVE INFLUENCED OUR LIVES, ENRICHED OUR experiences, and taught us helpful things. We would like to acknowledge some of them in particular:

- The students and faculty of the Graduate School of Business at Auburn University, especially Dr. Achilles Armenakis and doctoral students Lori Muse and Phil Chansler, who have consistently encouraged us in this effort, provided very helpful insights and criticisms, and stretched our thinking.
- Lee's colleagues at Responsive Organizations, Inc. (ROI), who not only have contributed dramatically as resources to the work at Harley-Davidson, but have continually provided personal support, counsel, and friendship to each and both of us.
- The employees of Harley-Davidson and the officials and members of the Paper, Allied-Industrial, Chemical, and Energy Workers International Union (PACE) and the International Association of Machinists and Aerospace Workers Union (IAMAW), whose courage and wisdom not only "made it happen," but also provided us with encouragement and support on our journey. We want specifically to acknowledge the extraordinary counsel, help, and research assistance that Flip Weber provided in the course of our writing.
- Kirsten Sandberg, senior editor at the Harvard Business School Press, whose professional wisdom, gentle guiding hand, and consistent encouragement gave us the will to start and finish this book.

- Jeff Cruikshank, whose extraordinary patience, competence, and skill helped us find our "voice," enabling us to say what we wanted to say more effectively.
- Ann Teerlink and Terri Ozley, who not only suffered through the peaks and valleys of our journey, but also provided unerring love, support, insight, and counsel as we struggled to write this book.

Authors' Note

As suggested above, many people have contributed to the processes and inventions described in this book. We are only two of those people.

In most cases, moreover, a number of people were involved in each process and should be credited with each invention. This creates a potential confusion: Who are "we"?

We (the authors) were tempted to sidestep this issue by a relentless use of the passive voice, but the Harvard Business School Press discouraged that strategy. We have therefore adopted our own convention. In this book, the first person plural ("we") is mostly reserved for that ever-changing collection of leaders in and around Harley, in both management and the unions, who helped make happen the things that are described in the following pages.

When the authors are mainly or solely responsible for the ideas or actions described, they will be referred to as "Rich and Lee," or "Lee and Rich," or "the authors." In some cases, it will be obvious that "we" or "us" refers to the team of Rich and Lee.

We have also tried wherever possible to let key individuals tell their own stories. (All quotes from Harley personnel, past and present, are from interviews conducted in the spring of 1999.) In that same spirit, when one of us has a point to make as an individual, that point is attributed either to Lee or to Rich. We hope this departure from joint-authoring conventions is helpful to you, rather than distracting.

MORE
THAN A
MOTORCYCLE

Introduction

ON AN OTHERWISE UNEVENTFUL DAY IN JUNE 1998, 150,000 visitors descended on the friendly midwestern city of Milwaukee, Wisconsin. They came prepared to enjoy themselves.

These were no ordinary partygoers. These were owners and enthusiasts of Harley-Davidson motorcycles, and they were returning to the birthplace of their favorite bikes to celebrate the company's ninety-fifth anniversary.

For many of these visitors, the journey began as one of five "reunion rides," each departing from a different location in North America. Each route was more than 1,000 miles. As these caravans wended their way to Milwaukee from five corners of the continent, they picked up more and more riders. Each additional Harley added its own throaty rumble to the chorus—a sound described by Harley lovers as something like *potato-potato-potato*, growled out in a gravelly *basso profundo* machine voice.

When the five rivers of riders converged, it was clear that something out of the ordinary was happening. "By the time the rides reached Milwaukee," as Harley's 1998 annual report later put it, "there was a feeling of something much bigger than all the people and all the planning put together. As an early morning sea of Harley-Davidson motorcycles paraded through downtown Milwaukee, the thrill of our anniversary was heard in the cheers of thousands of people lining sidewalks and streets, waving from office windows and parking garages, all jockeying for a view of the riders and their thundering two-wheeled machines."

Most of those 150,000 motorcycle fans and other visitors were no doubt celebrating the exhilaration and sense of freedom that comes with riding. A smaller group—including those who owned stock in the company, for example—surely was celebrating the company's stellar performance in recent years. In 1997, for example, Harley had racked up its twelfth consecutive year of record revenues and earnings. It had produced and sold more motorcycles than in any previous year in its history. One hundred dollars invested in Harley stock in 1986 was worth slightly more than $7,000 by the end of 1998.

But surely a minority of those visitors, as well as the company's local employees, were also celebrating the fact that there was still a company called "Harley-Davidson Motor Company," still making motorcycles and components in several U.S. cities. Fifteen years earlier, during the company's eightieth anniversary, this would not have been a sure bet. That was the year in which Harley's precipitous decline in market share reached such alarming, nosedive proportions—from nearly 80 percent of the 850cc+ category in 1973 to a meager 23 percent in 1983—that the Reagan administration extended tariff protection to the struggling domestic motorcycle industry. It was clear that Harley, beset by a high cost structure and poor quality, couldn't fight off its Japanese competitors on its own.

What changed at Harley between 1983 and 1998? The simple answer is: a great many things. Some—including a resurgence of interest in riding and a surge in discretionary spending that grew out of the sustained stock market boom—were completely external to the company. (Luck plays an important part in many corporate success stories.) Others, including several dramatic changes in the company's ownership structure, took place in very visible ways on the national stage. And still others went on mostly behind the scenes.

This book is about that last category of changes. This is a story of a corporate journey that began in 1981, although this book concentrates on the post-1987 period. This phase of the journey was initiated by one of the authors (Richard F. Teerlink, henceforth "Rich"), shaped and coached by Rich and the other author (Lee M. Ozley, henceforth "Lee"), and then joined by many hundreds of other individuals who worked in and around Harley-Davidson, Inc. ("Harley") in the late 1980s and the 1990s.

Rich and Lee joined forces in 1987 and worked together for the next dozen years. We provide a few basic biographical details here, to be supplemented later in the narrative when doing so becomes helpful to the telling of this story.

Rich joined Harley in 1981 and was a member of Harley's senior executive corps for most of the 1980s and 1990s. He participated in most of the key events in a notably turbulent period in Harley's history. He retired in March 1999, having served as the company's president and chief executive officer from 1988 through 1997, and as chairman of Harley's board of directors from 1996 through 1998.

Lee is an organizational consultant and theorist, with several decades of experience helping large companies initiate—and cope with—change. In 1979 he cofounded Responsive Organizations, Inc. (ROI), which specialized in designing integrated change processes for manufacturing organizations, most of which were unionized. Over the next decade and a half, ROI worked with some eighty organizations in North America and Europe, including Harley. After Lee went into semi-retirement and sole practice in 1992, he continued to work with Harley and a number of other clients.

We are writing about a series of changes that took place at Harley in the twelve-year span mentioned above. We do so because we believe they may be of interest to people who want to see America's great corporations—large and small, well known and unknown—perform more effectively, efficiently, and humanely.

Our basic premise, based on our shared and separate experiences, is that, in order for companies to be more effective, efficient, and humane, their leaders must have access to the wisdom and experience of their own people. To achieve that, they will have to engage in some radical processes of change.

We believe that traditional "command-and-control" hierarchies are of limited effectiveness and durability. These hierarchies were borrowed from the military by the American railroad empires of the late nineteenth century, and they have since been re-created by most of corporate America. Because they are "top down" and more or less unilateral in their decision making, command-and-control organizations can move quickly in a crisis. When Harley was in crisis in the early 1980s, it benefited significantly from just this kind of decisive, top-down leadership style.

But what happens when the crisis goes away?

We believe that, at that point, leaders have to stop taking answers to their people and instead take *questions* to their people. Leaders have to give up on some of the most treasured prerogatives of management, many of which were derived from the age-old "command and control." Instead of demanding compliance, these managers have to earn, and call upon, *commitment*.

We want to state at the outset that there are very few "new" ideas in the following pages. New ideas are extremely rare, especially in the context of human organizations, where so many talented people—academics, consultants, and practitioners alike—have tried so hard to make things better. Instead, what the reader will find in this book is a study of how change was initiated and sustained at one proud American company.

This introduces an obvious but important point. Single-company studies, even those with the kind of context that we have tried to provide in this book, have their limits. Yes, we believe that there are important lessons in this case study and that some of those lessons have broad applicability to businesses in the United States and elsewhere. On the other hand, neither of us accepts the "cookbook" approach taken by many business books on the market today: take a pinch of this, a dash of that, and a dollop of something else; stir things up vigorously, and transform your company. In our experience, it doesn't work that way.

In our experience, meaningful and positive change comes slowly. Rich talks about the activity of "pushing up a rope," by which he means to suggest the futility of applying energy in unproductive ways. Too much of management thinking today involves pushing up ropes—forcing change, measuring the wrong things, giving up on initiatives too quickly, and short-circuiting the processes whereby an organization could achieve *real* learning, growth, and development, if only it could get out of its own way. This is a book about planting seeds and encouraging other people to nurture the seedlings.

As should become clear in subsequent pages, we like nothing better than batting around ideas, thereby making those ideas clearer and more powerful. We hope that you'll enjoy learning what we've learned and join us in a dialogue that has been going on for more than a decade.

1

The Prelude

In 1965, sixty-two years after its founding in Milwaukee by William Harley and the three Davidson brothers—Walter, William, and Arthur—the last surviving solely domestic motorcycle manufacturer in the United States found itself in deep trouble. Under increasing pressure from foreign competitors, including several recent Japanese entries into the industry, the company needed cash for modernization and diversification. As a result, the company went public, and over the next three years, more than 1.3 million Harley shares were sold.

But public ownership had its perils. By late 1968, it was becoming clear that at least one company—Bangor Punta, a well-known "bottom feeder" with roots in the railroad industry—had hostile designs on Harley. Bangor Punta had a history of wringing cash out of its acquisitions and then scrapping the remains. This possible fate had little appeal to the founding families, who were still closely involved in the affairs of the company.

Acquired!

A possible solution to Harley's woes would be acquisition by a larger company, preferably one with deep pockets, manufacturing skills, and a compatible corporate philosophy. One potential white knight was American Machine and Foundry (AMF), headquartered in White Plains, New York. Until recently, AMF had been a fairly staid conglomerate, with most of its assets engaged in the manufacture of industrial products, such as tobacco processing and baking equipment. But, in an effort to diversify its portfolio, AMF in the 1960s had begun venturing into the "leisure products" industry. Its first move in this direction—an investment in automatic pin-setting equipment— had quickly become its primary generator of cash. AMF then went on to buy other leisure products producers, including companies that made golf clubs, tennis rackets, skis, and yachts.

In 1969 AMF acquired Harley. AMF got its desired toehold in a new sector of the leisure industry, and Harley began receiving a massive, multiyear infusion of capital that was desperately needed for improvements in its manufacturing processes. Even if this wasn't a match made in heaven, it was at least a successful marriage of convenience, and all parties declared themselves satisfied with the outcome.

At the time of the acquisition, all of Harley's operations were in Milwaukee, Wisconsin. Harley's plants were woefully outdated, and its quality standards suspect. The company's three most valuable assets— aside from the new AMF relationship—were a skilled dealer network, a powerful brand (which, fortunately, inspired astounding consumer loyalty), and a dedicated employee base. The company's hourly employees were all represented by local chapters of international unions: the Allied Industrial Workers (which later merged with the United Paperworkers International and will be referred to as PACE throughout this book) represented operating and maintenance employees, and the International Association of Machinists (IAM) represented the smaller skilled trades workforce.

When AMF bought Harley, it named a group executive located in White Plains, New York—site of AMF's headquarters—to oversee the motorcycle division. This change was a rude awakening for many longtime residents of Milwaukee. After sixty-five years in the heart of one of Wisconsin's oldest and proudest manufacturing centers, Harley-Davidson's headquarters were unceremoniously relocated to a white-collar suburb of New York.

More changes came quickly. Harley requested the necessary capital to expand production in Milwaukee; AMF responded by pointing out that the parent company had a huge, well-equipped plant sitting mostly idle in York, Pennsylvania. As a result, final assembly of the large bikes moved to York. True, AMF was sinking large amounts of capital spending into Harley, in both York and Milwaukee, and the motorcycle company's volume began to rise. But it would have been hard to claim that Milwaukee still "made motorcycles." In reality, Harley's Milwaukee-based operations had been reduced to the role of a major components supplier to the York factory.

Throughout this succession of wrenching changes—many of which stuck in the craw of Harley loyalists but were more or less critical to the company's survival—AMF officials assured their Wisconsin employees that the relocation of final assembly and other operations to the York plant would not lead to layoffs in Milwaukee. This soon proved untrue. And beyond the specifics of these kinds of broken promises, the people of Harley felt fundamentally betrayed. Harleys (*Harleys!*) were now being assembled by people from Pennsylvania who knew more about pin-setting equipment and bomb casings—two of York's leading products—than they knew about motorcycles. If there were such things as "Harley people," as the Milwaukee-based Harley employees saw it, they surely didn't live in York, Pennsylvania.

Partly as a result of these changes, relationships between PACE and Harley's management deteriorated steadily. The number of grievances escalated. Even though Harley badly needed to make productivity improvements, all management-initiated efforts to get the company's work done more efficiently were met with hostility and resistance. In particular, efforts to get Milwaukee-based employees—including managers—to interact and coordinate with their counterparts in York generated little more than stony silence. (This was ironic, in light of the fact that the IAM also represented York's employees.) A low point came in June 1974, when the Wisconsin-based PACE called a strike over the company's refusal to agree to coordinated bargaining across all unions within the larger AMF empire. (Absent that arrangement, to which AMF was loath to agree, it was impossible to control the movement of work from one AMF plant to another.) The work stoppage lasted more than one hundred days—an unprecedented rift in a company that for decades had prided itself on conducting itself like a "family."

Meanwhile, AMF was losing faith. Not only was Harley proving difficult to manage—divided as it now was between two states—but the motorcycle subsidiary was failing to respond to massive infusions of AMF cash. The Japanese conquest of the high-end motorcycle market continued unabated. And, although Harley's sales amounted to 17 percent of AMF's total revenues, very little of that dropped to AMF's bottom line. A study by the Boston Consulting Group suggested that an additional $60 million to $80 million would be needed to make Harley's proposed new engine line a reality.

Back in White Plains, enough was enough. By 1980, AMF let it be known that it was open to offers for its troubled motorcycle division.

From Honeymoon to Hard Times

On June 16, 1981, Vaughn Beals—formerly AMF's group executive for the Harley division, and now chairman and CEO of a newly independent Harley-Davidson, Inc.—rode his "hog" up Capitol Drive and into the parking lot of the Milwaukee plant. The ride was a highly symbolic one. Through his act, Beals made the point that Harley was returning to its birthplace and that Harleys once again would be made by "Harley people."

Three days earlier, Beals and twelve associates had purchased Harley from AMF in a daring and unlikely management buyout. How had this come to pass? To AMF's dismay, an aggressive effort to market the Harley division had elicited *no interested buyers*. When an internal management group led by Beals stepped forward with a proposal for a leveraged buyout, AMF had little choice but to negotiate. Several months and some $80 million later, Harley regained its former status as a private and independent company. The AMF logo was removed from Harley's trademark teardrop gas tank. Life, it seemed, could go back to normal.

Or could it? Beals and his adventurous associates faced some grim realities. The heavyweight-motorcycle market was contracting steadily. Even worse, Harley's share of that declining market was still plummeting—from nearly 80 percent of the 850cc+ category in 1973 to 30.8 percent in 1980. For the first time in fifty years, Harley lost money. As a result of the leveraged buyout, the company now carried a staggering debt load. Citicorp, the lender that had made the buyout possible, was already indicating that it might force Harley's liquidation in order to recover at least some of its investment in the motorcycle maker.

Meanwhile, of course, the company's internal problems had not gone away. Foreign competitors introduced new designs, but because Harley's product design and development processes were slow and unpredictable, the company had to stick with its traditional products. ("Traditional" was good in terms of visual appeal, but less good in terms of outmoded technologies.) Break-even points were high, making the company extremely vulnerable to even modest market swings. In terms of quality, the standard that the company embraced was not an improved product, but one that was "just good enough." Excessive in-process inventories and associated carrying costs sucked up the company's precious cash.

Beals and his colleagues knew that they had to turn things around. To their credit, they looked inside the company first. Yes, they were convinced that the external threats to the company were real enough—efficient Japanese competitors, a declining market, and so on. But even more responsible for the company's woes were its employees: management and labor alike. This, Beals and his colleagues decided, was where change had to occur.

During the next five years, Harley fought for survival. By most early measures, the company's performance and prospects were poor (see table 1-1). Efforts to stabilize and improve the company were hampered by severely limited cash, access to which was now limited by a strictly asset-based lending agreement. Desperate measures were called for and taken. In 1982 Harley chopped its overall workforce by 40 percent (with

TABLE 1-1: HARLEY-DAVIDSON'S PERFORMANCE IN 1982

U.S. market share (651cc+)	15.2%
Units shipped	32,400
Revenue ($millions)	210
Operating profit (loss) ($millions)	(15.5)
Employees	2,289

deeper cuts coming in the salaried than in the hourly ranks). All remaining salaried employees took a 9 percent pay cut and agreed to have their salaries frozen at the reduced levels for at least two years. It was not a close call. When management opened its books to the unions in May, the unions could only agree that drastic measures—measures that would hurt many longtime Harley employees—were needed.

The honeymoon that began when Beals and his colleagues brought Harley back to Milwaukee proved short-lived. Forced by circumstance into survival mode, Beals and his lieutenants adopted a highly traditional command-and-control style of management. The company's managers focused on top-down "fixes" and short-term financial results. All actions of consequence originated at the top of the corporate pyramid.

Of course, not all constituent groups felt compelled to take orders all the time. One example arose in late 1981, when management—having decided that operations in the existing warehouse were excessively costly—outsourced parts management and distribution to an external supplier. Arbitration of the resulting labor dispute returned this work to the unionized employees. A second example came in 1983, when a group of Harley dealers who objected to the way management was running the company formed the Harley-Davidson Dealer Alliance. They took their case to Harley's lead lender in an effort to force the company's management to change its ways. Although the effort ultimately failed, challenges were clearly emerging to management's command-and-control tactics.

Rays of Hope

But the name of the game was survival, and by the mid-1980s, it appeared that Beals and his colleagues might pull off the miracle that Harley needed. First, after several notable product development failures, Harley introduced the Evolution engine for model year 1984. This engine—combined with the exciting new Softail product line—quickly began making money for the cash-strapped company. The Softail was an elegant variation on the classic Harley look, and it stormed the marketplace.

Good products always make marketing easier. But Harley made extra efforts to make sure its improved products found their markets. The company initiated special programs to help its dealers attract and retain customers. Perhaps the most significant of these was the Harley Owners Group (H.O.G.), created in 1983. Begun as a way of communicating more effectively with the company's end users, H.O.G. quickly grew into the world's largest motorcycle club. In part because of this and similar efforts, dealers regained their confidence that the company could act as a dependable partner.

On the operating side, Harley executives pushed hard for improvements. Longtime manufacturing head Tom Gelb organized a group to study the current practices of the world's most effective manufacturing enterprises. Gelb and his manufacturing colleagues became convinced that, if the company's operations could be improved, both product quality and profits would increase dramatically. The manufacturing team therefore introduced into the Harley workplace three techniques borrowed from the Japanese: employee involvement (EI), just-in-time materials delivery (which at Harley became known as Materials as Needed, or MAN), and statistical process controls (which became known as Statistical Operator Control, or SOC). This "three-legged stool" served as the basis of significant productivity improvements in the mid- to late 1980s and remains a cornerstone of the company's manufacturing strategy today.

Operating costs kept a spotlight focused on the company's financial structure, which was shaky both before and after the management LBO. Harley restructured a major portion of its equity and debt in 1983 in an effort to relieve financial pressure and buy time for rebuilding. At the end of 1985—after the abovementioned brush with extinction—the remaining debt was restructured, with two new financial institutions taking the place of Citibank. These two restructuring events, coupled with marginally profitable operations, allowed Harley to show a small but positive net worth by December 1985.

One big step toward financial stability remained: going public. Beals and his associates had mixed feelings about a public offering. On the one hand, they *liked* being in control of their fate and running their own private company. On the other hand, they knew that access to the public capital markets would contribute to the long-term health of the company. Gradually, with the encouragement of outside advisers, Harley's managers warmed up to the idea of a public offering.

This meant waiting until Harley had recovered enough to command a good price in the marketplace. By 1986, all the relevant financial measures had turned positive. Manufacturing costs were declining. (Reductions in in-process inventories and associated carrying costs generated savings of more than $40 million a year.) Quality improved dramatically, which meant that riders made fewer warranty claims. The dealer network was revitalized and growing. When Harley-Davidson made a public offering in July of 1986, the gamble proved a resounding success. (In fact, it raised $25 million more than the underwriters had expected!) For the time being at least, the company had saved itself.

Introducing One of the Authors

One of the architects of Harley's financial recovery was the company's CFO, Richard F. Teerlink, who is also one of the authors of this book. Because Rich played a central role both in Harley's "survival" phase and in the subsequent developments described later in this book, we'll pause now to describe Rich's background and perspectives.

RICH: I'm from the first generation of my family that was born in this country. My dad was a tool-and-die maker from Holland, who came to this country because he knew that he could never have his own tool-and-die shop back home.

Dad believed in people and that everybody should have an opportunity. He implemented a profit-sharing plan at his small agricultural chain company back in the forties, for example. So I grew up steeped in the philosophy that everybody is important. But Dad also intimately understood the business of manufacturing. No matter that he had only a sixth-grade education. He could walk through the plant, look around, and say, "We've got too much inventory. Too many racks are full. Something is wrong."

I was trained as an accountant, but I always had my eye on

the bigger picture, perhaps because my dad had run his own shop and had trained me in that perspective. Some of my best preparation for leadership came when I was working for a gentleman named Earl Fester, at a small subsidiary of Miehle-Goss-Dexter in Racine, Wisconsin. The subsidiary had made the decision to grow. I signed on as plant manager and got into a whole realm of activities that I had never done before—negotiating contracts with our union, dealing with grievances, and so on. I then went down to Springfield, Missouri, where we built our new plant.

That experience, and others that came later, focused me on the importance of education and communication. Leaders have to be educated if they're going to be asked to educate, communicate with, and lead others. This doesn't happen by accident. It happens because an organization makes it happen.

But I also learned that there are limits on what you can do, even with educated and articulate leaders. At the end of the day, everybody isn't going to see things your way. They won't always want to do what you perceive to be the right thing.

So, although I was relatively successful as a traditional command-and-control leader, I learned to give the people around me a lot of latitude. I learned to let things evolve. Even when I want things to get done quickly, I still believe they've got to evolve. Some things just take six months to get done, no matter how much you want to get them done in three months. In particular, you've got to take the time to develop management. And that gets back to learning. When I look back on the various experiences that I've had, they always seem to add up to "Learn how people understand. Don't force them to understand. Help them understand."

Looking Forward

In the dark days of the early and mid-1980s, Harley's employees, salaried and hourly alike, found themselves on a scary ride. Many lost their jobs or lost opportunities for career advancement. Many very good

people left voluntarily, deciding that they had brighter prospects elsewhere. Departments were hollowed out, in some cases eliminating
bureaucracies, but in other cases crippling vital organizational functions.

As Harley's fortunes improved in the second half of the 1980s,
the company's leaders began to wonder if these improvements might be
a mixed blessing. What if the survivors, who had a lot to be proud of,
concluded that Harley was now "good enough"? After all, the company had beaten back its Japanese competitors and had asked the fed-
eral government to rescind its five-year tariff a year ahead of schedule.
President Ronald Reagan publicly praised the company (on a May 6,
1987, visit to the York plant) for its return to world-class competitiveness. "You've shown us how to be the best," Reagan said (as
quoted in Harley's 1987 annual report). "You've been leaders in new
technology. You've stuck by the basic American values of hard work
and fair play. . . . As you've shown again, America is someplace special.
We're on the road to unprecedented prosperity . . . and we'll get there
on a Harley."

By some measures, Harley was back in business (see table 1-2).
But was Reagan right? Was Harley the best? And was that good
enough?

TABLE 1-2: THE TURNAROUND, QUANTIFIED

	1982	1986
U.S. market share (651cc+)	15.2%	19.4%
Units shipped	34,000	36,700
Revenue ($millions)	210	295
Operating profit (loss) ($millions)	(15.5)	7.3
Employees	2,289	2,211

Note: The stability of the workforce between 1982 and 1986 doesn't reflect immediate
     prior experience. Between 1981 and 1982, the workforce was reduced by a full 40
     percent.

Among themselves, Rich and his senior colleagues at Harley wor-
ried that the answer to these questions might be no. Harley surely had a
great brand. If not a "leader in new technology," as Reagan had asserted,
Harley was now at least on the map technologically. Insiders knew,
though, that the company was not particularly skilled at innovation.

Most of Harley's profits came from parts sales and other ancillary revenue streams—in other words, not from the sale of new motorcycles. And those on the inside also knew that the company still had serious problems, including a high cost structure—the highest in its industry—inadequate quality standards, and an uncertain level of employee commitment to the continuing success of the company.

This last point proved difficult for Rich and his colleagues to gauge. Certainly Harley's employees had made heroic efforts to save the company. Every time they had been asked to make sacrifices for the company, they had done so—quickly, willingly, and effectively. And, despite an understandable antipathy for all things Japanese, they had embraced the manufacturing innovations that Tom Gelb and his manufacturing colleagues had imported from Japan. These changes had accounted for the substantial turnaround in the company's fortunes in recent years, a turnaround that was now being celebrated by the business press, as well as by the nation's president.

The company's managers, too, had made a vital contribution. During those troubled years when Vaughn Beals and his colleagues pulled Harley-Davidson back from the brink of extinction, a particular definition of "leadership" came to dominate the company. According to that definition, the role of leadership was to anticipate impending challenges, decide how to solve them, and then impose the prescribed solution on the organization. "Leadership" (according to this theory) resided in a few individuals around whom others within the organization would rally. In this view of the world, leaders had distinctive characteristics that uniquely qualified them to lead: charisma, technical and managerial knowledge, and the ability to focus on the big picture. Leadership was a personal trait, to be exercised in a top-down, hierarchical way.

Harley didn't invent this definition, of course. At virtually all of the more than eighty organizations with which Lee had worked, as well those with which Rich had worked and of which he was aware, the "command-and-control" model was (and still is) the dominant model for organizing industrial organizations. It was dominant in large part because it had *proven* itself, very recently at Harley, but also in countless other settings. When an organization is under extreme pressure—so much so that one wrong move can mean the death of that organization—then an authoritarian system of controls may be absolutely necessary.

We can make an analogy with a country surrounded on all sides by invading forces. The defending army looks to its generals for decisive leadership, and the nation prays that those generals are skilled and lucky. But what happens when the invading armies are turned back and that immediate pressure is relieved?

And what if the external threat isn't dramatic enough to serve as a compelling rallying cry? Invasion is one thing; a slow erosion of a competitive position is another. When faced by the latter kind of challenge, should the organization persist in its command-and-control ways? Or should it look for new ways of organizing and managing itself?

Rich learned that he would soon be asked to take more responsibility for the company's future. Accordingly, he began talking with his senior management colleagues, including Beals, about alternatives to the command-and-control style of management. Those colleagues were fundamentally in agreement with Rich's concerns, but no one had a clear sense of how those concerns might be *acted* upon. Had other companies faced similar decision points? What had *they* done? Who had helped them?

"Traditionally," recalls former Harley executive Jim Paterson,

> the company culture keyed around a very, very powerful president or CEO—from the Davidson generations right down through Vaughn Beals. You'd wait to be told what to do, and you'd go do it. If you did it right, you'd get promoted. The problem with that, of course, was that you wound up with a lot of Indians who don't know what to do without the chief. This was true not only in strategy and operations, but also in the way that people were treated. Rich identified these areas as the ones in which the changes were needed.
>
> He wanted to take out layers of management, for example. Of course, this would take out money, and make the company more profitable. But more important, it would make people feel like they belonged, and could make a contribution, and wouldn't have to go through ten levels of management to reach the leaders of the company.

During the lean years, from '81–'86, a lot of this stuff was done by necessity. We took out layers because we *had* to. And folks down in the lower levels of the organization stood up—they did their jobs, and more. They contributed ideas. They started to feel part of the organization, and part of its success. And we wanted to capitalize on that—not just protect it, but increase it.

In the old organization, you'd concentrate on building your fiefdom—reports, perks, secretaries, and so on. In the new organization that Rich was starting to visualize, you would succeed in very different ways. You were going to have to participate, be intellectually curious, go out and get your education, learn new management skills, be a team member and team leader.

"Easy enough to say," Paterson concludes. "But when you try to institutionalize this kind of thing, it's very difficult."

Inventing and institutionalizing a new approach to running Harley: that was the journey on which Rich set out as he prepared to assume the newly created position of president and chief operating officer of Harley's Motorcycle Division. By any measure, this was the flagship of the larger organization, which now included an Indiana-based manufacturer of recreational vehicles, Holiday-Rambler, acquired in 1987 as part of a planned diversification effort. Whatever Rich and his colleagues came up with in the Motorcycle Division (alternately called the "Motor Company") would be scrutinized for its company-wide implications.

RICH: I didn't have a deadline, but I had a great sense of urgency. I knew we had to get more competitive. We had to get costs out of our products, and in order to do that, we had to get more involvement. And in addition, I happened to believe fundamentally that people should have the opportunity to influence their lives and their workplace. It's all part of the same picture.

2

Getting Under Way

BEGINNING IN THE EARLY MONTHS OF 1987, RICH RAISED HIS
concerns about the organization with Tom Gelb, vice president of manufacturing, and John Campbell, vice president of human resources.
Together, at a series of informal and ad hoc meetings, they considered
various ways to keep the company moving forward.

One option, of course, was more of the same. Because Harley had
convincingly demonstrated its capacity to respond to crisis, perhaps the
solution was to ensure that a crisis atmosphere would continue to dominate throughout the organization. All three leaders suspected, however, that such a strategy would lead to burnout, rather than to sustainable high performance.

Building on his own long-held belief that *people* were the most
important resource in any corporation, Rich began wondering aloud
how Harley could provide new kinds of incentives which would stimulate a broad base of "ownership" (in the figurative sense) across the
company. That way, the company would be more likely to get the best
effort out of its employees. Employee involvement (EI), of course, was
far from new at Harley (see chapter 1). But what seemed to be needed
was broader and deeper involvement, across the entire company. In the
long run, Harley could survive and prosper only if every employee took
responsibility for leading the company.

These discussions gradually led the three executives to the conclusion that the company should consider implementing a formal program of "gain sharing," or enabling all employees to share in improvements made at the company:

RICH: We saw gain sharing as a possible toe-hold—a way to bring people together to focus on how we could get better together. It seemed to be a promising way to move ahead with a broader base of participation.

I had seen gain-sharing programs that I thought made some sense, and I had also seen others that didn't generate the kinds of improvements that we were looking for. Herman Miller's program, which I had seen firsthand, had both pluses and minuses. But it certainly helped create lots of commitment on the part of people.

Gain sharing wasn't the only thing we were looking at. We were poking, probing, and trying things on for size. In a sense, we were like old-fashioned product development guys, who would come up with a new product concept, make a prototype, then beat the heck out of it until it failed, and then figure out which piece of it broke and why. We were looking at this, and looking at that, and trying to make something work. Gain sharing was one of these things that we looked at and said, "Hey, let's see if this will get us there." It was our equivalent of "artisan engineering."

Introducing a New Resource: Lee Ozley

Based on this rationale, Rich, Tom, and John initiated a series of talks with Edward Lawler. Lawler, the head of the Center for Effective Organizations and a recognized expert on alternative compensation systems, listened carefully to the rationale that the Harley executives offered on behalf of a gain-sharing program. He surprised them by disagreeing with their conclusion. The issues facing Harley, he cautioned, sounded as if they might be too broad and too complex to be solved through a simple gain-sharing approach. He suggested instead that Harley have conversations with three consultants, each of whom might be able to help the company deal with broader issues.

And so, in October 1987, Harley held individual meetings with the three consultants whom Ed Lawler had recommended. The meetings took place in a first-floor conference room at Harley-Davidson's Capitol Drive facility. The three Harley representatives tried to give each of the interviewees a broad-brush perspective on the company. They were believers, they said, in employee involvement, and they were proud of the company's initial steps in this direction. On the other hand (they readily confessed), Harley wasn't anywhere near where it needed to be in terms of getting the best ideas out of its people.

Harley's leaders found the first of these discussions discouraging. The first consultant seemed to have a standard solution that he applied across all of his engagements. He made it clear that he was eager to implement the kind of gain-sharing plan that Rich, Tom, and John were contemplating. In fact, he said, he already had a good idea of what the plan should look like.

RICH: I've sat through many, many consultant sales calls. They all want to dazzle you with, number one, how bright they are and, number two, all these fantastic clients for whose success they have been solely responsible. And, in my experience, they'll almost never disagree with you. They'll almost never say, "Hey, if that's what you want, I'm not your guy." They'll generally accept the consulting assignment and then try to change the assignment after the fact. But they don't let the money get away.

The second interviewee was Lee M. Ozley, cofounder and president of Virginia-based Responsive Organizations, Inc. (ROI). ROI had an impressive roster of clients, including AlliedSignal Corporation, National Steel and the United Steelworkers, U.S. Steel and the United Steelworkers, and Cummins Engine Company, the Diesel Workers Union, and the United Auto Workers. We'll let Lee introduce himself.

LEE: I was born and grew up in Alabama. My father was a wholesale hardware salesperson—probably the most ethical person who ever played that role. He focused on getting his customers what they needed, rather than on padding his commissions. I recall going on a sales call with him, lugging those sixty-pound catalogs and watching him fill out forms for his competitors when their prices were better than his or their goods more appropriate for his customers' needs.

My mother—housewife, mother, and later a nurse—is the most remarkable person I have ever known. I don't recall her ever saying a negative thing about another person. She taught me that there is good in every person and that everyone is worthy of respect, and that it just takes longer to find the good in some people.

I did my undergraduate studies at Auburn University, where I also gained a commission in the U.S. Air Force through the ROTC program. After my early Vietnam-era stint in the Air Force, I did graduate study at the University of Wisconsin, where I studied the work of Abraham Maslow, probably the best Socratic teacher I have ever known.

During this time, I became involved with labor unions, which gave me a very different view of how employees experienced the organizations of which they were a part— including their union.

I then gained the perspective of organizations from the "other side," by serving in operating management positions for two manufacturing organizations. In one organization, we were faced with implementing Title VII of the Civil Rights Act of 1966 in the Deep South. This task was accomplished with remarkably little trouble. We just talked to all the people, explained what was and was not going to happen, and where we were trying to go. Quite frankly, we had no real problems in implementing what many, including myself, thought would be very difficult.

During this period of time, it became clear to me that, by restricting myself to working with either the "labor" or the "management" institution, I would not be able to have the kind of influence I wanted to have. At one point in my life, I thought about becoming a minister, because I wanted to help people make their lives better. But it hit me that the place where people spend most of their time is at work. If I could influence them at work, I decided, I would have a much better chance of really making a difference. So the workplace, from multiple perspectives, became the focus of the rest of my career.

I spent some time as an arbitrator and a mediator, which helped me understand and appreciate that everyone would be better off if we could get problems solved at their source—rather than at such a late date that a third-party intervener was required to help solve the problem.

I then joined Kurt Salmon Associates (KSA) in Atlanta. KSA at that time was focused on the implementation of a new manufacturing system and wanted to continue to develop the "human side" of its practice. Kurt Salmon was one of the most ethical men I've ever met. Working with him helped me to understand the basics of ethical consulting, and creating and maintaining mutually effective "contracts" with clients.

In 1975 I went to Washington, D.C., to serve as executive director of the American Center for the Quality of Working Life, a nonprofit foundation that implemented some of the earliest labor-management collaboration efforts in the United States. In late 1978 I wanted to go out on my own and apply some of the lessons I had learned. My wife and I founded Responsive Organizations, Inc. (ROI). By the time Harley contacted me through Ed Lawler, ROI was working with a number of unionized manufacturing organizations.

Ed and I have known each other for years. He was then living in Los Angeles and mostly restricting himself to work west of the Mississippi. He called me one day and said, "I gave your name to some people at Harley-Davidson. They say they're interested in a gain-sharing plan, but there's a bigger story there. I think it would be a very interesting challenge."

Again, the three Harley managers outlined their trial balloon: that an effective gain-sharing program might broaden the base of "ownership" across the company. They asked Lee whether he might be able to devise and install such a program.

Like Ed Lawler before him (but unlike his immediate predecessor in the room), Lee asked exactly which problem Harley was trying to solve. Rich, Tom, and John expressed their willingness to talk through the underlying issues that had led to their conclusions, but wanted to know why Lee felt he needed to go down one more level of detail. Lee responded that, in his experience, it was important to avoid settling on a solution to a problem before the root causes of that problem had been surfaced and talked out.

Too often, he said, corporations attempted to take solutions *to* their employees, rather than work *with* employees to solve a problem. It would be inconsistent with Harley's tradition of employee involvement, he pointed out, if the company simply implemented a gain-sharing program from on high.

And in any case, Lee continued, any proposed gain-sharing plan should be evaluated as part of a much bigger context. Many such plans were implemented in an effort to reduce overtime. But in cases where overtime amounted to 20 or 30 percent of base pay, a gain-sharing payout (typically in the neighborhood of between 3 to 5 percent) would be meaningless, and the plan would not achieve its stated goal. Companies that asked employees to trade 30 percent overtime for 3 to 5 percent gain sharing were almost always disappointed with the results.

Lee concluded these opening comments by saying that he probably wasn't the right person to plunge directly into the implementation of a gain-sharing plan. He would be happy to refer Harley to other consultants, if that was the direction they really wanted to pursue, but Lee and ROI were probably not a good fit for the job.

In Rich's experience, this was unusual. Most consultants with whom he had dealt in the past had been *hungrier* than this Ozley character.

RICH: It was the damnedest consultant sales call I've ever seen.

LEE: Quite frankly, we had plenty of work at that time. In light of that workload, we probably would just as soon not have gotten this assignment. In fact, I remember going into a planning meeting back home, after that first meeting in Milwaukee, and having one of my colleagues ask a pointed question. "OK, Lee," he said, "what the hell are you going to do if you sell it?" But it looked like such an interesting situation—as Ed Lawler had promised—and those three guys in Milwaukee were so obviously interested in getting it right, whatever "it" turned out to be.

Stimulated by this opportunity to focus on underlying issues and needs, Rich, Tom, and John filled Lee in on the gist of their conversations over the previous six months. They restated the questions that had so puzzled them: Does constant crisis management hurt a workforce over the long run? How could Harley, in the absence of a perceived crisis, strengthen its relatively fragile traditions of employee involvement and continuous improvement? What would motivate employees to do better and better? What would promote high performance without burnout?

From Sales Call to Dialogue

At this point, perhaps an hour into the conversation between the three executives and their guest, an interesting shift began to take place. The stated purpose of the meeting —to interview a possible candidate to help Harley implement gain sharing—receded in importance, and a new purpose came to the fore. Working at a "root-cause" level, the four participants in the meeting started working together as peers and colleagues, brainstorming and comparing notes. Lee served as informal facilitator of the meeting. But as an increasingly cohesive group, Rich, Tom, John, and their newfound colleague began batting ideas around and digging down into the real challenges that might be facing Harley in the months and years to come.

Each participant put perspectives on the table for discussion. Lee talked at some length about the ideas of organizational theorist Abraham Maslow, who had had a profound influence on Lee when Lee had studied with him years earlier. Maslow had argued, among other things, that, absent a crisis, people rarely commit to a program that is imposed on them. On the other hand, they willingly commit to a program that they help create. This, Lee suggested, had profound implications for the leaders of an organization. Perhaps a "leader" isn't someone who solves all of an organization's problems unilaterally. Perhaps a leader is someone who effectively identifies and brings together a broad range of people in a group problem-solving procedure.

LEE: We had kicked into a learning-together model. We'd be talking about something, I'd ask a question, and they'd say, "Maybe this concept would work." And then we'd reverse roles. It was more like a seminar than a sales pitch.

The Harley executives were familiar with Maslow's work and reflected aloud on how Maslow's "hierarchy of needs" had manifested itself in Harley's recent history. They also brought their own experiences, at Harley and elsewhere, to bear on the issues of leadership and effective problem solving.

Gradually, working with Lee, they reached consensus on a tentative redefinition of "leadership" for Harley. According to this new definition, leadership was the process of creating and sustaining an environment in which people work together toward the achievement of common goals—and not because they *have* to, but because they *want* to. Leadership was a process whereby *everybody* could make contributions to the success of the company. Leadership was a process whereby ordinary people could achieve extraordinary things.

Defining leadership this way would greatly accelerate the ongoing process of change at Harley-Davidson. Those occupying formal leadership positions would have to move away from command-and-control leadership and move toward acting as resources, facilitators, and coaches. They would continue to have primary responsibility for developing the overall strategic direction of the organization. But they would also help all the employees accept and carry out their individual responsibilities, in order to achieve mutually agreed-upon goals.

At one point in the discussion, Lee volunteered his opinion that expecting ordinary people to achieve extraordinary things was not an unrealistic goal. He was willing to bet, he said, that Harley's employees were just as talented as those in the other organizations where he had worked in the past. They almost certainly demonstrated extraordinary leadership skills outside of the workplace. They were leaders in their churches, in their fraternal and civic organizations, in the school systems that their children attended, and in countless other settings. The challenge was to manage Harley in a way that called upon these extraordinary leadership skills *in the workplace*.

Rich responded very positively to this line of argument. It tracked closely with his own background and professional experience, beginning with the lessons learned from his father's small manufacturing company and continuing through his experience with Michigan-based furniture manufacturer Herman Miller. And perhaps most encouraging from Rich's perspective was that these ideas tracked closely with Harley's recent history. If Harley went in the direction in which the group's discussion seemed to be pointing, the company would not be embracing an alien philosophy. Rather, it would be acting to reinforce the best and most fundamental values of the corporation.

Rich and Tom were in a particularly good position to articulate those values. Three years earlier, in 1984, they (along with other colleagues in senior management, in an effort spearheaded by then CEO Vaughn Beals) had put together a booklet on Harley's "business policies," which tried to capture and codify the company value system. The booklet was a compelling piece of work, in Rich's estimation. Unfortunately, it never saw the light of day. Very late in the process—in fact, after several thousand copies of the booklet had been printed—Harley's managers reluctantly concluded that they had to cut the effort short and "deep-six" the publication. Why? Because Harley was still effectively under the control of its prime lender, which was in a position to dictate terms to the company. It would be disastrous for the company to commit itself publicly to the kinds of behaviors outlined in the booklet and then to be overruled by a bank. If you can't be assured of living up to the standards you espouse, Harley's leaders reluctantly concluded at the time, don't celebrate those standards. The booklets were thrown away.

RICH: Why did we go public in 1986? All kinds of reasons, but one really good one was to get away from someone else telling us how to run our business. I'd rather face shareholders than bankers, any day.

After about three hours of this freewheeling discussion, Lee offered to summarize what he had heard about the problem that Harley faced and what steps Harley might take to solve that problem.

First, he said, Harley had achieved a dramatic turnaround in its fortunes, admired in management circles around the world. The turnaround was a significant accomplishment, which deserved to be celebrated. It had been accomplished predominantly through a command-and-control leadership style that was absolutely appropriate for the particular challenges of the 1982–1986 period.

Second, the zeal demonstrated by employees during the recent times of crisis would be difficult to sustain as the air of crisis receded. This troubled Rich and Tom, because they saw real market and financial challenges ahead—challenges of such complexity and urgency that Harley needed an even greater level of commitment from its employees in the future than it had enjoyed in the past.

Third, a consensus was emerging among Rich and a few key colleagues that the people of Harley-Davidson constituted the company's best and most distinctive competitive advantage. This idea originated in Rich's personal beliefs, and also in the company's remarkable accomplishments in recent years. Yes, the Harley brand was a powerful one, all around the world. But *people* had pulled off these miracles, Rich emphasized.

Fourth, Harley's management in the near term needed to persuade the company's employees to "take ownership of" (that is, be individually responsible and accountable for) the success of the company.

Fifth, the company's leaders had to replace the command-and-control approach with something else. Command and control would not help Harley achieve the results it now needed to achieve—nor was it consistent with the company's values or with those of Rich and other leaders. The shortcomings of command and control included a lack of acceptance of personal responsibility, a focus on narrow tasks and duties, frustration, limited or narrow input into problem solving and decision making, a not-my-job syndrome, and—most dangerous of all for the company's long-term health—*compliance* rather than *commitment*. The new approach to managing Harley was as yet unknown. Based on that afternoon's conversation, however, that new approach surely would be grounded in employee involvement and personal responsibility.

And, finally, the people of Harley had to settle on a direction for the company. Lee quoted a saying attributed to Yogi Berra: *If you don't know where you're going, you'll end up somewhere else.*

Rich, John, and Tom agreed. They also observed that *acting* on the implications of that summary would be a daunting task, focusing in particular on the topic of *change*. Rich pointed out that people are instinctively resistant to change and that changing the "winning formula" at Harley would be a particularly tough sell. People were very likely to cite the old cliché: If it ain't broke, don't fix it.

Rich then articulated a paradox that was emerging in his mind. It was possible, he reasoned, that he and other leaders at Harley could impose the necessary organizational changes by fiat. Simply by virtue of their hierarchical authority, they could substitute any kind of management system they wanted for the one that was now in place. But wouldn't this be counterproductive? Wouldn't this just reinforce the very command-and-control mentality that they were trying to dislodge?

How, Rich asked aloud, can you get people to want change—or even to *demand* it?

Getting There from Here

Keying off this question, the meeting turned to the kinds of practical steps that might get a productive change process under way. Midway through this discussion, Lee took this opportunity to describe a process that he used with other organizations.

First, Lee suggested, the leadership of the organization, including the union leadership, had to sit down together and discuss the future they wanted to achieve. On a flip chart, toward the right-hand side of a blank page, he drew a single rectangle. Under this he scrawled the phrase "Vision of ideal future."

Vision of ideal future

These discussion sessions, he said, had to be well planned and facilitated, to allow the full airing of opinions, especially differences of opinion. "People will be looking for signals at these meetings," he explained. "They'll be looking for congruence between what you say you want and what your behavior says you want. If you tell them that you 'value differences,' for example, they'll watch you closely the first time those differences hit the table."

This vision-setting exercise, Lee continued, rarely turns out to be the kind of free-for-all that a manager might anticipate. Instead, when employees have the opportunity to freely express themselves and describe their ideal organization, the vision they come up with is often *quite similar to* that described by the organization's leaders. In other words, despite all the complicating factors of organizational life—including level in the organization, functional specialization, educational background, and so on—*people within an organization want more or less the same things from and for that organization.*

LEE: And what's really interesting, in my experience, is that the shop stewards and the rank and file tend to be much more aggressive in their expectations of the organization than the typical manager. Not every time, but more often than not.

The convergence of values within an organization is a natural and powerful phenomenon, Lee continued. People don't *have* to be where they are, for the most part. If the hopes, dreams, and values of an organization's leadership differ too much from their own, one of two outcomes tends to arise. Some of those "outliers" simply hunker down and become compliant. Others leave. They find someplace else to work where they're more in synch, and over time, there is an increasing congruence of values among the people who remain. "They may not talk about it," Lee commented, "but it's there."

Again, Lee's comments resonated with Rich's own experiences. At Herman Miller, where Rich had worked before coming to Harley, Chairman Max DePree had stressed that all employees were "volunteers." People only volunteer to help an organization that they admire and within which they feel comfortable.

Tom Gelb concurred with the premise that people throughout Harley had similar hopes for the company. He knew his managerial colleagues well and, as head of manufacturing, also had a good feel for the rank and file. "I'm convinced," he said, "that *any* employee in our company, given the same information and the same *understanding* of that information that we in this room have, would come to the same conclusions and make the same decisions that we would."

If that was true, Lee responded, then the real starting point in an organizational change process ought to be the vision of the ideal future (as symbolized by the rough square he had drawn on the board). "I'm constantly amazed," he said, "at how much energy is spent on fighting over 'how to get there,' rather than 'where we're going.' People spend all their time fighting over process, and they never get to the vision. And because that process battle was so hot and heavy, the various groups simply assume that they could never reach agreement on something as important as a 'vision.'"

Conversely, if people succeed at the visioning process, this creates a far better context for solving the how-to-get-there problem. "How to get there" doesn't go away, Lee cautioned, but the problem becomes far more manageable.

Keeping the process manageable was a continuing concern, Lee said. He generally recommended that a core group of individuals from across the organization be assigned the task of drafting a preliminary "vision of the ideal future." Once this representative group reached a consensus, they would share that vision with the larger organization. They would also engage a much broader segment of the employee population in a second key step of the change process: describing where Harley was *now* in relation to the desired future.

At this point, Lee went back to the flip chart and drew a second box to the left of the "vision" box. This box he labeled "Where we are today."

Where we are today   Vision of ideal future

By diagnosing where the organization was today compared to a desired future, people would feel far more free to own up to shortcomings—both their own and the organization's—than if they were asked to diagnose the current situation compared to any other benchmark (for example, yesterday, or another organization). Such other comparisons, Lee said, almost always prompt defensive reactions, including excuse making and blaming, and rarely lead to helpful insights.

Once the vision of the ideal future was juxtaposed with a clear depiction of "where we are today," Lee continued, the really hard work would begin. In this stage of the process, the members of the organization would have to develop an integrated, comprehensive "strategic thrust for change," as well as a series of supporting action plans. These would move the company from where it was today toward the desired future. Again, Lee scribbled on the board, this time generating a dramatic, rightward-sweeping arrow.

The fourth step in the process, Lee said, scribbling once again on

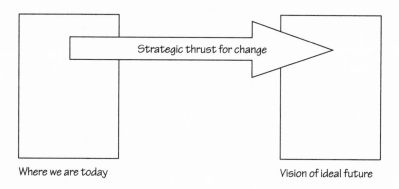

the crowded flip chart, would involve examining and, if necessary, modifying all of Harley's existing policies, procedures, and systems toward two ends. First, all would have to reflect the values, principles, and philosophies inherent in the envisioned future. Second, all would have to be supportive of the *specific changes* that would be needed to get to that desired future state.

At the end of this round of scribbling, the flip chart looked something like this:

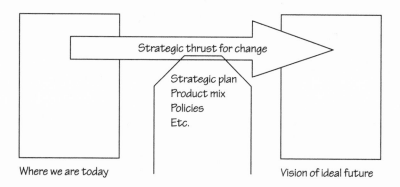

One more important piece needed to be added to this model, Lee said. Finding some room on the flip chart, he drew a crude set of stairs going upward from lower left to upper right. On one of the steps in the middle of this rough staircase he drew a stick figure, the top of whose head didn't quite reach the bottom of the next step:

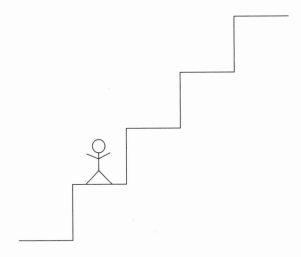

This poor fellow, Lee explained, is living through an organizational change. In real life, change is neither linear nor smooth. It tends to come as a stair-step function, often after a relatively static period. Someone standing on the tread of a step is usually unable to see what's ahead and may well be apprehensive about the impending change. This underscores why a shared vision is so important: people are more likely to tolerate the near-term unknowns if they've helped chart the overall course of action.

Then Lee moved up the chart and superimposed the stair step on the model, placing the stick figure on the staircase halfway between the "today" and "ideal future" boxes.

When an effective change process happens, Lee explained, it takes change a step at a time. "We're not talking home runs," he explained. "We're talking a scratch single here, a stolen base there, and then another scratch single." Small day-to-day actions, skillfully chosen and successfully implemented, persuade people that everyone is on board and that things are moving forward.

At the same time, Lee said, people "on the staircase" must learn to look backward as well as forward. All too often, people in the process of large-scale organizational change lose track of the very real progress they have already made. They get discouraged and lose faith in the process. Being able to point behind them, to some place from which they and the organization have come, can be extremely reassuring.

RICH: We've been through lots of problem-solving efforts at Harley. In retrospect, I see this model as by far the most effective of all of them. Its power derives, in large part, from this stair-step idea. I think that's because it causes you to think where you've come from.

Making Change Welcome

Rich and his colleagues said that they were intrigued by the model that Lee had walked them through. Rich compared it favorably with the traditional "gap" analysis conducted by the strategic planners in many corporations. The gap analysis scrutinizes the company's strengths, weaknesses, opportunities, and threats. (For this reason, the gap analysis is also referred to as "SWOT" analysis.) The "envisioned future" approach seemed more dynamic than the gap analysis, and that was all to the good, Rich stated. However, Rich continued, he wasn't sure he had gotten an answer to his original question. Change is threatening, and in some ways, planned change is the most threatening change of all. So how can an organization expect its members to welcome change, and even demand it?

In response, Lee outlined a simple conceptual framework he had developed, based on work done by the late Richard Beckhard at MIT and Michael Beer at Harvard. Starting with a clean sheet on the flip chart, Lee wrote out the following formula, which he labeled "the mathematics of change":

$$\text{Change} = (E \times M \times P) > \text{Resistance}$$

$$E = \text{Engagement}$$
$$M = \text{Model}$$
$$P = \text{Process}$$

This framework (Lee explained) helps people understand change, understand where resistance to change comes from, and create the circumstances within which resistance can be overcome. It begins with

Rich's question. People perceive change as something that will move them to a new place, which is likely to be uncomfortable and perhaps even painful. When they are confronted with a proposed change, therefore, people find great comfort in the status quo (even if they weren't previously great fans of the status quo). Absent a recognized crisis, therefore, a dramatic departure from the status quo won't happen unless it is imposed on people.

But this creates its own problems. Rich had already pointed toward the biggest of these problems. A change that is imposed through command and control not only creates anxiety, it also creates a second kind of resistance: People don't like being pushed around. They don't like change, but they especially don't like *being changed*.

But, Lee suggested, we can look at change another way. This alternative was captured in the formula on the board. Change can be self-motivated, rather than imposed. This happens when the product of three factors is greater than the resistance to the proposed change, and when none of the factors is at zero.

The first of those three factors is *engagement*, represented by E. Engagement arises when people see and understand the need to do things differently. Rich, Tom, and John clearly saw a need for employee involvement and continuous improvement at Harley. Many structures and processes designed to foster that kind of involvement and improvement were already in place. But, before dramatic changes could occur at Harley, people across the organization would have to share that perception. Engagement would be achieved when employees throughout Harley saw the world in similar ways and agreed that continuing in the current mode was *not in their own best interests* over the long term.

Resistance to change, Lee continued, grows out of a fear of the unknown. In order to launch a successful process of change, therefore, the organization had to create new vehicles for education and the sharing of knowledge. In an ideal world, employees would have exactly the same information (concerning critical topics such as market share, competition, dealer and rider satisfaction, and so on) that was available to Rich, Tom, and others in management, and they would have a similar *understanding* of that information.

The second factor for encouraging change is a *model* (M in the formula). This was the "vision of ideal future" described previously as the first step in the four-step process. Such a model had to be developed with the thoroughgoing involvement of employees. When sketched out in adequate detail, it would provide everyone in the organization with a clear goal. If the goal inspired people sufficiently, the model would reinforce engagement, thereby helping to transform the shared goal into a reality.

The third factor in the formula, represented by P, is *process*. Again, this linked directly to the four-step model that the group had already explored. *Process* was a catchword for all the many systems, procedures, and programs that would have to be brought into alignment for change toward the desired goal to take place. Process also includes ways of giving people the help they need (in terms of training, coaching, and so on) to make changes. The company would have to provide these supports both to individuals and groups.

This framework was far from a precise formula, Lee stressed. It wasn't a matter of plugging in hard-and-fast variables and calculating an optimal recipe for change. Instead, he said, the framework provided a useful approach to making change welcome. It emphasized a rich and subtle interplay among three key variables: engagement, model, and process. It also put authority over the change process where it belonged: in the hands of those who would be most affected by any envisioned change.

Again, Rich and his colleagues agreed with this line of argument. Of course, they did not suspect that the model and mathematics of change under discussion would serve as a foundation for dramatic changes at Harley for more than a decade to come. But they *were* becoming persuaded that Lee was a valuable resource. Unlike some other consultants, it seemed, Lee would fit in with the particular culture of Harley and this could only help the kind of change process that he and they were advocating.

Rich asked Lee to talk about time frames. Lee responded that Harley's managers probably should expect to spend between twelve to eighteen months working with Lee and his associates in order to prepare for this kind of change. For Rich and Tom, however, spending up to a year and a half simply getting *ready* for change was unacceptable. The schedule of upcoming collective bargaining, for one thing, argued for a shorter timeline. And, looking more broadly, in light of the urgency of the realities facing Harley, the company couldn't wait a year or more for management to get comfortable with change. By that time, they said emphatically, *all* employees had to be deeply engaged in the process.

LEE: To me, it was a perfect example of how the demands of the present can overwhelm the best of long-term intentions. "We have to hurry up and get people to get to the right answer." Yes, they had compelling reasons to get things moving. And, yes, it was up to them to get things moving. There was no alternative system in place. But getting things moving in the wrong way might be coun-terproductive in the long run. We talked a lot about this tension in our subsequent discussions.

RICH: In a vacuum, Lee's timetable would have been fine. But we had a union contract coming up, and it was going to be a three-year agreement. I felt that, if we didn't have something in place before that next three-year agreement was put in place, the company was going to be in deep, deep trouble. I didn't think we could live with-out some kind of change process that had the blessing of all parties.

The meeting drew to a close. The question of a shorter time frame remained open, with Lee promising to talk with his own colleagues in Virginia about possible ways to accelerate the process. Rich, Tom, and John thanked Lee for contributing to an extremely interesting session and promised to share the gist of the meeting with other key executives.

This they did over the next few weeks. They also conducted infor-mal meetings with the union leadership to discuss those organizations' concerns about the future. Most people agreed that the ongoing employee involvement effort had generated some real benefits, but that Harley still faced difficult challenges. From the unions' perspective, get-ting *everyone* focused on the long-term success of the company was the biggest challenge that lay ahead.

LEE: I went back to Virginia and told my colleagues about this delightful four-hour meeting I had attended. "That's the good news," I said. "The bad news is, they can't give us the twelve to eighteen months they'd need to do it right." We struggled with that. We seriously considered disqualifying ourselves, because we believed it would be very difficult. At the same time, however, we were excited at the prospect of working with this interesting client.

First Steps and Missteps

Within a month of the original October 1987 meeting, Lee was invited back to Milwaukee to visit again with Rich, Tom, and others. These discussions would explore how Harley could move forward along the lines that had emerged during Lee's initial visit.

"I think that Lee Ozley came on the scene because he was very good at intervention," recalls HR manager Filippa "Flip" Weber. "And he was a *process* guy, which is what we needed.

"Originally," she elaborates, "we thought we wanted somebody who knew all about gain sharing. But we were more interested in building a relationship with the employees, which was what Lee was very good at."

Harley's executives found this second round of discussions equally promising. They increasingly felt that they had happened upon the right resource for the difficult tasks at hand. Accordingly, they decided to arrange a series of meetings with key union and management leaders, at which they would share the emerging plan. Because it was important for all parties to feel comfortable with Lee and his ROI associates, Lee undertook to meet with about forty-five key union leaders in the Wisconsin facilities on three different occasions.

Lee later recalled the first of these meetings as a "disaster."

LEE: The Milwaukee Grand Hotel. I'll never forget it. I made some fundamental errors, starting with a tailored shirt with my initials embroidered on it, and cufflinks. My hair was a little shaggy, and I had some gold jewelry on.

I was a little nervous, so I talked too fast. I was trying to sell an idea to them, and I know I came across as some sort of southern chicken thief or snake oil salesman. Later, a union member who became a friend said, "Hey, man, you were talking about nine kazillion miles an hour."

Dumb, right? But it happened, in part because, by now, I really believed in this thing, and I wanted it to happen.

Aside from stylistic problems, the unions also harbored doubts about Lee's mission. After all, he represented a proposed initiative that had been blessed by management. The initiative had been shaped in part by management, and if it proceeded, management would pay for it. From the unions' point of view, skepticism made sense.

RICH: We had some concerns when the word got back to us about the unions' response. To say we were "shook" would be exaggerating, though. We wanted to find out what went wrong. And Lee made it easy for us. He stepped up and said, "I blew it. I need another shot." So we arranged it for him.

But managers, too, seemed to have concerns, although those concerns were harder to get at. When Lee held his meetings with groups of second- and third-level managers, he encountered surprisingly few challenges. Instead, he found a pervasive attitude of compliance. He heard regular references to an unspecified "they": If that's what *they* want, that's fine with us. This convinced Rich and his colleagues that they had put their fingers on a real problem at Harley. The insidious effects of command and control at Harley were coming into view, and the first and best evidence could be found among the ranks of management.

Meanwhile, Rich and Tom visited the York facility and asked leaders there to consider a similar process. But York quickly expressed its disinterest in the initiative. The managers and employees in Pennsylvania would continue their own continuous-improvement efforts, designed to achieve more efficient operations and build more harmonious labor-management relations.

York's rejection was a setback, of course, but it didn't derail the process that was being set in motion. A small cadre of top-level managers had hired an unusual resource from the consulting world. That resource was prepared to help them recast an organization that, to many onlookers both outside and inside the company, didn't need recasting. Skeptical unions in Milwaukee had yet to be won over, and the huge York facility, which comprised more than a thousand skilled employees, had opted out of a process that hadn't yet begun. As Rich and his colleagues had suspected all along, they faced a formidable challenge.

RICH: My philosophy is, pick your battles, pick your beachheads, and never push up a rope. We never tried to force York—or anybody else, for that matter—into doing something they didn't want to do.

No, it's never easy. It's never obvious. If it were, we wouldn't be dissecting it today for lessons and learning. It all goes back to that fundamental belief—that people are the only sustainable competitive advantage. And a key element in realizing that advantage is participation. So how were we going to get participation based on commitment rather than compliance? The big, big question.

3

Agreeing on a Road Map for Change

THE FIRST STEP TOWARD CHANGING THE UNION-MANAGEMENT relationship at Harley, as Lee had discussed at the October 1987 meeting with Rich, Tom, and John, was *envisioning a desired future.* This process, which the group had endorsed at that time, would involve leaders from across the organization—management and union alike. Harley's leaders decided to take this message to the broader organization.

In the late fall and early winter of 1987, therefore, Lee, Tom, Rich, and John—both individually and together—met with managers and union groups to explain the proposed plan and try to enlist the cooperation of those groups. Some of these meetings succeeded; others were disappointing. In at least one case, Lee went back to a union group that had not been receptive to his message and tried again.

While this introductory process made slow headway, another parallel process was raising the stakes for the company. The labor agreement covering Wisconsin employees would expire on April 1, 1988—only a few months away. This deadline put significant pressure on the timetable for change.

In this chapter, we describe how individuals from across Harley came together to create what Harley ultimately would call the "joint vision" for the Wisconsin operations of the company.

"Lee told us that it could be done," recalls Director of Labor-Management Relations Flip Weber. "I don't think he ever told us exactly *how* it was going to work. He did have some of the 'how-tos' and a sense of the process you had to follow to work together. It doesn't just come out of the blue. He had the *process*. But still, he couldn't tell us exactly how it would go, in part because it had to be for us. We had to 'Harleyize' it."

Getting Started

At Harley, three-year labor contracts were the norm. Rich (along with other managers of the company) was convinced that real change could not occur at Harley unless an explicit commitment to substantive change could be built into the next round of union contracts. From the vantage point of early 1988, Rich felt that Harley couldn't afford another three years of only incremental change. And changes could "stick" only if the collective bargaining process sanctioned and reinforced them. On the other hand, Rich didn't believe the company could commit to a full-blown transformational process in the upcoming three years.

> **RICH:** Given where we were starting from, we decided that we wanted a one-year contract. To negotiate a three-year contract that involved that kind of commitment, given where we were starting from, probably wasn't doable.

Accordingly, management representatives decided to abandon the standard management approach to bargaining. They decided not to approach the table with a long list of proposed work-rule changes aimed at improving productivity. Instead, they began the negotiations of early 1988 with only one demand: support for the joint visioning process that Lee had described to them. Management also expressed its preference for an interim, one-year agreement.

RICH: By saying, "This is the only thing we want," we were sending a very strong message. We were saying, "This is extremely important to the company."

LEE: You might ask whether there was any way that some process of joint visioning could have been worked through without being embodied in the contract. In my experience, the answer is, "Probably not." In the case of every group we've worked with, there's been a formal memorandum of agreement. Otherwise, you set the elected union officials up to get killed, politically. The deal can be in the contract, or a side letter of agreement. But you don't want the rank and file asking, "Who the devil authorized you to get into bed with management?"

For their part, the unions approached the table with a fairly conventional set of demands. After substantial back and forth, the parties—who included PACE Local 7209 (Milwaukee), IAM Lodge 78 (Milwaukee), PACE Local 7460 (Tomahawk), Flip Weber, and the plant managers from both Milwaukee (Capitol Drive) and Tomahawk—reached a one-year labor agreement that included a more or less typical pay increase, as well as the all-important language supporting the joint visioning process. In retrospect, the one-year term of the agreement helped both union and management to take a risk. No matter how badly things went, people on both teams reasoned, it would last only a year.

Also in retrospect, Rich's and Tom's strong personal relationships with union leaders helped make these successful negotiations possible. As a result of years of straight talk with both management and union, they had earned a high degree of personal credibility. In conversations before, during, and after the formal negotiations, Rich and Tom offered credible assurances that they were not out to sacrifice vital interests.

LEE: What you tended to hear about Rich and Tom was "Well, I may not like what they're saying, but they're straight shooters, and they don't dance around the issues." There was never any sub-terfuge, spin control, hidden agendas, or all that PR stuff; it was just straight from the shoulder. The union folks believed that Rich and Tom were being straight with them. Now, whether the union people thought what Rich and Tom were advocating was doable or not was another question entirely. But they never doubted Rich's and Tom's commitment.

Together, management and labor made their first critical decision: to go forward.

Designing on the Fly

The first step involved creating a structure and a facilitated *process*. One of Lee's associates from ROI took responsibility for each partici-pating Harley location, after winning approval from both the local union and management leadership. Lee, for his part, took on the role of de facto backup resource for all the site groups and also served as facilitator at the center of the process.

Lee and his colleagues, working with individuals at Harley's Mil-waukee and Tomahawk plants, set out to engage everyone who occu-pied union and management leadership positions in these locations. These meetings began on an intensive basis in the first week of April 1988. All told, more than 100 union and management leaders partici-pated in these discussions. The overall goal was to enable people to articulate their hopes, fears, concerns, beliefs, and feelings about Harley as an organization and about their role as employees at Harley.

Rich and Lee had agreed that an organization's leaders couldn't tell people what to believe, or how to feel, about anything. People had to meet and discuss these critical issues together and reach their own con-clusions. At the same time, however, Harley needed a *structure* to ensure that something coherent would emerge from all of these discus-sions. At each site, therefore, participants experienced the "boxes" exer-cise through which Lee had led Rich, Tom, and John in the previous fall:

the future, where we are today, and how to get from here to there. Lee and his colleagues developed a structured outline for use in all of these facilitated sessions. Using the same outline across all of the facilities helped all participants provide their input into the vision process in a uniform manner—one that would allow for consolidation at a later point.

RICH: The outline was extremely important. To succeed at this, you have to frame the issues. For example, you have to ask: What is the appropriate relationship between the union and the company? What is the appropriate relationship between unions? What should the financial performance of the company be?

LEE: You begin by saying, "Okay, if this company were functioning the way you'd like it to be functioning, what would the various stakeholder groups have to say about the company? What would the financial community say about the company? What would your customers be saying about the company? What would the shop floor worker be saying about the company along the following dimensions: quality, financial performance, interpersonal relations?"

You give the visioning process a structure. And, in the case of Harley and others, you want to get a standard format, because some day you're going to have to pull it all together. It's like a translation process: At the end of the day, you'd like it all to be in English, rather than sixty different languages.

The Joint Vision Process

The Joint Vision Process (it soon became capitalized) developed site by site on a series of different levels, in a prespecified sequence. First, each individual used a worksheet to wrestle with the challenge in his or her own mind, and to arrive at a personal vision for the company and its union-management relationship. All of these individual visions came together in the context of a work group of employees, and each work group fed its vision into its respective leadership (union or management) for that site. Finally, these two perspectives were brought together into a joint vision for the plant as a whole (see chart).

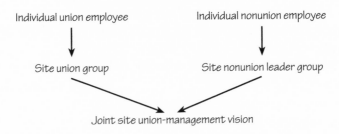

Information Flow

As this complicated process unfolded, the clock ticked away, with the one-year union contract defining the outside time limits. This created both negative and positive pressures. On the negative side, Lee and his colleagues were trying to squeeze a year's work or more into three months. Many hours had to be worked in around the edges of production, which the Joint Vision Process was designed not to disrupt. (All told, the company committed some 6,000 person-hours to the meetings associated with the Joint Vision Process.) Different sites needed to come along at roughly the same pace, so that no facility would decide that it had been left behind.

On the plus side, deadlines served as a useful stimulus to the process. Lee and his colleagues applied subtle pressure to groups that were lagging behind. Gradually, momentum built at the separate facilities. Lee and his ROI colleagues met regularly with union leaders ("who, predictably, were getting hammered," Lee recalls). They also met frequently with Rich, Tom Gelb, and other leaders. Keeping all the leaders informed on the rapidly evolving design of the Joint Vision Process was a huge challenge. Partly due to the time pressures, the ROI team improvised day by day.

LEE: Most of the time, it was, "Well, here's our best guess. What do you guys think?" It gave a whole new meaning to the phrase "designing on your feet." When it started moving, it moved very fast. It was diagnose as you go: talking to our team members, talking to the key leaders, and constantly asking, "Does this make sense? What do you think of this?" So we were molding it with their input as we went along. No one wanted command and control from the consultants! So we were working in that mode of constant questioning, and checking off. It was a lot of long hours, and it was hectic.

RICH: The cost of all of this effort was readily included in our budgets and forecasts. Did we get our money's worth? Absolutely. These activities laid the groundwork for all of the changes that were to follow.

Management, too, struggled with changes during this hectic period. Rich needed a successor as president of the Motor Company and settled on his colleague Jim Paterson, who had both a breadth of experience in finance and marketing, as well as strong people skills. But how would this change affect the Joint Vision Process? "In March of '88," Jim Paterson recalls, "Rich took me aside and said, 'I want to name you president of the company.' We talked about that, and I finally said, 'Okay.' And then a couple of weeks after that, he said, 'Oh, by the way—we're starting this Joint Vision Process, and you've gotta help make it work.' That's how I got thrown into this thing."

Bringing the Vision Together

After three months of work at all Wisconsin locations (York, again, was not involved), more than 130 union and management leaders came together in May 1988 for a three-day session at the Ramada Inn at the Milwaukee airport. In internal ROI documents, this meeting was dubbed "the May Big One," indicating the great significance that Lee and his colleagues attached to it. The goal was to produce the final Joint Vision of the company, based on the separate, plant-based visions that the various groups had produced during the previous three months of work.

The only rule governing the May Big One was that *nothing would be included in the final vision statement that wasn't the product of complete consensus*. No idea that failed to generate unanimous support would survive the final cut.

The three-day session consisted of a series of extensive, exhausting, and sometimes heated discussions. By the time the May Big One's participants arrived in Milwaukee, each had worked very hard to articulate his or her deepest feelings about where the company should be going. The process of moving from an individual vision to one that was institutional (either union or management) had heightened the sense of ownership that the participants felt about their articulated visions. These feelings of ownership were strengthened further as the people from each site then worked together to arrive at a *joint* consensus vision (a "site document") for the site as a whole.

The result was that each plant produced its own vision of Harley, and these particular visions—although not worlds apart—were different enough that some substantial brokering was needed to achieve common ground. Naturally enough, some intraplant rivalry also arose, with each plant assuming that its own vision of Harley, so carefully worked over, was the "correct" one.

Often during this process, a participant would demonstrate a natural and expected reluctance to depart from the *particular* site document he or she had struggled to produce. This constituted a very positive signal that the developmental process was already succeeding: people at the May Big One were showing a sense of personal ownership in company matters. Through a continuing dialogue (mirroring the dialogue processes used to date), the meetings brought individual participants from point A ("*my* ideas") through a series of steps ("my *institution's* ideas," "my *site's* ideas") to point B, where the individual's ideas became "my *company's* ideas." This was a rewarding process for all involved, and an outstanding portent for the future.

In some cases, despite the structure that had been provided by the outline, individual plant visions included sections that were too local and specific for inclusion in the companywide document. "We envision Harley-Davidson becoming more involved in community projects and events," read a section of the vision submitted by one group, "including Veteran's Day ceremonies, participation at sports night, and being a corporate season ticket holder of sporting events, with events raffled off to employees." Participants concluded that this vision was not "wrong"—in fact, it was probably "right" for the circumstances of that plant—but it didn't speak to overarching goals and principles.

Even aside from the far-ranging nature of the subject matter, getting 130 people to reach a consensus presented a huge challenge. The participants at the May Big One ranged from the CEO of the company to senior operating and functional leaders to international union officials to local union and management officials to rank-and-file union members who also served on a part-time basis as union stewards and Executive Board members. To complicate things further, groups tended to fracture at different times along different fault lines: by plant, by function, by institutional affiliation, and so on.

LEE: Well before we got to the stage of the signing by the 130 people, we took the union people off by themselves, and we took the management folks off by themselves, and we put it to them: "Listen," we said, "if you've got any unresolved crap among your people about what's going on, we've got to learn about it now, because nobody wants this to pop up at the last minute, and in front of the other party."

Through these informal, off-line discussions, Lee and his fellow process managers identified both areas of apparent agreement and areas of apparent disagreement. To address the areas of disagreement, the ROI team set up the equivalent of congressional "conference committees," designed to broker between management and labor and among locations. Depending on the seriousness of the issue, the members of the "conference committees" could include the most senior managers and labor leaders in the company.

Among the most contentious issues: sourcing and manufacturing in Wisconsin. (Overseas sourcing made up one piece of this; so did the issue of whether or not to move some motorcycle assembly back to Wisconsin. At this time, final assembly was carried out solely at the York, Pennsylvania plant.) Sourcing and the location of manufacturing processes were critically important to the company, and the roster of the relevant "conference committee" reflected that importance: Rich Teerlink, Tom Gelb, the two international union representatives, and the local union presidents.

The sourcing and assembly committee's deliberations went to the eleventh hour, and the group almost failed to reach consensus. At one point, Lee entered the room where these discussions were going on and announced pointedly that everyone else was on their way to dinner. "It's now or never," he said, pushing both sides toward the middle. Shortly thereafter, the two sides settled on a carefully worded sentence: "We seek new product opportunities for Wisconsin facilities as well as for all facilities to manufacture and assemble products in house." The sourcing and assembly committee nearly failed, but at the last minute reached consensus.

LEE: Really, the only problem we had in the Joint Vision Process up to this point concerned the assembly issue. Other than that one tough issue, it came together very rapidly.

And that's what we've come to expect from a healthy organization. If it doesn't happen, in fact, the organization probably has a real big problem. But when it succeeds, as it did at Harley, it provides a wonderful vehicle for asking the question: Well, why do you suppose you needed this intervention to find out that you all agreed on these fundamental issues? You can push back on them, and challenge them to think about how the organization is functioning.

Participants in the invention process also focused on structures, although the topic was considered outside of the Joint Vision Process itself. Drawing on his previous experiences in more than two dozen other joint collaborative efforts, Lee suggested that the assembled management and union leaders consider creating a network of temporary structures to help move the Joint Vision Process forward.

In response to this advice, the participants in the May meeting called for the creation of a Joint Leadership Group (JLG), composed of union and management leaders from all the Wisconsin locations (as well as Rich Teerlink and Tom Gelb), to guide the process. The JLG was defined as the "caretaker of movement toward our vision." It would identify who the "appropriate decision makers are for any given subject." The JLG would also take responsibility for integrating the Joint Vision–related activities across the company and ensure "effective joint communication about our progress toward the vision."

At the same time, the working group called for the development of an infrastructure of Local Site Committees (LSCs) to take primary responsibility for identifying obstacles to change. (The identification of these obstacles, or "barriers," soon emerged as a crucial part of the change process at Harley.) As they worked through these structures, the participants agreed on three guidelines to use for deciding which groups should work on which problems:

- *Problems and issues would be dealt with by the people most directly affected and knowledgeable.* This guideline captured the spirit of the broader effort: to allow and encourage everyone at Harley to take responsibility for the success of the company and not to wait for answers from on high.
- *Only the top-level joint group could identify issues as off limits to the Joint Vision Process.* These included subjects that remained the exclusive province of management (acquisitions, executive compensation, and so on) or were subjects of collective bargaining (wages, benefits, working conditions, and so on). Nothing in the Joint Vision Process, in other words, would undercut fundamental management prerogatives, and nothing would contravene labor's rights as contained in existing local labor agreements.
- *Any joint group could form task forces to do pieces of work within the charter of that joint group.* Again, flexibility and local decision making were central tenets of the effort.

On the last day of the three-day session—May 20, 1988—all participants signed their names to the final document. That document (which was later printed and distributed as a vest pocket–size, twelve-page brochure, with the roster of signatures taking up the last four pages) addressed twelve topics: financial performance; quality; product; customer satisfaction; management effectiveness; union effectiveness; relationships, compensation, and benefits; safety, health, and housekeeping; work environment; and communication. In keeping with the spirit of envisioning the desired company, all statements were cast in the present tense: "we see," "we market," "we pursue," and so on. The only exception came in the preamble to the Joint Vision which, in simple but strong language, explained the purpose of the unusual document:

> The men and women of Harley-Davidson have learned from our turbulent experiences of the '70s and '80s that change is inevitable. To survive and prosper through the next decade and into the 21st century, we must continue to adapt to the changing environment and strengthen our company to excel in the new worldwide competition.
>
> This document was produced by some key union and management employees in the Spring of 1988. It is our vision of the kind of company we want Harley-Davidson to be. As the environment continues to change and new opportunities become apparent, our vision may also have to change.
>
> Today's Harley-Davidson (Summer 1988) does not measure up to this vision. This vision is our road map for change. The components of this vision are all interrelated. As we work to change our company, at times we will focus on selected pieces of the vision. However, we recognize that the total vision must be achieved.

The preceding description of the Joint Vision Process necessarily omits the many small dramas that went into this process of consensus building. Participants made mistakes, and those mistakes were discussed, corrected, and forgiven. During the closing session, for example, a union official asked Executive Vice President of Manufacturing Tom Gelb what would happen if managers under Tom's supervision failed to behave according to the terms of the agreement which was then in the final stages of drafting. "Easy," Tom said, deadpan. "We'll just shoot them!"

Although Tom made his offhand comment in part to demonstrate his real commitment to this risky new process, it was a joke in classic command-and-control mode; in other words, the kind of management response that the Joint Vision Process aimed to eliminate. The union leader might well have wondered if the next shooting victim would be a wayward union leader, perhaps even himself. But in the spirit of the May 1988 meetings, missteps were forgiven, and the group maintained its forward momentum.

Hunting Down Barriers

The next phase of the Joint Vision Process involved a far broader population. Referring back to Lee's "boxes" model, the company's leaders could now share the vision of the desired future (the first box) with that broader population, and invite their reactions and modifications. Meanwhile, the leadership group could work on squaring the Wisconsinwide joint vision with the local site–based visions, to ensure that details in the site-level visions didn't work at cross-purposes with the larger vision.

At the same time, the broader population had to take responsibility for the next challenges: defining "where we are today"(the second box) and the "strategic thrust for change" (the arrow connecting today and tomorrow). The "stair-step" aspect of the model—incremental steps upward on the metaphorical staircase toward the envisioned future—now would become real.

Once again, the ROI team fanned out to the separate Harley facilities. This time, their goal was to help build internal competencies among the union and salaried employees who had volunteered to design and deliver a vision orientation and training program. The ROI team members trained these volunteers in delivering the program content—the Joint Vision Process, techniques for joint problem-solving, and so on. When the orientation and training programs were completed, they were jointly delivered by paired teams of union and management representatives.

Of particular importance in this phase was the task of identifying the barriers to change that were first described at the May Big One. Now the time had come for the Local Site Committees (LSCs) to find them. Such barriers might include a product mix problem, a skewed compensation plan, or an outdated policy—any aspect of the business, in fact, that encouraged people to take *less* responsibility, rather than more. The LSCs identified hundreds of such barriers, ranging from the trivial to the extremely important. The LSCs also took on the tasks of running local problem-solving groups and creating appropriate orientation and training modules, intended to help employees at all levels of the corporation "live" the Joint Vision.

LEE: Reactions were predictably mixed. You could have plotted them on a bell curve. A small number of people thought this was the greatest thing since sliced bread; a whole lot of people thought, "Hmm, interesting, I'll see what happens"; and a small group thought, "No way!"

Meanwhile, of course, design mistakes surfaced, some of which demanded prompt attention. For example: during the first orientation session, which included primarily nonrepresented salaried administrative and technical employees, a salaried supervisor asked an unexpected question. "Rich," he inquired, "exactly who represents people like *me* in this process?"

No one had a good answer. Despite all the hard work invested in the design of the Joint Vision Process, no one had focused on the needs of this particular group of employees. The union and management leaders charged with the joint leadership of the process quickly admitted this oversight. They took steps to restructure the process, providing for more involvement on the part of nonmanagerial salaried employees. Specifically, they created two additional Local Site Committees (LSCs) to represent the Juneau Avenue site's salaried employees.

RICH: We just stepped up to the bar, and said, "Oops—we made a mistake."

LEE: Right. "We screwed up. We should have done it differently, and we didn't."

Ironically, though, this well-intentioned effort to remedy an oversight created new kinds of problems. The Joint Leadership Group (JLG) decided that these two additional LSCs deserved seats at the JLG table (along with all the other LSC representatives). But this addition to the JLG created a numerical imbalance: there were now more nonunion representatives than union representatives on the JLG, a circumstance that the unions didn't appreciate. After some discussion, the JLG decided to merge the two new LSCs into one, as well as to add a member who was also a union member, thus bringing the JLG back into "balance."

The schematic diagram below depicts the "temporary" governance structure of this process:

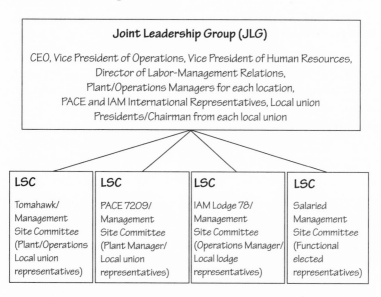

Joint Leadership Group (JLG)			
CEO, Vice President of Operations, Vice President of Human Resources, Director of Labor-Management Relations, Plant/Operations Managers for each location, PACE and IAM International Representatives, Local union Presidents/Chairman from each local union			

LSC	LSC	LSC	LSC
Tomahawk/ Management Site Committee (Plant/Operations Local union representatives)	PACE 7209/ Management Site Committee (Plant Manager/ Local union representatives)	IAM Lodge 78/ Management Site Committee (Operations Manager/ Local lodge representatives)	Salaried Management Site Committee (Functional elected representatives)

RICH: What happened here? Both sides reverted to the traditional view of things. Management said, "Here's the fix." The unions said, "We don't like your fix." One lesson is that old habits die hard. And another is, you really do have to think through all of the implications of everything that you propose to do.

LEE: At the early stages of a change process, appearances can be extraordinarily important, especially to those people who haven't yet been directly involved in that process. So this kind of balance, which stands for fairness, is extremely important.

Around these kinds of problems, the Joint Vision Process gathered momentum, in all three Wisconsin locations. Participants identified hundreds of barriers to progress and in many cases proposed methods to overcome the barriers. A specific barrier was identified: *We don't have enough boring machines.* A possible solution was proposed: *Buy more boring machines!* The proposed solution raised new questions: *Can we . . . should we . . . buy Japanese boring machines?* Sometimes these questions got asked and answered locally; other times, they floated up in the organization and prompted guidance on a policy level. Sometimes policies changed as a result.

Modeling Appropriate Behaviors: The Ops Committee

For many years before the Joint Vision Process began, Harley was organized in a very traditional and hierarchical way. The Executive Committee (which included Rich, Tom Gelb, Vice President of Parts and Accessories Jeff Bleustein, and then–Vice President of Marketing Jim Paterson) made all policy-level decisions. The individuals reporting directly to members of the Executive Committee constituted another group called the "Operations Committee," which was formed to encourage information exchange and to begin involving them in the decision-making process.

When Jim Paterson took over as president of the Motor Company in the spring of 1988, he became an active member of the joint oversight committee for the Joint Vision Process. In addition, he and Rich revived the long-dormant practice of holding "Town Hall" meetings for all employees, to discuss the state of the business, market conditions, and so on. Jim and Rich worked closely with union and management leaders to ensure that the Town Hall meetings touched on issues of genuine interest to employees. All too often, management had failed to disclose useful information to employees, and at the same time disclosed reams of information that employees found useless. The new Town Hall meetings represented a first step toward an over-all communications plan (see chapter 10) that would avoid these two traps, but they were nevertheless still limited in their effectiveness. They occurred only every two or three months, depending on the location. The information shared in this context tended to be delivered by management in a top-down manner. And, although these meetings always included a question-and-answer session, there was a good chance that someone from management would respond to a given question with a stock answer: "Someone will get back to you on that."

In his new role as president of the Motor Company, Jim began to chair the meetings of the Operations Committee. (The majority of that committee's members reported directly to Jim.) Rich and Tom participated in meetings of the Operations Committee when the topics under discussion seemed to call for their participation.

From the inception of the Operations Committee, its role and purpose was very clear. Participants agreed to ground rules that would serve as guidelines for the conduct of meetings. They also agreed to a set of expected behaviors for those present at these meetings.

Despite this advance work, Jim quickly recognized that the Operations Committee wasn't functioning as well as it could. Its members shared information reasonably well, but didn't solve problems together very effectively. Jim reluctantly concluded that the Operations Committee—composed of key leaders on the management side of the Joint Vision Process, who were supposedly key role models for the envisioned organization—was coming up short. Its members weren't performing as effectively as they had when they were working on the Joint Vision Process.

In and of itself, these shortcomings troubled Jim. But they also had profoundly troubling implications for the larger organization. If the key operational leaders on the management side of the house—leaders who knew each other well and communicated regularly with each other—couldn't serve as effective role models, could the members of the larger, geographically dispersed, and more disparate organization do any better?

Jim therefore asked Lee Ozley and Bob Landies (an outside consultant then working on team building and group process issues at York and other Harley locations) to sit in on some Operations Committee meetings and to provide the group with feedback and suggestions for improvement.

After observing a few meetings of the committee, Bob and Lee summarized their observations as follows:

- These meetings worked well for information-sharing purposes. They did *not* work as well, however, for involving people in problem solving and decision making.
- Operating Committee discussions tended to be limited to a reporting function: a member of the group would provide a status report, in response to which colleagues would ask minimal questions for purposes of clarification. There was little true debate.
- Operations Committee members tended to be very passive. When it came to problem solving and decision making, they deferred to Executive Committee members who happened to be present.
- Decisions made by the Operations Committee didn't "stick." Members agreed at the table, but during the next coffee break, small groups gathered in the hallway or lunchroom to complain about either the process or the outcome. "I can't believe they made such a dumb decision," one person might say. "Boy, I can't agree with what just occurred," another might interject. "Did you see how Joe was acting? Terrible!"
- Individuals on the Operations Committee made private appeals to Executive Committee members, in an effort to overturn decisions made by their own committee.
- Individuals on the Operations Committee talked about each other in each other's absence. This amounted to governance by rumor. Members A and B talked about member C in C's absence, attributing motivations to him or her. This led to a large number of what Lee and Bob referred to as "third-party attributions." The third-party attribution problem proved particularly damaging to the conduct of business.

As agreed at the outset, Bob and Lee presented their observations to the Operations Committee. At the end of this presentation, the two consultants also made a series of recommendations about how the committee could address its problems.

First, they said, the committee should employ someone with facilitation training to help its members abide by the guidelines and ground rules laid out when the Operations Committee was created. Thanks to the training programs associated with the Joint Vision Process, a number of Harley employees could step forward to play this role.

Second, committee members had to agree to speak their minds at the table. As a corollary, if they refrained from speaking at the table about a particular subject, they then had to refrain from addressing that topic *away* from the table. "If you don't say it at the meeting," Lee and Bob prescribed, "you can't say it after the meeting."

And, third, committee members had to refrain from third-party attributions. "If someone starts talking to you about somebody else in that person's absence," Lee explained, "you have to ask, 'Well, what did this person say when you talked to *her* about it?' And if the person you're talking to admits that he hasn't actually talked to her directly, you have to say, 'OK then, I can't talk to you about that. Go talk to *her* about it.'"

The Operations Committee took this feedback relatively well. Members made jokes that implied that the suggestions had merit. "We can't agree to that," one member said with a straight face. "Our meetings won't be fun any more!" Another seconded the mock objection: "Wait—you mean we have to begin acting like adults??!!"

The Operations Committee agreed to abide by the three suggestions that Bob and Lee had offered. (The Executive Committee, for its part, also signed up.) A process of informal but extensive coaching began, with Bob and Lee coaching the members of the Operations Committee and with the members of that committee coaching each other. The dysfunctional behaviors that had plagued the committee declined quickly and dramatically. From time to time, individuals reverted to their old (bad) habits, but in most such cases, their colleagues steered them back on track.

Management, in other words, began to *model* appropriate behaviors for the larger organization, which is why this long-ago interlude involving the Operations Committee is still of interest today. Through their actions, these individuals injected new models of behavior into the organization. Over time, people across the enterprise picked up on them and imitated them. Again, no quick fixes or panaceas emerged, but individuals and groups made important progress.

Today, if someone at Harley engages in second-guessing, back-stabbing, or similar behaviors, he or she is likely to be called on it. By and large, people don't put up with these behaviors, which are seen as "outside the culture." As we will emphasize in later chapters, small investments in fixing behaviors can return big payoffs over time.

Negotiating amid Change

Meanwhile, joint groups in all of Harley's Wisconsin locations continued to identify and address barriers to the Joint Vision. They succeeded abundantly—and this abundance gradually became a troublesome issue.

"There were hundreds of barriers," recalls Flip Weber, director of labor-management relations. "But we never got to the point of saying, 'Hey, could this be broken down into ten big categories?' That piece did seem insurmountable."

Slightly less than a year into the Joint Vision Process, Harley and its union had to reopen contract negotiations. (The one-year agreement signed in the spring of 1988 would soon expire.) Several of the management representatives involved in these negotiations suggested that this round of bargaining be conducted in a problem-solving rather than an adversarial mode, and that the skills then acquired by all parties as a result of the Joint Vision Process be called into play.

Leaders on both "sides"—union and management—greeted this suggestion with skepticism. Both sides agreed, however, to conduct an experiment in consensual bargaining. In that spirit, the union representatives framed their demands as "questions." The management representatives came to the table with "problem statements."

The ensuing negotiations proceeded in a substantially different way than in previous rounds. Although they were far from a true problem-solving effort, they resembled consensual bargaining far more than had any previous round of negotiations. The two sides reached a new two-year labor agreement with little acrimony, especially when compared with past negotiations.

A Suspension

So far, we have documented a process of incremental progress: small investments and small payoffs, but with steady progress in the right direction. In other words, the Joint Vision Progress was working as it was supposed to work. In the first year and a half following the inauguration of the Joint Vision Process—roughly from mid-1988 through early 1990—management and union groups at Harley helped to identify and begin to remove barriers to the envisioned future.

Then, early in 1990, this process went off the rails. A key constituency unexpectedly turned away from the joint path, temporarily casting doubt on the potential of the whole process. On February 26, 1990, Flip Weber received a letter from the executive board and bargaining committee of PACE Local Union 7209. The letter requested a "suspension" of the Joint Vision Process. The rationale was as follows:

> The Leadership [of PACE Local 7209] feel that the Process as we know it, is running completely out of control. The "7209" part of the LSC has repeatedly raised some issues over the past 8 months and no one listened. Local Union leaders have problems either in the shop or at the process meetings and no one listens unless it is a Company problem. With these and other issues that the Leadership of Local 7209 see, we came to the conclusion that we can no longer continue to participate in the Process as we know it today.

She immediately contacted Jim Paterson, Rich Teerlink, and other management officials to discuss the implications of this bombshell. Jim formally advised Local 7209 officials of his (and other managers') interest in discussing the union's concerns. A combination of schedule conflicts and other factors (Jim had to undergo a previously scheduled back operation, for example, and then recuperate) delayed a meeting for several months. Meanwhile, Jim, Rich, and other leaders heard reports from salaried and management people. Many of these people also were frustrated with what they perceived as an overall lack of progress. Some of these managers expressed their conviction that the union leadership didn't appear to be fully committed to the nontraditional approach of the Joint Vision Process, and that this "suspension" was evidence of that lack of commitment.

When the meeting finally occurred, in July of 1990, the union leaders took the opportunity to clearly articulate their concerns and spell out the issues that required them to suspend involvement in the Joint Vision Process. They put six specific issues on the table:

- Managers didn't listen and didn't seem to recognize that the "small things" were also important.
- Some in the union suspected that management's real intent was to weaken the union and then push for decertification.
- The Process was causing strife within the union, which would also weaken the union (whether or not that was the intention of management).
- The formation of salaried site groups (which the unions had initially sanctioned) was now perceived as a "union without dues," which was threatening to traditional union prerogatives.
- Union members felt that the structures associated with the Joint Vision Process (the JLG, the LSCs, and so on) were mostly a waste of time, featuring lots of talk about changes, but no action.
- Management was not "waterfalling" its stated commitment through the organization, nor demonstrating that commitment adequately.

The two sides discussed each of these issues in depth, with both sides presenting their respective positions on each. Neither Lee nor any of his ROI colleagues were present at this meeting. As one union official phrased it at the time, "This is a problem within the family, and we need to keep it within the family." Clearly, Lee and his colleagues were still "outsiders" in the eyes of this union group. The Local 7209 leaders then went back to their membership for further consultations. As explained in a July 15, 1990, letter from union president Gerald Knackert to Jim Paterson, the upshot was that the union still wanted a suspension of the Joint Vision Process.

> While we believe we can work with all Harley-Davidson employees, we are not interested in the bureaucracy that the JLG and LSC brought to our organization. . . . The future of our cooperative

efforts to involve our members in the success of the Company will be developed through a more traditional structure.

This reinforced the standing perception of many salaried and management people that the local union leadership wasn't up to the challenge of operating in a nontraditional environment.

LEE: Could the suspension have been avoided? Probably not, at least without the comprehensive training of leaders. And the pressures of business precluded such a comprehensive preparation of leaders. The practical business realities required that everyone "learn as they went along."

Obviously, those of us who had already made a major investment in the Joint Vision Process were greatly disappointed. Making the best of what would otherwise be a bad situation, we (Rich and Lee) decided to look for positive aspects in the larger experience. To our surprise and satisfaction, we discovered that there were quite a few, including the following:

- Union and management officials had learned a great deal more about each other and their respective institutions, such as the dramatically different political systems between the two organizations, the complexities of business economics and so on.
- People could and did work together toward common goals for improvement, even in the absence of a perceived crisis.
- All agreed that neither Harley nor the unions representing its employees could succeed by doing things the "old way."
- Generally speaking, all parties agreed that collaboration and cooperation were better than adversarialism.
- The people of Harley really did want the same things for their future.

Of course, we (Lee and Rich) also tried to identify the shortcomings of the Process as we had conducted it. Again, we found we could draw up a good-sized list:

- We hadn't adequately prepared the leadership of the union or management organizations to lead and support a change of this order of magnitude.
- No one adequately understood or addressed the differences in the respective political processes within the union and management organizations.
- Parallel structures created problems. "We had dual structures: the Joint Vision Process and the traditional management/union structure," recalls Flip Weber. "And Lee told us that wasn't a good thing. We decided that we needed it to be that way, and that was probably a mistake."
- Allowing involvement in the Joint Vision Process to be voluntary, rather than mandatory, created imbalances. Some union and nonunion employee groups were "in the process," and others were "out of the process."
- Conducting the Joint Vision Process orientation and training programs by filling training sessions with volunteers from across the organization, as their workloads would permit on an "as available" basis, rather than by work groups (including union and management leaders of those work groups), led to uneven understanding of and commitment to the concepts and principles of joint cooperation.

Without a doubt, this adds up to a mixed report card for the Joint Vision Process. Collectively, we committed tactical errors that hurt the effort. "Going right to the barriers," says Margaret Crawford, director of training and development and a member of one of the salaried site groups, "was probably a mistake. Maybe focusing on the opportunities would have been a better idea. Maybe the emphasis on 'barriers' ought to come a little farther down on the list."

Collectively, we had failed to keep everyone on board. Our process was imperfect, and implemented imperfectly. We (union and management leaders alike) failed to make the day-to-day realities faced by union and nonunion employees congruent with the vision we had jointly developed.

Nevertheless, we felt that on balance we had made substantial progress. This conviction grew over time, after the initial shock of the suspension wore off. Despite the "suspension," for example, many of the structures and practices initiated during the Process continued to function. Harley's two other unions, moreover, stayed with the Joint Vision Process. The members of these two continuing unions used the Joint Vision Process very effectively until a new and far-reaching "partnership" arrangement replaced it. (See chapter 11.)

"Building relationships takes time," concludes Flip Weber. "It's a very slow process. It doesn't always work the first time. You've got to come at it from a lot of directions."

We should note, too, that Local 7209's concerns about a diminution in the power or size of its membership have proven unfounded. (See table 3-1, below.) In fact, its numbers, as well of those of Harley's other unions, have increased dramatically. And while the union has surrendered none of its traditional rights and responsibilities, it has gained far more control over key aspects of the workplace.

TABLE 3-1: UNION EMPLOYMENT LEVELS: 1988–1998

Location	1988	1998	Change (#)	Change (%)
York	1,184	2,340	+1,156	+98
Milwaukee	646	1,372	+726	+112
Tomahawk	139	236	+97	+70
Kansas City	0	319	+319	NA

An Early Look at Lessons

In the summer of 1991, Rich Teerlink made a brief presentation to the Harley board of directors, summarizing the tentative lessons that he and other company leaders had learned from the Joint Vision Process. Rich saw this as an interesting juncture for taking the pulse of a large-scale change effort: too early to know how things would "turn out," but early enough to know that real mistakes had been made and that real successes had been recorded.

We must be wary of our success, Rich began. We must be aware that change takes time. We have to build commitment, by developing an environment that encourages and rewards learning. We have to remember that, in the beginning at least, process is more important than structure.

And, he continued, we can't just *hope* that people will change eventually. We have to take active steps to *help* them change.

The process of change, he concluded, reflecting on the journey that he and his colleagues had begun years earlier, can be an arduous one, especially if the change leader is unwilling to resort to command and control to make it happen. As Lee had pointed out in their first meeting in 1987, for every two steps forward, there is likely to be a step backward. But that seemed to be the nature of the beast. Harley would live and work with this reality, and even turn it to its advantage.

"The Joint Vision Process wasn't an overwhelming success," concludes former Motor Company President Jim Paterson. "In fact, it was a painful process. We were trying and failing to meet people's expectations. We were thinking that we were at point C when we were really only at point A. We spent a lot of time on hand-holding and on jumping over little hurdles.

"But did it move us in the right direction? Yes. Definitely. It got a lot of people to sign up. It got other people to realize that they couldn't get on board, and persuaded them to get out of the way."

"To me," says Flip Weber, "the Joint Vision Process set the foundation. You could say it wasn't successful, because we didn't get as far as we wanted to take it. But I think of these things as a journey. Any step we take is a step closer to where we want to go."

4

Awareness Expansion
Testing the Commitment

LET'S BACK UP ABOUT SIX MONTHS BEFORE THE SUSPENSION OF the Joint Vision Process, to mid-1989, to begin the story told in this chapter. At that point in time, we felt strongly that we were making progress. On the shop floors, at the negotiating tables, and on other informal meeting grounds, we perceived a subtle but important shift taking place. People at many levels of the organization were starting to take more responsibility. People seemed less inclined to look "up the ladder" for answers; more and more, it seemed, they were helping to shape the questions.

Strangely, though, despite Lee's successful work with the Operations Committee, we had far less confidence that this shift was occurring in the upper ranks of management. After considerable discussion, we concluded that we had to take extra measures to reach this important group.

This chapter tells the story of the first such measure. It recounts an intense and sometimes difficult episode in both the evolution toward a changed Harley and the evolution of the CEO-consultant relationship. On balance, the long-term results of this activity were positive. But there were painful moments when, separately and jointly, we had our doubts.

The Idea

In the summer of 1989, Harley's Executive Committee began discussions about ways to engage the company's key executives in the initiative we were trying to promote. These executives included Wayne Dahl, president of Holiday-Rambler; Bernie Witzak, president of Utilimaster; John Campbell, vice president of human resources; Jim Paterson, the president of the Motor Company; Jeff Bleustein, executive vice president; Tom Gelb, vice president of manufacturing, and Rich. Lee sat in on and occasionally facilitated these meetings.

The group's mandate was to find ways to get the key managers from both Harley-Davidson and Holiday-Rambler (in this chapter, HDMC and HRC, respectively) "on the same page" in terms of continuous learning and also in terms of their absolutely critical role in the change process. This appeared to be a substantial task.

RICH: The fact was, we didn't have a group of intellectually curious people.

LEE: It wasn't exactly "fat, dumb, and happy." It wasn't that bad. But it wasn't all that far away from that, either.

Rich and Lee had identified a central challenge during Lee's first visit to Milwaukee. How could Rich (with help from Lee and others) create opportunities for learning, without resorting to the kind of command-and-control authority that he felt was counterproductive? After wrestling with this paradox for a while, Rich decided that, at least up to a point, leadership involved *creating opportunities*. He therefore felt free to convene the first session and (with guidance from the Executive Committee, Lee, and other outside resources) to decide what subjects would be covered. Subsequent sessions, if any, could be convened and scripted by the participants themselves.

And so, on a Tuesday evening early in October 1989, fifty-five executives converged on a Marriott hotel in the Chicago suburb of Lincolnshire, a location halfway between both divisions' home bases, allowing people from both locations to drive to the site. In addition, the hotel had enough elbow room for the activities we had planned. And, finally, the nearby golf course would give us the opportunity to relax between working sessions.

The executives had been told that they would be attending something called an "Awareness Expansion" session. This event would last from Tuesday night through Friday morning and would require casual clothes. We suspected that the phrase "awareness expansion" would provoke some interesting discussions between husbands and wives on that preceding Monday night, as the executives were packing their bags for who-knows-what. We decided, though, that getting people's curiosity aroused would be a good idea and might help the sessions be more productive.

HDMC and HRC were substantially separate organizations. (See the organization chart below.) Because their businesses were very different (HDMC made motorcycles, and HRC made large recreational vehicles) there so far had been little reason to assemble all their executives for working sessions. In fact, this was the first time that all top HDMC and HRC executives would be coming together in a working session.

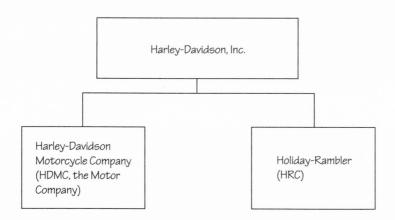

Just among ourselves, we confessed to having a few reservations. The HRC representatives were from Amish country in Indiana, a nonunion setting in which people saw themselves as pretty different from their HDMC counterparts in urban and unionized Milwaukee. At the same time, the HDMC managers would bring their own complications, in part because of the company's highly visible successes in the motorcycle business. As one concerned member of our planning team phrased it one day, "So exactly how are we going to keep these arrogant Harley know-it-alls from blowing away the Holiday-Rambler people?"

The answer, it seemed, lay in the design of the experience. Lee and his Virginia-based colleagues, working in conjunction with Holiday-Rambler's consultant Dick Axelrod, wanted to create a series of interactive and experiential learning activities that would put the company's key leaders into challenging situations with peers outside their respective functional areas. We planned to intersperse these activities with presentations by provocative scholars and practitioners of management. The design had grown iteratively out of discussions with the Executive Committee, which was particularly interested in presentations that would stimulate debate, shared learning, and organizational cohesion.

The outside presenters were a distinguished group. Ed Lawler, for example, was a nationally respected authority on the subject of large-scale organizational change. James Brian Quinn, author of numerous books and articles on managing innovation (through what he called "controlled chaos") would push us to think about the core functions of an organization. Jerre Stead, then the CEO of electrical equipment manufacturer Square D, Inc., agreed to challenge us by talking about his experiences in a successful and celebrated "learning organization."

At the Wednesday morning welcoming session, Rich explained that the purpose of the meeting was to "expand awareness of senior management of Harley-Davidson and Holiday-Rambler." The group's objectives, he continued, were to

- provide insights and concepts to assist senior management in leading their organizations more effectively.
- demonstrate continuous learning as a way of life.
- get better acquainted.
- exchange ideas and information.
- elicit ideas for the content and process of future sessions.
- have fun.

We soon learned that these objectives added up to a daunting assignment. We knew we expected a great deal from our participants, but we didn't realize how much.

Fun with Tinker Toys

We felt we should prove fairly quickly that having fun would be a core part of the experience. In that spirit, and also to initiate the larger purpose of continuous learning, Lee and his colleagues decided that Wednesday morning's activities would include a creative reuse of an old toy: Tinker Toys.

The Executive Committee, with help from Lee, divided the participants into five-member teams, which consisted of purposeful mixes of HDMC and HRC employees. From among its membership, each team had to identify two "designers," two "builders," and a "salesperson." Their collective job was to draw on a fixed inventory of parts (spindles, spools, and so on) to design, build, and "sell" a Tinker Toy bridge that could support a four-pound brick in the middle of its span.

LEE: We were prepared to be told that this was dumb. We were even prepared to admit that it might be dumb—but that it was worth an investment of time on their part. As it turned out, people jumped right into it.

The Tinker Toy exercise was, in effect, a pared-down simulation of what manufacturing companies are supposed to do every day. And just to keep "teamwork" in the front of the minds of our participants, we imposed a number of arbitrary rules on them. For example, we told the builders that they could use only one hand in putting their inventions together. This meant that, to be successful, the builders had to convey that message to the designers, and the designers had to take that constraint into account.

All of the "construction sites" were set up in the same room, so that each team could see what its competitors were doing, using exactly the same materials. This created ample opportunities for "industrial espionage" but also illustrated how quickly a powerful idea could spread across an "industry." One group, for example, was having trouble getting a particular spindle to go into a spool using only one hand.

A team member discovered that dipping the end of the spindle into a glass of water made it slide easily into the hole in the spool. This discovery, and others like it, flashed around the room with amazing speed.

LEE: One sidelight: After the exercise was over, my colleagues and I had to take these bridges apart so that we could put the pieces back in the boxes. But the wet spindles had swollen up so much that there was no way to get them out of the spools.

The teams worked on their bridges right up to the deadline, at which point the "sales presentations" began. The "clients" who listened to these presentations were senior people from both HDMC and HRC, and the sales pitches ranged from the earnest to the mock sleazy. (One salesman let it be known that there were cases of scotch in the trunk of his car for those clients who made the "right" choice.)

The Tinker Toy exercise turned out to be an effective icebreaker. And, although the simulation was far from a true-life representation of a real work experience, the participants seemed to enjoy talking among themselves about the significance of the experience. What did it mean? Was there some lesson to be extracted from it?

From Fun to Work, and Back

The next activity had a more serious intent. With guidance from the Executive Committee, Lee and his colleagues regrouped the participants into new six-person teams. All participants met for a plenary session, at which guest speaker James Brian Quinn made a presentation. Quinn presented a forceful, even extreme, version of his idea that most functions of most corporations could be outsourced successfully. If this was true, Quinn asked rhetorically, what was a "corporation," anyway? What was its purpose?

Then Quinn circulated from small group to small group, answering questions that the group posed to him. While they waited for

Quinn's arrival, the groups were supposed to prepare questions and comments with which to challenge Quinn and each other.

Rich and Lee moved from group to group along with the speakers. At this juncture, though, things started to go slightly awry. Rich began to get signals that the Awareness Expansion might not provide the payoff he had been hoping for. He had hoped to hear energetic back-and-forths among the participants and between the participants and the experts. At the very least, he had hoped to hear some expressions of interest in the ideas that were being floated. But, by and large, that wasn't happening.

RICH: I wasn't hearing anybody asking Brian, for example, how you could possibly outsource something as fundamental as product design. He had made what some people would surely consider to be an outrageous proposal—and yet no one was saying "boo" in response.

LEE: You'd hear folks saying, "Hmm. Interesting. Might be right for some folks, but of course it doesn't apply to us."

Although some storm-warning flags were now flying, we forged ahead to the next stage of our plan. Once again, we divided the participants into new groups, designed to be diverse in terms of both functional orientation and base of expertise. Each group accepted the responsibility of preparing a three- to five-minute skit acting out a real-life scenario in which an HDMC or HRC manager might find himself or herself. The topics, ceremoniously drawn out of a hat at lunchtime, had been developed by senior managers at both organizations. They included, for example,

- dealing with a dissatisfied customer.
- responding to an employee's suggestion for an improvement.
- justifying a capital expense overrun.
- conducting an employee appraisal interview.
- responding to a sexual harassment complaint.

Once again, all groups got the same inventory to draw upon: in this case, things like wigs, makeup, and other theatrical props. And once again we imposed a constraint on the participants. This time, we asked them to do their job *as badly as possible.* In other words, they were to demonstrate the *worst possible way* a manager could carry out the assigned task.

During a golf "scramble" in the early afternoon, the teams pulled together their respective skits, which they presented to the entire group that evening. Not too surprisingly, the skits made their points by appropriating one or more recognizable HDMC and HRC "organizational character traits" and then exaggerating them wildly. We had already talked among ourselves about the perils of arrogance in an organization that had (as the popular press tended to phrase it) "beaten the Japanese." Now we could see that, at least to some extent, our colleagues also understood that problem. In one skit, a trio of particularly obtuse Cone Heads (managers) rejected a series of thoughtful work process improvements proposed by a delegation of skilled craftsmen. A blundering, self-important human resources manager conducted an abysmal performance review of an employee with some very complicated problems.

We had rented an old-fashioned applause meter to gauge audience reaction to the various skits. Based on the meter readings, Rich awarded honey-baked hams to the members of the best team and ham bones to the members of the worst team—although we had to remind ourselves that, in this case, "best" was truly worst.

Once again, the experiential learning proved enjoyable and promoted a high level of camaraderie among the participating managers. But once again the serious sessions that followed the fun proved less than satisfying—particularly to Rich, who was emerging as Awareness Expansion's toughest critic.

Participants were asked to reflect on the possible lessons that might be gleaned from the speakers to whom they were being exposed. What had they learned that had surprised them? Which lessons might they be able to take back to work and apply productively?

Once again, these kinds of questions went unanswered. At least to Rich's ear, Thursday's small group discussions were flat and unadventurous. People had energetic and positive responses to the skits, but the discussions of the speakers' presentations were flat, uninspired, and one-dimensional. Rich became increasingly impatient with what he was hearing.

RICH: The question I kept hearing was "Okay, so what do you want us to do?" And I kept saying to myself, "That's the question that I'm trying not to answer."

From Unhappiness to Commitment

At around 10:00 P.M. on that Thursday, Ed Lawler sought out Lee to give him a heads-up. In formal terms, Ed was only a distinguished guest at Awareness Expansion. But he had steered Harley toward Lee in the first place, had been a participant in the first phase of this event, and felt some responsibility for its success. Ed knew that, during the preceding hours, Lee had been intensely focused on coordinating the work of his colleagues and probably hadn't been keeping track of the bigger picture. That picture wasn't good, in Ed's estimation: Rich was unhappy.

Lee called a quick huddle with Rich, who explained the source of his dissatisfaction. Once again, Rich said, he didn't see much evidence of people trying to think in new ways. Instead, he saw the effects of many years' reliance on top-down, command-and-control management. People were accustomed to getting the answers from on high, and these habits appeared to be very difficult to break.

RICH: I was frustrated because I had expectations of new learning. Not that it was going to change anything overnight, but that we were going to start to click in people's heads, and they might start to say, "Aha! There might be something to this kind of change!"

Were my expectations unrealistic? In retrospect, probably yes—because I'd spent much more time tussling with these ideas than others had. But I had caught glimpses here and there of a new way of managing an organization—even a different way of looking at the world—and I urgently hoped that others would see the same thing.

After a brief discussion, Lee and Rich agreed that Rich should share his frustrations with the entire group on the following morning. "When all else fails," we reminded ourselves, "tell the truth." This was a catch phrase that Rich and Lee had started to use which had grown out of their frustration with corporate tendencies to obfuscate and apply spin control. When you're up against it, give your audience the unvarnished truth.

The next morning, Rich presented a series of overheads to the participants. Uncharacteristically for Rich, he stuck closely to the language of the prepared materials. Those in the room who knew him well understood that he was working hard to control his frustration. "Participation is an important element of Harley-Davidson's long-term success," he began, "and must be so recognized by the operating units.

> We are not going fast enough. We seem to fear employee reactions if we make a mistake and have to adjust or change. I have confidence that employees will understand.
>
> We have too much bureaucracy, which prevents involvement.
>
> We aren't effectively communicating that this is the way we are going to run this business. Everyone must understand that this is how we're going to run the business. It won't be the same everywhere, but the basics will be the same.
>
> We are throwing people and money at our problems, rather than applying the intelligence of those who are currently doing the job. Managers still feel that they are the only ones smart enough to identify the problems. This attitude concerns me, because it undermines our efforts to empower all employees.

"Up to now," he concluded, "our approach has been evolutionary. The time has come for a revolution, and one led by the *managers* at this meeting. And be clear on one thing: I am *not* going to lead the revolution!"

LEE: I was in the back, watching the group, and observing their reactions after Rich finished. And the most common reaction was, "Well, looks like we screwed up. We let Rich down." Or worse— "Uh, oh! Daddy's mad at us!" And that only made the car ride back to the airport worse.

On their way to O'Hare, Lee and Rich agreed not to engage in faultfinding or recriminations, although Lee ventured to say that Rich's remarks might have been made by General Patton—a comment that Rich didn't much appreciate. A cooling-off period seemed like a good idea. They set a time to meet toward the end of the following week and went their separate ways.

After a gloomy weekend, Lee called his Virginia-based colleagues together for a post mortem. They focused on figuring out what could have been done better and, more importantly, what should be done next. Among the options that they seriously considered was resigning the account. This alternative gained momentum as the post mortem proceeded. Lee and his colleagues concluded that they had done their job as well as they knew how. If that wasn't good enough, how could they justify continuing?

LEE: Don't forget that I'd been doing this sort of stuff for more than three decades. I'd learned that these crises happen. They're in the very nature of the beast. You can't predict them, and you can't necessarily avoid them. All you can do is work through them.

But knowing all that doesn't make you feel any better when things do go wrong!

Rich, meanwhile, arrived at his Juneau Avenue office on Monday morning and soon perceived a low level of tension in the air. After several hours, a colleague finally came into his office and gave him some honest feedback: "You know what you did, Rich? You got up there and stuck a pin in our balloon. We felt we were learning something, and you told us that we weren't." After all, these executives had opened themselves up to something new and felt they had "played by the rules"—only to learn that the boss was very disappointed with the sessions.

Rich was dismayed; this wasn't what he had intended with his candid comments. He decided to circulate a copy of those comments to everybody who had attended the session. His purpose in circulating the notes (as he explained in a cover memo) was to make it perfectly clear what he had said and what he had *not* said. If he had said something that was inaccurate, or overstated, people should feel free to say so. In fact, he earnestly hoped that the dialogue would continue.

RICH: There was no reaction. Nothing. And that, too, was discouraging.

When Rich and Lee got back together in Milwaukee, a week after the end of the Awareness Expansion session, both of them were still struggling with their thoughts and emotions. Each felt inclined to take all the blame for what he saw as a failure. Rich blamed himself for giving his speech. Lee blamed himself for not anticipating and heading off the kinds of problems that had so frustrated Rich. Each spent a lot of time letting the other one off the hook.

Over the next few hours, the two commiserated, engaged in ghoulish scenarios about the "efficient" ways they could solve their problems ("Are there bullets that don't hurt?" Rich asked at one point), and talked about how Awareness Expansion fit into the larger change process. Should they call the whole thing off? Should they jump back in with all four feet?

Gradually, they reached a shared conclusion: They were on an important journey—together. Neither was the kind of person who would write something on a wall in big letters, but each believed deeply that he was engaged in something of great importance to a particular human organization (and maybe even to other organizations). Yes, they were quite capable of making mistakes, alone or in combination. And yes, sometimes they charted a course that involved taking two steps backward for every step forward.

But it was the *combination* of their skills, and the opportunity for blunt, no-holds-barred discussion, that would make the journey possible. Up to this point, Lee and Rich had left these sorts of things mostly unsaid. Now these ideas were getting on the table, explicitly, and both felt reaffirmed by this candid expression of commitment to the larger process and to each other. No, Rich wouldn't throw in the towel, and Lee wouldn't quit. They would push on together and do a little better the next time out. Or, preferably, a *lot* better.

In a ceremonial gesture of commitment, both got out their date books and started looking for a good time to schedule Awareness Expansion II.

LEE: Regardless of whether Rich or I was pleased or not with it, Awareness Expansion was a watershed event, because it broke the egg open a little. It cracked the shell of the egg, if you will. And it changed our relationship. Rich said, "If this is going to work, you're going to have to get more deeply involved. You're going to need to know a lot more about what's going on." From that point on, we started talking about things that, quite frankly, sometimes I wished I didn't know. So it was a watershed event. It was like we had been going together for ten months, and we were finally deciding that this was serious.

RICH: Organizational change doesn't happen like a thunderstorm which—after lots of thunder, lightning, and rain—is then completely done. In fact, abrupt changes frequently do more harm than good. With organizational change, the effects take longer to emerge. It's more like a gentle rain that is absorbed into the ground and later produces beautiful flowers. You have to be patient.

Yet here I am—a guy who's talking about "revolutions." I want it done now. That's always been a tension for me in organizational life, and sometimes it gets me into trouble.

At Harley, we had some long gentle rains—the Joint Vision, the beginning of what would eventually be called the Business Process, and now Awareness Expansion—but the flowers had not yet blossomed.

We should forewarn you at this point. The episode just recounted included some relatively intense and emotional moments, at least by the standards of organizational life. Subsequent chapters of this book focus less on interpersonal drama and more on *process*. This reduction in the emotional quotient may frustrate those of you who want more examples of "high highs" and "low lows," but it accurately represents how our journey together took shape. In the wake of Awareness Expansion I (as it later came to be called), we agreed to act like partners—toward each other, and toward our colleagues. We succeeded in that assignment, for the most part. As a result, we were able to respond to subsequent challenges far more effectively. And, more important, we had many more colleagues helping us find good solutions.

5

The Business Process

Awareness Expansion took place in a rapidly changing context. The Joint Vision Process that began in the spring of 1988 sparked a brushfire of change. What happens when you invite people across a complicated and tradition-rich organization to look for "barriers to change"? Most likely, they start finding those barriers—and in large numbers.

Some barriers are removed easily; others seem immovable. Inevitably, some people involved in the Joint Vision Process became frustrated. Some felt that things weren't moving fast enough. This was particularly true for some managers, who suspected the unions were dragging their feet. At the same time, many union employees felt that the Joint Vision Process was overly bureaucratic and that management was using the process to undermine the legitimate role of organized labor. The hunt for barriers raised questions of both *pace* and *process*, with the result being Local 7209's request for the suspension of the Joint Vision Process in 1991.

The suspension gives us an opportunity to depart from our chronological narrative and present the first in a series of thematically organized chapters. The risk in this approach is that the reader may lose the thread of the narrative or may not feel the sense of forward momentum at Harley that we are trying to convey. But our content now calls for a new approach. In most of the remaining chapters, we will trace a key theme forward from the late 1980s through to the recent past.

In the 1988–1991 time period, the Awareness Expansion sessions, the Joint Vision Process, the beginnings of organizational learning, and related initiatives released *energy*. Those who had been pushing for this kind of organizational shake-up (Rich, Lee, and others) realized that they needed to invent structures for channeling this energy in productive directions.

The most important of these channeling devices, in retrospect, was the "Business Process." This is a complex structure that today helps define much about the way Harley does business. It is shown in its entirety in the figure that follows.

In this chapter, we will discuss the top three tiers of this schematic—the corporate "Umbrella," the operating unit, and the work unit ("My Area")—in the order in which they were invented: operating unit issues, the Umbrella, and work unit considerations. In chapter 6, we will complete this discussion with an in-depth look at the Performance Effectiveness Process (PEP), which ties the individual's efforts into the work unit, the operating unit, and the corporation as a whole.

RICH: The real value of the Business Process is that it provides an understandable framework for dialogue within the organization. It ensures that everybody has the appropriate level of information, as defined by them, to allow them to do their job to serve the organization. That's what it's all about.

As you've no doubt already guessed, terminology was a problem, at least at first. "There was a lot of confusion about the 'Joint Vision Process' and the 'Business Process,'" recalls former Motor Company President Jim Paterson. "In terms of a visible and concrete program, the Joint Vision Process came first, starting in March of '88. And although pieces of the Business Process were in place before that, the 'Business Process' as such didn't really get a public face until late '88 or '89. So terminology sometimes got in the way."

The roots of the Business Process actually predated the Joint Vision

Business Process

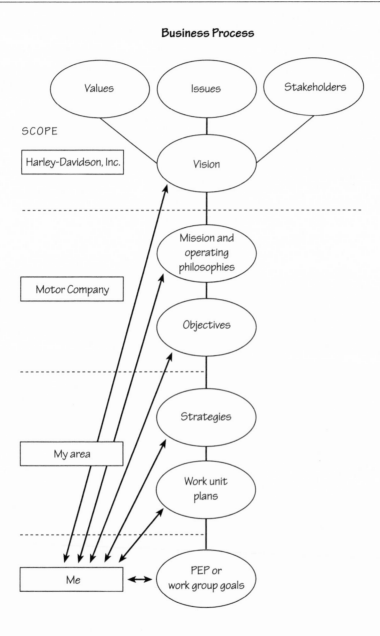

Process. And although the Joint Vision Process was suspended and later was transformed into other structures, the Business Process emerged as an enduring tool in the larger reorientation of the company—away from command and control and toward shared responsibility.

One reason why the Business Process assumed great importance to Harley was that, in the late 1980s and early 1990s, the company had precious few management resources and processes in place. Tim Savino joined Harley's human resources (HR) department in April of 1990, after six years with Bell Labs in Chicago. It was, Savino recalls, a severe culture shock:

> Remember that Harley had been through tough times. There had been 40 percent layoffs. So there was almost nobody *here*. The technical ranks were very thin. Except for Margaret Crawford, there was no HR staff to speak of—they had two contract recruiters at the time, a handful of administrators, and nobody who was skilled in employee relations. In fact, *everything* was thin. I remember standing at a bulletin board, trying to figure out who was *in* this organization. There were no org charts. There was no documentation. There was no new employee orientation. I mean, I came out of AT&T, and there we had a six-week orientation!
>
> On one of my first days at work, a guy came up to me in a hallway and said, "I saw you talking to Jeff Bleustein," who at the time was VP of parts and accessories. And I said, honestly, "Who's Jeff Bleustein?" There simply weren't any clues. The phone directory was a single eight-and-a-half-by-eleven sheet. All it gave you was a last name and an extension. You were simply supposed to know who did what.
>
> What I'm describing is an organization that was relationship-centered, and didn't value discipline. The Business Process was the first effort to instill some discipline and logic in the organization. Before that, Harley really didn't *have* any discipline.

Because we believe that the Business Process has proven to be of real value to Harley, we will recount its development in some detail. The chronology is somewhat confusing, because different pieces of the larger process developed independently and only came together into a coherent whole after several years of invention and reworking. And, as was typical for many innovations from this period—especially those that had Rich as a primary sponsor—the components of what became the Business Process were introduced, discussed with the affected parties, redefined, and then allowed to "percolate" (Rich's word). Nothing happened faster than it "wanted" to happen.

From Mission to Strategies

Leadership changes also affected this process. In March 1987, Rich became president of the Motor Company, where he launched the Joint Vision Process and other initiatives. His responsibilities at the Motor Company soon persuaded him that Harley needed a more systematic approach to business planning.

In a cover note prepared for the December 1987 board of directors meeting, Rich wrote, "This is really the first formal approach to strategic planning that has occurred at the new Harley-Davidson." Attached was a three-year plan that included a mission statement, operating philosophy, and selected strategies.

Although he didn't know it at the time, this approach was destined to become the foundation of the Business Process. The piece of the schematic depicting this first step in the larger evolution looks like this:

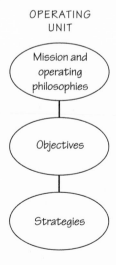

OPERATING
UNIT

Mission and operating philosophies

Objectives

Strategies

Each element of this schematic can also serve as the answer to a question:

- Why do we exist? (*mission and operating philosophies*)
- How do we measure success? (*objectives*)
- What must we do? (*strategies*)

We will review each of these in order.

Mission: Why Do We Exist?

In his December 1987 board presentation, Rich described what the Executive Committee had developed for the Motorcycle Division's mission:

Through continuous improvement in organizational and business planning and in work practices, we will strive:

- To increase our customer's satisfaction and thereby our market competitiveness within the large-displacement pleasure motorcycle and related product lines
- To strengthen our ability to diversify our business through

    - Extensions of our existing products and/or markets
    - Development of contract manufacturing

Through this approach, we will:

- Improve job security for all our employees
- Provide appropriate rates of return to maintain the health and growth of the business, and
- Achieve mutually beneficial relationships with our various constituencies.

Rich explained that the Executive Committee had also generated a number of statements about operating philosophies (considered a coequal with the mission statement) which comprised issues such as business emphasis, customer service, dealer/distributor relations, employee relations, supplier relations, and financial goals.

By the time Rich and his colleagues prepared the company's 1991 strategic plan, they had the benefit of a sustained exploration of *values*, *issues*, and *stakeholders* (see the subsequent "Umbrella" section). As a result, they restated the mission as follows:

- Preserve and perpetuate the Harley-Davidson institution through continuous improvement in the quality of our goods and services, and achievement of our financial goals.
- Provide motorcycles, accessories, and services to motorcycles in selected niches.
- Provide the general public brand-identified products/services to enhance Harley-Davidson's image and attract new customers.

 - Engage in manufacturing or service ventures that can add value (not only profit) to the motorcycle business.

Some of the changes between 1987 and 1991 reflect the fact that several key concepts "migrated" out of the corporate mission statement into other documents (again, described in a subsequent section). Others reflect a general refinement of thinking in the intervening three years. But the changes are less significant than the continuities. Absent significant changes in the operating environment, technological advances, government regulation, economic dislocation, or a legitimate and substantive change in how the business was viewed by the company, Harley's mission would not change.

At the same time, Rich and his colleagues placed a great value on flexibility. When Harley began designing a learning module on the subject of mission in 1995, for example, the company's senior managers began to feel a significant level of discomfort with the mission statement. The existing statement, they argued, was too constraining and ignored a key aspect of Harley's business and culture: giving people opportunities for fun and pleasure. A new mission statement, rolled out at a management meeting in February 1999, read as follows:

We fulfill dreams through the experiences of motorcycling—by providing to motorcyclists and to the general public an expanding line of motorcycles, branded products, and services in selected market segments.

The new mission statement recognized, in effect, that "making smiles" had been a major element in Harley's success, and therefore was an important piece of the institutional mission.

Of course, Harley wasn't the only company worrying about "mission" during the 1980s and 1990s. Many companies in this period sought ways to provide clarity of purpose to their employees. At times, in fact, we debated whether Harley should adopt a different terminology to emphasize that the company wasn't just signing up with yet another corporate fad. Ultimately, we decided that we should use the common terminology and at the same time keep stressing that this was part of a larger effort to help people ask and answer two key questions:

1. Where are we going?
2. How can I help?

Objectives: How Do We Measure Success?

"Objectives" were a subset of the package that Rich presented to the board in his December 1987 presentation. Rich and his Executive Committee colleagues had developed these objectives through a series of management discussions, and the result was similar to what one might have found at a number of corporations at that time: fairly general, with a principal focus on financial factors.

By 1991, the Executive Committee was thinking about objectives differently. It had concluded that Harley's objectives should cover a five- to ten-year time frame and comprise more than simply financial factors. The risk in focusing solely on financial objectives, the committee felt strongly, was that the needs of one stakeholder group (the investors) could quickly dominate. In addition, the committee felt, financial results represented the far end of a complex calculation: the efforts put forth by all people at all levels in the organization, every day, to deliver on the company's mission.

The Executive Committee also argued for more specificity (in terms of both timing and goals) than had been the case previously. A new objective added in 1991 reflected this new emphasis: "Develop the global market potential of 100,000 units by December 31, 1996, and develop the capacity to meet that demand while continuously improving quality." In December 1994, a new manufacturing plan was presented to the Board of Directors: the capacity objective was increased to 200,000 units by the year 2003.

The Executive Committee also suggested that no operating unit within Harley adopt more than five objectives. It encouraged all such units to establish objectives that were specific to their operation and at the same time would contribute to accomplishing the objectives set for the total organization.

RICH: If the operating unit leader's efforts wind up with that work group's adopting 73 objectives, then that's a failure of leadership. You can't go in 73 directions at once.

Strategies: What Must We Do?

Operating units are guided in general terms by objectives and in specific terms by strategic plans. At Harley (and many other companies) objectives are based on a five- to ten-year time horizon, whereas strategic plans are based on a three- to five-year time horizon. In most cases, changes in objectives call forth corresponding changes in strategies.

The 1991 objective described above—developing the capacity to deliver 100,000 units by December 31, 1996—definitely called for a new strategy. This time, the leadership of all Harley plants determined how this objective would be met. This discussion led to an integrated manufacturing strategy that the plant leadership presented to the Board of Directors in 1992.

The following year, Harley began a longer-term planning process, which resulted in "Plan 2003," the new manufacturing plan that was presented to the board in December 1994. On a rolling basis, this plan has served as the foundation for all strategic planning since that date.

Building the Umbrella

When Rich became chief executive officer in August 1988, his authority now extended to the entire corporate enterprise and therefore included Indiana-based Holiday-Rambler, the manufacturer of recreational vehicles and various other products that came into the Harley fold in 1986. As a result of that acquisition, two companies of approximately $350 million in revenue each were joined together. For the first time in Harley's history, large and substantially different businesses coexisted under the same corporate "roof," and Rich decided that Harley needed new mechanisms to help these businesses work together effectively.

In other words, he perceived the need to tie together the organization on the level of *values*, *philosophies*, and *vision*.

RICH: Now I'm looking at two different businesses, and the newer business had a whole range of activities of its own: a company that produced trailers, a kitchen cabinet company, an injection-molding company, and so on. If we wanted to integrate these companies under one grouping—Harley-Davidson, Inc.—we had to identify our values, constituents, key measures, and so on. We didn't want different values popping up in different parts of the organization.

There was certainly lots of progress associated with the Joint Vision Process. But that was an initiative within only a piece of the larger Motor Company. Now there was a larger context, with different challenges.

Rich therefore initiated a series of brainstorming sessions in 1988 at the Juneau Avenue headquarters facility. Participants at most of these sessions included the members of the Executive Committee: Rich Teerlink, chairman; Jeff Bleustein; John Campbell; Wayne Dahl; Tom Gelb; Jim Paterson; and Bernie Witzak. This group included high-ranking managers from both the Motor Company and Holiday-Rambler.

Rich led these discussions, the focus of which could be summarized as follows:

- How will we behave in our interactions with others?
- What is truly important to Harley-Davidson?
- Whom does Harley-Davidson serve?
- How will we describe success in the future?

To sidestep the trap of endless wordsmithing, the group agreed on the following one-word "signposts":

- How will we behave in our interactions with others?
  Values

- What is truly important to Harley-Davidson?
  Issues

- Whom does Harley-Davidson serve?
  Stakeholders

- How will we describe success in the future?
  Vision

We will discuss each of these signposts in the order that Harley's leaders tackled them.

Values: Determining Our Interactions with Others

The Executive Committee found it difficult to reach agreement on a concise statement of a set of values summarizing what Harley stood for as a company. It was tempted to include more words, rather than fewer; but wisely recognized that long lists of values (many of which sound similar) quickly lose their impact.

At one point during this discussion, Rich recalled a presentation he had seen by an ethics professor, Dr. Alex Horniman, a faculty member at the University of Virginia's Darden School. Horniman had presented a short list of values, succinctly stated, that seem to suit the purposes of many different kinds of businesses:

- Tell the truth.
- Be fair.
- Keep your promises.
- Respect the individual.

Ultimately, the Executive Committee adopted this list for provisional use by Harley. But reflecting the goal of the larger change process that Rich advocated, the Executive Committee added a fifth value:

- Encourage intellectual curiosity.

This fifth point struck the group as an essential guidepost for the kind of company Harley sought to become.

RICH: Embracing these five imperatives was a step forward for us, although many of the words sound like the words that get used at other companies. Rather than starting with a high-flying statement of a "vision," and then moving on to values, we started with values. What do we value, in this company? It forces you to think very differently.

Issues: Determining What's Important for Harley

With Rich's strong guidance, the Executive Committee next focused on five issues that Harley would have to address consistently and well, if it was to become the kind of company it was envisioning:

- *Quality.* In the company's recent near-death experience, poor quality had created Harley's vulnerability and enabled competitors to get a foothold in the U.S. market. No one doubted the importance of quality.

- *Participation.* Good ideas and strenuous efforts had pulled Harley through its recent hard times; this kind of joint effort now had to grow exponentially.
- *Productivity.* The realities of the competitive marketplace spoke loudly and underscored the importance of eliminating nonvalue-added activities that increased Harley's costs without improving customer satisfaction.
- *Flexibility.* The rapidly changing international operating environment compelled the company to develop new systems that could respond to challenges and opportunities quickly and easily.
- *Cash flow.* Harley had only recently escaped the heavy hand of its bankers; it did not want to go back to a dependent status. The company had to generate the cash flow required to sustain the business, or it would again lose control of its fate.

Stakeholders: Whom Harley Serves

With values and issues defined, the group next tackled the question of stakeholders. Rich, somewhat provocatively, defined a stakeholder as "anyone who can put us out of business." The group argued instead for a definition of "anyone inside or outside the company who has an interaction with Harley's products, services, or representatives."

Rich agreed with this more positive definition and then began listing those groups whom he thought it comprised. His list began with the most obvious stakeholder: the *customer.* To serve the customer, Rich asserted, the company also had to serve other constituencies. And, depending on how specific the list became, it could be an almost-endless accounting.

At the end of this discussion, the committee agreed on six key stakeholders:

1. Customers
2. Employees
3. Suppliers
4. Shareholders
5. Government
6. Society

The Executive Committee recognized the difficulty of paying attention simultaneously to a diverse set of stakeholders, all of whom have their own motives in their relations with the company. But the fact was that each of these key stakeholders could influence the company's future considerably—for better or for worse. By definition, Harley had to attend carefully to the needs of *all* stakeholders, even when that created conflicting tugs on the organization.

In part because of the "near-death" experience of the 1980s, Harley always retained some focus on stakeholders (although different terminology was used at different times). The 1989 annual report, for example, quoted Harvard Business School Professor Rosabeth Moss Kanter to the effect that "service to all publics . . . is the principal reason for being in business. Evidence suggests that this orientation enhances long-term economic value." The goal now, however, was to push the stakeholder concept front and center.

The stakeholder concept was and is open to refinement and revision. In 1994, for example, Rich began making the argument that *shareholder* was too narrow a term to encompass all of those who backed Harley with money and other assets. As a result, *investors* was substituted for *shareholders* on the list of key Harley stakeholders.

Vision: How Harley Will Define Success in the Future

The definitions and decisions described in the previous three sections (values, issues, and stakeholders) were, in a sense, a preamble and prerequisite to what came next: a definition of the company's vision. Rich suggested that his colleagues agree on a "vision" of the company, a vision that would represent the collective view of senior management. In response, they arrived at several key ideas that would have to be included in any vision statement about Harley. These included

- the importance of relationships.
- the imperative for action.
- the international nature of the company's future markets.

They then combined these ideas into a sentence that captured most of the ideas they had laid out up to that point:

Harley-Davidson is an action-oriented, international company—a leader in its commitment to continuously improve the quality of profitable relationships with stakeholders (customers, employees, suppliers, shareholders, governments, and society).

This statement was an adequate description of what the committee thought Harley should be in the future. But committee members were concerned that it didn't quite capture the gist of the large-scale organizational change that was then getting into full gear. Rich therefore suggested the addition of a second sentence:

Harley-Davidson believes the key to success is to balance stakeholders' interests through the empowerment of all employees to focus on value-added activities.

In effect, this closing statement provided a means whereby every employee could determine, daily, whether he or she was working effectively toward the vision.

"The value system and relevant issues were the basis for this short statement," Rich wrote to the Harley board in July 1989. "While the words are few, the implication on the process by which we run the business is overwhelming. This vision will become the driving force to ensure dedication to our values and focus on relevant issues. As a result, there will be a legacy of responsible future leadership."

The Executive Committee dubbed this package of ideas the "corporate umbrella" (later shortened to "the Umbrella"). As its name implies, the Umbrella was intended to accommodate a number of complementary ideas under one roof. It would provide meaning to any organization that was already a part of Harley or any other organization that became part of the Harley family. The Umbrella, depicted in chart form, looked like this:

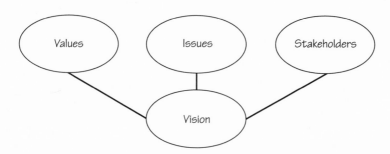

Unless Harley faced dramatic changes in its operating environment, the elements of the Umbrella would not change. Individual words might be modified for clarity. An example of this can be found in the original vision, which included the term *profitable relationships*. As time went on, we became uncomfortable with that term, because it gave the impression that we were focused mainly on profits. This caused us to rethink that section of the vision. We realized that what we were really seeking was to develop win-win relationships with all the stakeholders who helped to make Harley successful. With that in mind, the vision was changed in 1994 as follows:

> To be a leader in continuous improvement in mutually beneficial relationships with all our stakeholders.

In retrospect, this accomplished what we were trying to accomplish initially: an integration of the concepts set forth in our values, issues, and stakeholders.

A second, less dramatic change came when we replaced the word *shareholders* with the word *investors*. (This seemed like a more inclusive term that better reflected Harley's changing financial structure.) But these changes only underscore that change can live comfortably alongside a fundamental continuity. Individual words changed, but the concepts *behind* the words did not. In theory, at least, the time horizon of the Umbrella was forever.

In subsequent weeks, Rich, Jim Paterson, and other senior managers presented the Umbrella to all 2,000 employees of the company, assembled in groups of about 40. (This committed Rich and his colleagues to a total of some fifty meetings, mostly run by pairs of senior managers.) In response to the suggestions heard at these meetings, the Executive Committee modified descriptions of some of the component parts of the Umbrella.

The dynamics of these meetings varied considerably, based on who was participating. In almost all cases, though, the groups engaged in spirited dialogue, with lots of debate about specifics, but very little disagreement on principles. This reinforced a key lesson emerging from the Joint Vision Process: On the most fundamental levels, Harley employees tended to think very similarly about what they wanted their company to be like.

In many of these meetings, the dialogue focused on gaining an understanding of what key words meant, both in a broader context and to individual participants. The disagreements that arose focused on process issues—*What do we need to do about the fact that we aren't there yet?*—rather than on the validity of specific elements in the Umbrella.

LEE: Bear in mind that the Joint Process is running parallel to this, and by this time, people in the organization had things to draw upon. And when the Executive Committee went out, it wasn't a case of "Here they are: the values and issues of the organization." It was, instead, "This is a beginning point—a way to ensure that you'll get the information you need to do your job effectively. And we need some help in figuring out how it's all going to work."

RICH: People really did shape our thinking in these meetings. Someone did get up and say, "I think your definition of quality is a manufacturing definition. You haven't really considered the customer's perspective." So we thought about that and added the phrase, "while striving to meet or exceed customers' expectations." So it was both top down and bottom up, in that sense.

The Umbrella, and the learning related to the Umbrella, have been remarkably durable. For the past decade, an introduction to the Umbrella has served as an integral part of the orientation program for new employees. Until his retirement, Rich usually led this discussion, underscoring the importance that the company attached to this process.

In 1996 Rich and Jeff Bleustein suggested that the company's Functional Leadership Group (see chapter 7) create four-hour training modules covering each of the four Umbrella topics (values, issues, stakeholders, vision). These modules are presented to all work groups by their direct supervisor or leader.

Taking the Next Step

Even before Lee arrived on the scene at Harley, Rich was convinced that the people of Harley had to commit themselves to a particular conception of the company—one that would focus on *processes*, *actions*, and *behaviors*, rather than structures, and one that would concentrate on *renewal*, rather than survival. This would be a company that would allow all of its employees to take personal responsibility without waiting for directions from on high. It would be a company that did the "right thing" not because it *had* to in response to some external crisis but because doing the right thing came naturally and organically, to the best informed and most skilled people throughout the organization.

To accomplish this, people across the organization would have to understand how what they were doing fit into a larger picture. They needed the tools to balance "local" responsibility with the larger needs of functions, divisions, and departments.

RICH: Take a real-life example, only slightly disguised. The folks in engineering come up with a plan that requires thirty new engineers. It's a good plan, in and of itself, thought up at the "local" level to move a good agenda item along. But over in human resources, no one budgets for the cost of recruiting those thirty people. The company needs some kind of process that ties together autonomy with shared purposes.

The Umbrella served as a useful starting point for sketching the larger picture, especially in combination with the earlier work that focused on mission, objectives, and strategy. In the early 1990s, the Executive Committee began thinking about a process that would serve as both an integrating device and an iterative tool for agenda setting and autonomy building across the organization. Individuals and groups that understood and employed this process—whatever it turned out to be—would have the tools they needed to operate independently, without ongoing guidance from corporate. In this spirit, the Executive Committee began looking for a structure that would extend responsibility beyond the executive ranks of the company.

RICH: We started saying to ourselves, "Hey, once you've got an effective umbrella in place, you're in a pretty good position to give true autonomy to the operating units, because they'll never go too far astray from the corporation's fundamentals." So we leveraged the Umbrella to work out the rest of the process.

In other words, the top two tiers of what later came to be called the Business Process began to be tied together in a conscious way. Schematically, this looked as follows:

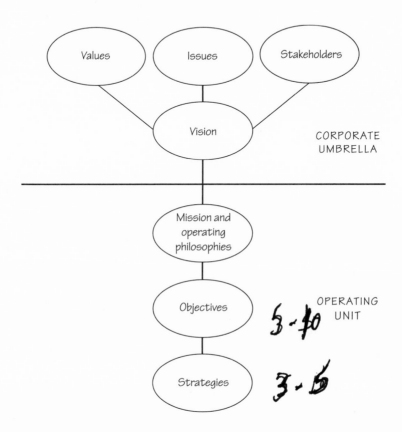

The Executive Committee therefore worked its way through the challenge of bringing this process home to the operating units of the company and to the individuals within those operating units. They looked for ways to enable groups (or individuals) to answer three questions. Here are the questions, and the answers, that Harley eventually arrived at:

Question: *What does our group have to do to deliver the strategies?*

Answer: *Individual work unit plans.* Initially, a "work unit" was defined as the smallest group over which there was a direct supervisor.

Today, it is defined as an organizational unit that operates as a "natural work group" (in other words, one for which there was either a direct supervisor or a work group adviser). The work unit would prepare plans annually during the development of the annual operating plan.

Question: How can we personally ensure that each and every employee understands both the strategic and operating plans, so that he or she can develop her own plan?

Answer: The Performance Effectiveness Process. Each salaried employee would develop an employee-driven Performance Effectiveness Plan (PEP).

Question: What is the critical underpinning for this process?

Answer: Two-way communication. The Executive Committee chose two-way communication with a clear purpose in mind. Many leaders of organizations use printed pieces, video presentations, or large meetings to get their message across to employees. All of these approaches reinforce the idea that these senior leaders represent the source of all wisdom. They cast managers as the *knowers*, to whom people go for the answers. This kind of communication benefits neither party.

Communication certainly was already occurring at Harley, in part thanks to the employee involvement (EI) programs described in chapter 1. And more improvements in the realm of communication—what got distributed to whom, and how—were still to come. (These will be described in later chapters of this book.) But the Executive Committee in this context aimed for an *active, easy,* two-way communication across all levels and functions of the organization. All were exposed to the organization's plans and had the opportunity to focus their efforts toward effective implementation of these plans, while developing their competencies for future growth.

Obviously, Harley's leaders still had an enormous amount of work to do to pull these disparate pieces together into a coherent whole. (Some of that work is described in the next chapter, where we describe PEP in greater detail.) But by the early 1990s, Rich and his colleagues were talking confidently about something called the "Business Process," which comprised all of the separate structures and processes introduced in this chapter. In schematic form, this time with time frames included, the Business Process looked like this:

Business Process

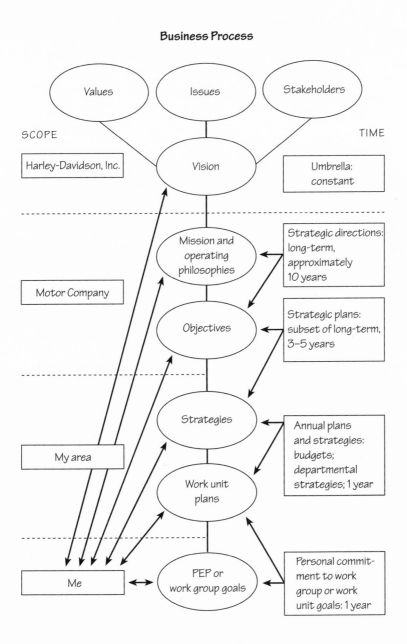

Assessing the Business Process

The previous pages lay out, in a more or less linear way, the development of what Harley eventually called the Business Process. What they *don't* provide is a flavor of the human challenges inherent in getting people to embrace the Business Process at all levels and in all areas of the company. Winning people over was neither quick nor easy, and that aspect of the story deserves some special attention.

We've already described Rich's and Jim Paterson's efforts to explain and win people over to the Umbrella. The larger Business Process had the benefit of the same missionary effort. Rich and Jim Paterson took personal responsibility for winning over as many employees as possible. Rich had always asserted that the traditional "CEO plant tour" amounted to an artificial exercise (although, schedule permitting, he never turned down an invitation to go meet with a group of Harley employees). But he took to heart these meetings in support of the Business Process. Over the course of several months, Rich and Jim spoke with more than 100 union leaders about the means and ends of the Business Process. Rich personally ran eight two-hour sessions with Harley's York-based employees. And, once a month throughout this same period, Rich and Jim each spent an hour and a half with new employees, proselytizing for the Business Process.

"The key word here is *process*," says Jim.

> That's what this whole thing was about. I remember a session at the Marriott on Moorland Road. Rich and I were teaching it. We'd take turns. There was one employee in the back row who was really having trouble with this. This guy said, "You know, I really can't get behind this whole thing. It's just another program—the program of the month. I can't take this crap seriously. It'll be gone next year." And he then went through a whole list of programs that had gone by the wayside.
>
> I said, "OK, first, what we're dealing with here is a *process*. It's not a program. It has no end. It's made up of a lot of programs. Yes, you'll have a program over here that will be shut down, or changed. But you'll continue to build, and build." Then I asked him if he considered the 883 Ride Free program a success. This

was a marketing program in which we guaranteed full trade-in value on an 883 Sportster if the owner traded it in within two years on a Big Twin. It was tremendously successful, and our guy in the back row absolutely agreed with that.

And then I asked him, "So why aren't we doing it now?" Silence. I answered my own question. "Because we don't *need* to. And it's the same thing with all these programs. We have to change a whole culture, a whole mindset. It's hard work, but it's worth the effort. It *will* make a change, it *will* have an impact, and the organization will be the better for it. This process will not go away. A program may die, but something will be right behind it to take its place. Don't waste your time waiting for the Business Process to go away, because it won't."

Paterson's interrogator—the "guy in the back row"—had a point. Like lots of organizations, Harley had implemented a number of improvement programs, most of which had some value in and of themselves. But they weren't well *integrated*. This lack of integration led to duplication and confusion. Some programs lived well beyond their natural lives; others were terminated prematurely. The Business Process provided a way of killing off the unproductive programs, and expanding and extending the productive ones.

Through the 1990s, Harley's senior leaders also took the word to the company's dealer network and key suppliers—to any stakeholder group, in fact, that would have them. What motivated them to make this major commitment of senior management time? They had become convinced that only a thoroughgoing process—taught to all, visible to all, and adhered to by all—would enable Harley to get through the immense changes that still lay ahead for the organization.

The enormity of the change represented by the Business Process can be seen only in retrospect. "I remember very well the first time I got wind of this," Jeff Bleustein says.

We were at a meeting in Florida, which brought together some key people from both Holiday-Rambler and Harley. At one point during that meeting, Rich handed us a paragraph and said, "I want us all to think about a vision for this company."

I think the general reaction was, "Well, uh, sure; the CEO

wants this, OK." Given that we were executives, we couldn't just leave it alone, of course. So we agreed to do a little wordsmithing. I think that, if we had understood at that time how important this all was going to become in our lives, we surely would have paid a lot more attention to it.

But Rich didn't stop there, of course. Next we had to get a "mission" together. This started looking serious. We had to ask ourselves, "What are we trying to *do* in this business?" And we began to understand that this was a way to communicate to a lot of people and get them to help move the business forward.

As we got into it deeper, we began to understand that this was the whole point: empowering people, by getting common values out there for people to use. I don't think any of us knew how far it was all going to take us. But looking back, I can see that it provided an important road map.

Ron Hutchinson, currently vice president for parts, accessories, and customer service, adds another perspective:

> This was a vision of the way people needed to be engaged in an organization, and developed a structure—the Business Process—that allows for theoretical alignment of an individual's job with the long-term direction of the company. No other organization that I'm aware of has built a whole process and structure around that.
>
> In the final analysis, I'd say the Customer Service department, where you spent eight hours a day taking phone calls from unhappy campers, is a true test of whether the Business Process works or not. I'm convinced that we wouldn't have the reputation that we have today in the marketplace if we didn't have front-line people excited by charismatic, visionary leadership, who can see exactly how their little piece of the organization fits into the long-term strategy and direction of the company.

This is the Business Process, and because it underlies so much of what Harley has become, it is a subject to which we'll return in later chapters.

6

Evaluation and Development

THE BUSINESS PROCESS, DESCRIBED IN THE PREVIOUS CHAPTER, provided a structure that Harley could use to communicate to every employee exactly what the company was trying to accomplish. Although the Business Process started with some top-down, command-and-control attributes, it soon evolved into an iterative and participatory process.

In chapter 5, we introduced the two parts of the Business Process that were invented last: the components that dealt with work units and individuals. The Performance Effectiveness Process (PEP) pulled together these components. It gave all individuals the opportunity to participate actively in determining how their work units would function and how they themselves could make a difference in the company's fortunes. We'll take a closer look at PEP in this chapter, emphasizing both its performance evaluation and its career development aspects.

Inventing PEP

Shown as the "bottom" component in a logical-looking flowchart, the Performance Effectiveness Process (PEP) might seem to be the product of a logical and linear process. This wasn't the case. PEP did not arrive fully developed. Instead, like almost all of the innovations we describe in this book, PEP emerged over several years, with individuals and groups adjusting tactics as necessary to fix unexpected problems or to deal with new realities.

"The push for what became PEP came primarily from Rich," recalls Margaret Crawford.

> I'd love to say, "Oh, yes, it was clearly thought out." But it wasn't so clear. The beginning was in 1991, shortly after Bill Gray joined the organization as head of HR.[1] Bill came to Tim Savino and me and said, "We need to get started on this."
>
> It was a very organic process. Rich had the corporate Umbrella idea clear in his mind. But the Executive Committee hadn't yet done its work on the values and associated behaviors. So Rich simply said to us, "Be sure that the performance plan connects the individual to the broader goals of the organization, and that it's within the framework of the corporate Umbrella." And he told us that many, many times!

"It felt very iterative at the time," adds Savino.

> Rich and Jim had already done some work on the foundations of the Business Process. Margaret and I started working on the performance system. Along the line, we agreed that for this to work, we needed to have a plan whereby these efforts could be aligned.
>
> Once the leadership group agreed to this performance system, they also agreed to put together plans. I'm not suggesting that the performance system drove the planning process, because of course Rich was putting pressure on them from that end, as well. It was all part of a bigger picture, being sketched by many hands.

In its first iteration, PEP combined new and old elements, and the result was uncomfortable. "We had a performance-management system already in place," recalls Crawford. "It was what was called a

---

[1] Gray succeeded John Campbell, who moved over to Holiday-Rambler.

'360-degree system.' But it mostly considered your boss, your peers, and your subordinates, and not other stakeholders. And in terms of really having to enter into helpful dialogues around performance, it really didn't have a systemwide component to let that be done well."

There were other problems with the existing system. "There was no alignment between what the individual was doing and what the rest of the organization was doing," explains Tim Savino. "So we started to redesign the performance system to get an alignment between the individual and a core set of emerging organizational values."

Part of the previous performance evaluation system that the HR staffers carried forward into PEP was a performance rating form. Although performance ratings at first seemed more like a housekeeping issue than a policy-level concern, Rich and his colleagues (both in senior management and in HR) soon realized that this particular form (and the logic behind it) represented a real impediment to changing the review and compensation system.

The problem lay in the *source* and *content* of the established performance measures. Historically, a few key Harley executives had established these measures, with additional input only from a small number of executive colleagues and outside compensation specialists. The measures were presented in terms of nonspecific traits and characteristics: *effective communicator*, *global thinker*, *effective problem solver*, *gets results*, *acts as effective role model*, and so on.

The nonspecificity of these measures posed two additional problems. First, neither party to the review dialogue could figure out exactly how to apply these measures. Which *specific* behaviors demonstrated, objectively and conclusively, that an individual was an effective communicator or a global thinker? No one knew. If an employee wanted to improve along a given dimension, such as problem solving, what exactly would he or she have to do? Again, no one knew.

LEE: We developed a little piece of jargon around this problem. It was HWIKIWISI— pronounced "hee-wee-kuh-WEE-see"—and meaning "How will I know it when I see it?" How do I get this trait, or this characteristic, down to the level of observable behaviors?

If someone says to me, "Lee, you're a lousy listener," that will offend me, and it won't help me change my behavior. But if some-body says to me, "Lee, you constantly interrupt me when I'm talking to you, you're always shuffling papers on your desk, you're always looking past me at the people walking by in the hallway, you don't ask any follow-up questions," well, those are specifics. I may be offended, but at least I can act on them.

And, second, no one was asking—or perhaps had ever asked—whether these traits and characteristics were the right ones for Harley to be recognizing and rewarding. Certainly, no one had asked whether they were aligned with, and supportive of, the values of the recently envisioned Harley.

Going First

Recognizing that the lack of a clearly defined group of desirable behaviors was a major barrier to change, Harley's leaders in January 1993 assembled a group of ten executives, including Jeff Bleustein, who had been appointed president of the Motorcycle Division, to work with Lee to develop specific lists of expected behaviors. Drawing on a list of more than 250 behavioral descriptors that Lee provided, based on his work with many companies in previous engagements, the ad hoc group selected a list of 90-plus descriptors. These included, for example:

- Values diversity in people in the workforce.
- Openly provides his/her opinion if a higher-ranking individual has a different opinion.
- Actively supports decisions made by consensus.
- Acts in a genuine manner with others.
- Protects trust placed in one by others.
- Communicates in a way that permits full understanding.
- Does what he/she says he/she will do.
- Properly delegates to the appropriate level in the organization.
- Responds in a positive manner to criticism.

- Respects the opinions of others.
- Shows appropriate concern for his/her employees' problems.
- Listens actively to a person when he/she is speaking.[2]

The group's members agreed that, if the organization actively embraced this set of behaviors, it would make realizing the "envisioned corporation" a far easier task. The individuals who practiced these behaviors, moreover, would serve as role models for their colleagues in the company.

The ten-person leadership group took an unusual next step. In an effort to test the validity and usefulness of this list of 90 descriptors, the group decided to convert the descriptors into a data collection instrument, which each member would then use to anonymously evaluate each of his nine management colleagues. Alongside each behavior was a 1-to-5 scale, with 1 standing for "never" and 5 for "always." (A sixth choice was "unknown.") To ensure more reliable results, some behaviors were recast as negatives. "Acts in a genuine manner with others," for example, became "Acts in an artificial manner with others." "Listens actively to a person when he/she is speaking" became "Interrupts a person when he/she is speaking."

At the end of the data collection process, therefore, each of the ten executives wound up with a pile of nine unattributed surveys, each of which evaluated his behavior along 90-plus distinct axes on a "never" to "always" scale.[3] An outside data analysis bureau was hired to process the data (and thereby retain anonymity). That bureau prepared a summary version, which compiled the results of the nine separate responses into one aggregate survey. Lee then talked through those results with each "reviewed" individual.

These discussions differed from all previous methods of feedback that the participants had experienced; for example, supervisors' appraisals, career development discussions, and annual merit review discussions. Among the key differentiating factors:

---

[2] These dozen behaviors are numbers 17 through 28 from the longer list of 90 behaviors and are representative of that longer list.

[3] This is a variation on the five-point Likert scale, pioneered by the Institute for Social Research at the University of Michigan and widely regarded as an effective method for capturing and analyzing statistically significant data.

- The participants themselves selected the items on which they would receive data.
- The survey items articulated specific behaviors, not "characteristics" or "traits."
- Respondents to the survey represented a much broader peer population than would normally be the case.
- The individual leading the individual feedback reviews—that is, Lee—didn't belong to the chain of command. He therefore was able to serve credibly as a *coach*, helping promote individual learning, rather than an evaluator.

Each executive had the option to share whatever portion of his aggregate results he chose to share, if any. Jeff Bleustein volunteered to go first, and also decided to share every item on his "behavioral review" with his colleagues.

LEE: The thing to realize is that everybody gets dinged, in one way or another, on these things. Nobody comes out looking perfect. So Jeff gets kudos for going through his line by line, including the tough parts. That was wonderful.

According to those who participated in this unusual process, the results had a significant impact. Most indicated that this experience was the first time in their years with Harley (or elsewhere) that (1) they had participated in defining their performance measures; (2) they clearly understood how their colleagues perceived them; and (3) they knew exactly how to improve their performance in the eyes of their colleagues. No one liked everything he learned, but all felt the learning to be invaluable.

"That was a huge *aha!*" recalls Jeff Bleustein. "It was a revelation for all of us. We finally began to understand what was making the rest of the team tick. Up to that time, we had just looked to each other for functional performance. When we got together as a group, we weren't really understanding each other. But in this process, a lightbulb went on for all of us. We started to coalesce as a team."

Most survey respondents found the *specificity* of the described behaviors extremely useful as they assessed a colleague's performance. And the assessed individuals prized the survey's focus on *specific, observable behaviors*. The company's former emphasis on traits and characteristics didn't lend itself to action in any obvious way. (What, exactly, should I do if my reviewer says I'm inadequately global in my thinking?) The new focus on behaviors marked a significant and very helpful change, for both the reviewer and the reviewed.

The outside service bureau also provided a summary version of the survey that compiled all ten managerial profiles into a single overall profile of the group. This composite allowed the group to focus on areas in which the group as a whole either shone or seemed weak. This summary defined an overall learning agenda for the group.

LEE: Again, this summary picture proved very helpful. I've never seen a group yet that scored well on giving and receiving negative feedback. A second problem area, in most cases, is fostering broader involvement in decision making. This is always tough when you're in the middle of changing the culture of an organization. So along comes this survey, and here's the evidence in black and white. What are we going to do about it? Invariably, someone suggests doing a workshop on this particular topic.

The success of this "mutual performance review" among the group of ten managers led eventually to the adoption of a similar technique as part of the PEP system. The HR managers modified the formal performance appraisal system so that a general heading—such as "Communicates effectively"—comprised between three and five specific behavioral descriptors, such as "Communicates in a way that permits full understanding" and "Listens actively to a person when he/she is speaking." And specific functional areas were encouraged to add specifics that reflected priorities in their own areas.

Overall, the larger company's experience resembled that of the pilot group: both the reviewers and the reviewed felt that the new focus on specific, observable behaviors contributed significantly to broadening the base of responsibility and accountability across Harley.

PEP at Work

PEP went through many iterations, and is still being fine-tuned today. Crawford, Savino, and the others involved in inventing PEP began their work by imagining some truly radical approaches to achieving alignment between corporate and individual goals. "One version we dreamed up," recalls Savino, "was completely customer driven. The supervisor would have been completely out of the loop, and the assessment would have been performed entirely by the individual's customers, inside and outside of the organization."

Senior management listened to discussions of these more or less radical approaches and rejected them. ("The word came back," recalls Savino with a smile. "*Wrong!*") Today, in some of its aspects, PEP resembles a traditional "management by objectives" performance system, although it operates in the very untraditional context of the Business Process. It aims to give every employee the opportunity—and the responsibility—to influence what happens in the organization. The employee earns this influence in four ways:

1. By having a complete and accurate understanding of how information flowed within and across organizational units.
2. By participating in the dialogue during the development of work unit plans.
3. By participating in the meetings and formal presentations that finalized (and revised) these plans.
4. By helping to define a desired performance on the individual level.

Maybe the best way to illustrate how PEP works is to lay out an illustrative example in some detail. Let's imagine that I'm a work unit leader—say, an accounts payable supervisor. I'm about to put together my work unit plan.

Well, I've already met with my leaders, and we've discussed what our strategies are, based on their meetings with their leaders. So, based on this dialogue, I talk with my work unit members. I make sure that they understand and support the Business Process, from the generalities of the Umbrella to the specifics of these strategies. (If they don't, of course, we need to discuss their reservations openly.) Assuming that they support the strategies, I then ask them, "OK, how are we going to deliver the activities that support these things?"

Based on our discussion, we come up with a work unit plan that identifies our key results areas. Maybe it involves processing 5,000 invoices a day. Then I ask the individuals in the unit, "OK, how are you going to deliver your piece of that? What are your *commitments*? [See chart.] How do you want to be measured? What's necessary for your personal future development?"

And, looking at the same process from the work unit member's point of view: "It's clear to me what the work unit is going to do and

The Commitment-Setting Model

Activities (input)

Results areas —————— What's the job?

Annual —————— What is this year's
commitments   contribution to success?

Indicators and —————— How will I know when
specific   success is achieved?
measures

Actions and —————— What do I need to do to make
plans   the commitment happen?

Output —————— Actual result

how I'm going to contribute to it. I can meet with my unit supervisor as necessary, and I will meet with him or her at least quarterly. I know how my work meets the agreed-upon strategies, how the strategies serve the objectives, how the objectives help meet the mission, and how the mission serves the vision."

RICH: It all sounds complicated, but it's actually designed to be as simple and effective as possible.

LEE: Until you get to the work unit plan, it's all kind of floating out there—which is where it remains, at a lot of companies. As an employee, I know I'm doing something, but I'm not sure why. Through the work unit, I learn the direct ties. I learn why what I'm doing is important. In fact, I can help define something important for me to do.

Performance Evaluation and Career Development

The HR department also tailored PEP to serve as the principal vehicle for career development at Harley. As an employee handbook later summarized this objective:

> Employee development increases employee satisfaction and sense of self-worth by providing challenge, variety, and growth opportunities.
>
> All employees are expected to demonstrate a willingness to continually learn. Improving job performance, competencies, and ability to contribute is a long-term condition of employment.
>
> Harley-Davidson is committed to creating a work environment designed to maximize each individual's ability to contribute, and will provide access to resources and opportunities for all employees to acquire and develop their skills, knowledge, and abilities.

In January 1992, Harley's leaders met with all management and union leaders to discuss the concept of basing salary increases on demonstrated capabilities. Attendees at that meeting raised many questions, which can be boiled down into two larger categories:

1. What kinds of competencies will be required?
2. How will varying levels of competencies be differentiated?

As a follow-up to these January meetings, the HR staff began working with Novations, a Utah-based consulting group, to develop a competency matrix. This work, which began in the summer of 1992, continued through 1995. When the participants completed their work, they agreed on the following structure of competencies:

Interaction. Build strong commitment through:

- Personal example
- Communication
- Conflict resolution
- Teamwork

Execution. Getting results through:

- Stakeholder focus
- Problem solving/decision making
- Planning
- Performance management

Demonstrated competence. Achieving competence through:

- Technical expertise
- Continuous improvement

In this context, employee development has two objectives: (1) to provide for growth in one's current position and (2) to prepare for the future. The career development plan prepared as part of PEP provides the individual with opportunities to work on both of these objectives at the same time.

And finally, as an important part of both performance evaluation and career development, the group also adopted Novations' "four stages of leadership" model. In ascending order of scope and complexity, they are:

1. Working with others
2. Contributing independently
3. Contributing through others
4. Leading through influence

The team's conclusion was that, as one ascends this "leadership ladder," one draws less on purely technical skills and more on interpersonal and strategic skills. In chart form, this looks as follows:

Skill Requirements: Leadership

Individual and technical skills

Interpersonal and strategic skills

| Working with others | Contributing independently | Contributing through others | Leading through influence |

Beginning in the spring of 1996, Harley introduced these competencies to all salaried employees during the Leadership Business Process Module (see chapter 9). This module included an "upward-feedback" component, based on the competency matrix. This upward-feedback instrument was employed through 1997. Although this program never became an explicit part of the salaried compensation system, it continues to be used in many areas of the company as part of performance evaluation.

Bumps in the Road

PEP encountered plenty of bumps in the road. "At first," recalls Margaret Crawford,

> people were hostile to PEP because they thought it was bureaucratic. There was, and is, a rebel spirit here at Harley. To lots of people, PEP felt too much like going to school. "Don't we trust each other? Don't we know if we're doing the right job? Don't we talk to each other every day?" So I came across tremendous resistance.

Seen from another perspective, the company was experiencing a major cultural change, and many people resented that change. "In the old days," continues Crawford,

> it was all hands on deck, and do whatever it takes. After PEP was put in place, everybody had to figure out exactly what their group had to accomplish. I work in this work unit; what are we supposed to *deliver*? To answer that question, my boss has to talk with us about the kind of work we're doing, and what he or she wants us to get done. I have to know what my results are supposed to be, in terms of key result areas. I have to identify the things that are important for me to do this year, in the form of commitments. I have to write down these commitments. I have to write down the people who can give me good input, and tell me what I could do to do a better job. I have to take *personal responsibility* for my development.
>
> Well, that's a lot of work. You have to talk to a lot of people, and go to a lot of meetings. The meetings generated resistance, too. But on the tail end, people who resisted this now champion it. Employees who have taken the time to do it find there's less confusion, more clarity, less conflict. They know what they're supposed to deliver, and when.

RICH: Nothing works perfectly all the time. But PEP works well a lot of the time. When it does, the individual knows with clarity how he or she can make a difference. That's good for the individual, and it's good for the company.

7

Upending the Pyramid

FROM TIME TO TIME IN OUR JOURNEY, WE (RICH AND LEE) TALKED seriously about the need to make changes in Harley's organizational structure.

Neither of us had illusions that a structural change would represent a cure-all for the company. In our respective experiences, organization ("org") charts have more often been a representation than a cause of problems. In fact, both of us had long been convinced that the reporting relationships codified on org charts—relationships to which many people attach so much importance—are basically irrelevant. At this point in our journey together, we still felt that way (in fact, more so than ever). We believed that if the right combination of shared leadership and individual responsibility were in place, *any* form of organization could be made to work, whether it be matrix, divisional, functional, or whatever.

And, just as important, we didn't want to send a confusing signal. If Rich simply announced a significant change in reporting relationships, people in the organization would most likely interpret that change as just another case of top-down, command-and-control decision making. Giving this impression would only reinforce the kinds of mind-sets and patterns that we were trying to undo.

At the same time, however, we realized that the existing organizational structure was beginning to get in the way of the kinds of changes that were in process. Structural change had to come, sooner or later, and we had to lay the groundwork for that change.

LEE: The guideline we set our ourselves was "Don't mess with the organizational structure until we've been down this road enough, and people begin to understand what this change process is all about, and begin to tell us that the current structure is starting to get in the way."

Starting around the end of 1990, we began to see indicators of organizational trouble.

In addition to these signals, Rich felt another spur to action when Jim Paterson, president of the motorcycle company, requested a job change. Jim explained that, for personal reasons, he wanted to return to his previous post as vice president of marketing. Rich agreed and, rather than foreclosing options by appointing a successor too quickly, stepped in as temporary president of the motorcycle company. He would hold that post for eighteen months, during which many of the changes described in this chapter took place.

One more spur to consider an organizational change came when the York plant experienced a two-week strike in 1991. The immediate cause of the strike was a suggested management-imposed change in the paint system used at the plant. (The quality of Harley's paint finishes is one of its most important differentiators in the market, so the stakes were high.) Below this surface dispute, however, lay a more significant tension. York's management had announced that it planned to implement a team-based work system at that plant. York's organized workforce was quick to register its unhappiness with the plan.

In this chapter, we recount the changes that led to the creation of a new organizational structure at Harley.

Exploring the Alternatives

Those changes began with a series of discussions between Lee and Rich and, periodically, among other participants. As we talked through the question of organizational structure, we gradually settled on two guiding principles. First, we agreed, great wisdom resided in a maxim from the field of architecture: *Form follows function.* In other words, *the Harley organization should be only as complicated as it absolutely needed to be.* The organization should derive "organically" from the functions the organization needed to carry out. We didn't want to draw boxes and lines on org charts until it was clear exactly what the organization needed to do.

And, second, we concluded that, when the time came, *the employees themselves should decide on the specifics of those boxes and lines.* Managers and union members at Harley's Wisconsin facilities were then working hard to identify barriers to organizational improvement. In the course of this work, they were identifying structural barriers to the realization of the future company that we had collectively envisioned.

Even with these two principles (minimal structure, employee-driven structure) as our starting point—principles that argued for a light hand on the tiller—we felt we still had a lot of homework to do. Rich and his colleagues in Harley's leadership surely had to contribute to the "organizational invention" phase when that time came. (In fact, one could argue that the organization's formal leaders should take the lead in any such effort.) We therefore focused over the next several months on the universe of organizational structures. Specifically, we looked for viable alternatives to the organizational form that Harley was then using.

At that time, Harley-Davidson, Inc. (HDI) was organized in a traditional multidivisional manner, with two subsidiaries (the Motor Company and Holiday-Rambler) reporting to the parent company. Within the divisions, reporting relationships also were very traditional. The Motor Company, the focus of our organizational review, seemed to be chafing within the confines of its organizational structure. Specifically, the then-current organization

- encouraged functional independence and competition, instead of interdependence and collaboration.
- impeded project start-ups.
- fostered "process" problems.
- failed to reflect and meet customer needs.
- vested responsibility and authority in the *hierarchy*, rather than in the individual.

RICH: You didn't have to go far to find evidence to support these conclusions. Our projects were chronically slow getting started. Our technological "fixes" usually involved cost overruns, and even then often didn't work as they were supposed to. Our new-product introductions were late and ran over budget. You couldn't miss the evidence, if you went looking for it.

With these problems in mind, we reviewed the organizational forms that were in general use among companies similar to Harley and catalogued what we took to be the pros and cons of each. At the end of our joint review, we decided that we had been digging a dry hole. No existing organizational structures fit the Harley-Davidson that managers, salaried personnel, and union members had envisioned.

Why Not Teams?

An example may help illustrate our thought processes at that time. During the late 1980s and early 1990s, many organizations seized upon *teams* as the solution to all their problems, including problems related to boxes and lines. Would a team-based organization suit Harley?

We soon decided that it would not. For most of those Harley employees represented by labor unions, *team* was already a very loaded term. (The most recent and vivid example was the reaction of York employees to management's embrace of a "team-based organization"!) Both of the international unions that represented Harley workers had experienced the team concept elsewhere and held strongly negative opinions about it. They felt that management often used teams to undermine the functions and even the legitimacy of organized labor. The union leaders told us that, as they saw it, team-based structures were part of a bigger fabric of top-down–imposed programs, such as the Total Quality Movement (TQM), which were almost always developed and implemented without any real involvement on the part of union leadership and membership.

So we were on notice that Harley's labor relations could be jeopardized if the company embraced a team-based structure. But there were other disincentives to going this route. Our observations of all the reported "leaders" in team-based organizations (ranging from Cummins Engine Company to NUMMI to Kellogg), as well as a comprehensive review of all the literature on teams, suggested that these kinds of organizations were *no more or less effective* in meeting the needs of their customers than any other. In fact, it appeared to us that teams—acclaimed by some as the foundation for the flexible corporation of the future—could sometimes be quite rigid.

Over time, we observed, team members tend to develop complementary skills to deal with the specified task at hand, especially if the task stays constant. (Indeed, that's why team members perform so well together.) They become tightly knit, even insular, groups, with principal allegiance to each other. But what happens when outside circumstances change? Many teams tend to close ranks and defend the status quo, and defending the status quo is what kills companies.

LEE: The problem arises when we let the "team" become an end in itself, as opposed to a means to the real end: serving the customer, who may be internal or external to the organization. So we realized that we wanted to focus people on the principle behind the "team" label, rather than on the label itself. We wanted people to buy into something good that they understood and endorsed.

And, finally, we noted with interest that teams consisting of senior managers were very hard to find. It seemed that managers tended to impose a formula on the vast majority of employees in a team-based organization, but not on themselves. This struck us as odd, and not representative of the kind of organization that we wanted Harley to be.

Beginning at the Beginning

We returned to our starting point. Mirroring the sequence of steps in the Joint Vision Process, we decided that we first had to describe exactly what the organization needed to do. Then we had to figure out what was working well and what wasn't. If something wasn't working well, what was wrong with it? And how did this analysis square with the envisioned organization then emerging through the Joint Vision Process?

Our discussion of these questions, as well as our observations of other ongoing processes, led to the following answers (as originally set forth in a memo written by Rich).

The organization was expected to

- reflect and meet internal and external customer needs.
- support individual growth and excellence.
- develop interdependence and cross-functional collaboration.
- position the company to be successful in a rapidly changing environment.
- create flexible groupings of functional leaders who could provide a common leadership direction.
- support personal responsibility and accountability.

Note the emphasis on *customers*. Harley's people had learned in recent years that customer needs can change *dramatically* and *quickly*. Just getting good at solving last year's problems was no longer acceptable. (In the difficult days of the early 1980s, Harley had lost huge amounts of market share by solving last year's problems to the exclusion of more proactive steps.) What Harley needed was to get the *right* people together, at the *right* time, to do the *right* work *right*. We stated it this way purposely, both to emphasize the simplicity of the concept and to underscore that achieving it would not be easy.

We should emphasize again that we believed that the existing organization had done many things very well. Harley had risen to the serious challenges of the early and mid-1980s. It had created structures to provide for a certain degree of employee involvement. But at the same time, we knew that some things were amiss.

RICH: There were plenty of examples within the organization of people who did things right. Jim Lucas, the plant manager at York, was one. He was a big believer in the wisdom of the guy on the shop floor. He was always telling people in Assembly, "Hey, when you've got a problem with a part, call the damn supplier and tell him about it!" In other words, he created a setting in which employees could solve problems without worrying about the hierarchy. But we wanted people to make that call on their own, without waiting for a Jim Lucas to tell them it was okay.

We knew of an interesting innovation that was already in place at Harley. This was the creation of outgoing Motor Company president Jim Paterson, who returned to his former position in sales and marketing with a novel idea in mind. "When I went back into marketing," Paterson recalls, "I talked to Rich about setting up a rudimentary kind of circle organization. I remember sketching out a little atomlike model that had little electronlike functional balls sitting out around a core, which I labeled 'customer satisfaction.' We went at this for a couple of months, and one day Rich said, 'Great! This fits right into what I want to do.'"

The 1991 annual report included a schematic drawing of this new approach. The report said in part

> Our separate "domestic," "international," and Parts and Accessories operations have been eliminated to enable us to become a unified, empowered organization which views the world as a single market. . . . With "improving customer satisfaction" remaining as the Organization's primary goal, a leadership team identified seven key functional areas to ensure long-term success in our globalization. The seven functional areas . . . will be "responsible" to each other, thus improving lines of communications within the company and speeding our response times.

The focus— internationalization—was different, but the prescription was promising.

Natural Work Groups

The *right* people, together at the *right* time, to do the *right* work *right*. What did this catch phrase really mean? It meant that we wanted the best of all worlds. For Harley, we wanted something really unusual: *teamwork without teams*.

We began by describing what was dubbed "customer-flow" organization. Every person within an organization "receives" something—a subassembly, a form, information—from someone (the "supplier"); that person takes some action on what he or she has received—produces another part, makes a decision, researches data, answers a question—and then moves the results of that action on to someone else—the "customer."

With this in mind, we could see that work should be organized around the natural customer flow for a particular function and should be flexible enough to respond in size, composition, skill sets, and so on, to the inevitable changes in demands from the customer.

Those people involved in the partnering process (described in chapter 11) arrived at the following definition of a "work group":

> A group of employees, both salaried and hourly, who produce products and services. The work group has the authority, within predetermined boundaries, to make decisions supportive of their activities and is accountable for the results. Work groups are expected to transform themselves quickly and smoothly in response to the changing needs of the work group's customer(s).

To move forward with this emerging concept of natural work groups, we first needed a clear definition of the core processes of the organization, around which we could organize groups of people in some new kind of way. Next, we needed to organize things in a way that would make it *easy* for employees to come together and perform these core processes. And, by logical extension, when those activities were completed, the organization had to make it easy for employees to regroup for the *next* set of "customer-driven activities."

We then went on to identify four such core processes:

1. Creating demand for the products and services of the organization
2. Producing those goods and services
3. Supporting the demand-creation and production processes
4. Coordinating these activities, both internally and in relationships with external stakeholders

It is tempting to translate each of those terms into a traditional functional label. "Creating demand," for example, might sound like marketing; "producing" might sound like manufacturing. But we really were thinking of something more flexible, more customer driven, less hierarchy oriented, and less etched in stone. In other words, we wanted terms that would fit the definition of a natural grouping of people appropriate for the task at hand—again, a means of getting the right people to come together to do the right work and do it right.

Challenges demand responses. Ideally, those responses would come from the group of people most qualified to design and implement them. The phrase "natural work group" eventually emerged as the best way to describe what we had in mind and as a way to distinguish our ideas from a team concept.

Work groups would come in all sizes. The people who created demand, for example, would comprise a "natural work group" on a large scale. That large grouping would contain many smaller natural work groups. And, most importantly, natural work groups would also form across functional and divisional lines, to the extent that they still existed; and when they completed their work, they would "unform" themselves.

RICH: In the seventies, I was in an organization that had to downsize. It was a troubling process, to say the least. But most troubling was the fact that no one knew how to do it right—if it could be done "right" at all.

In that context, we developed something that we called "accountability center analysis." We identified the smallest work unit over which there was a direct supervisor and defined that as an accountability center. We then asked each of these units a series of questions: Why does your accountability center exist? How does it add value? How is that value delivered by the people in that accountability center? How do the individuals measure what they do?

This kind of analysis didn't make the downsizing painless, of course, but it made it *rational*—based on something real and meaningful to the organization. This long-ago experience implanted an important question in the front of my brain, where it has remained ever since: What is this unit's task? If we know unit A's task, and unit B's task, and unit C's task, and so on, we can probably figure out how the structure should go.

Creating demand, we agreed, was a "natural work group" of all of the people and activities that created, increased, and sustained the demand for Harley's products and services. To be sure, this included such traditional promotional activities as marketing, sales, and public relations. But it logically could include additional activities borrowed from other functional areas, such as styling and customer service.

Producing products and services was a natural work grouping that included not only manufacturing, engineering, and new product development, but also purchasing, quality/reliability, logistics, and so on.

Supporting would encompass all traditional "staff" functions, such as finance and accounting, human resources, strategic planning, government relations, information services, legal, and so on. Any individual or group that helped the first two natural work groups (creating demand and producing products and services) would be part of this group.

Coordinating would be the responsibility not only of the president, but also of representatives of the other three natural work groups.

RICH: When you have a senior vice president, he or she almost inevitably becomes the local god. The people who report to that person may get together and communicate across functional lines, but for the most part, they know who they're playing to: they're playing to the local god.

We were talking about policy making at the senior levels of the organization. We were talking about having many more people deeply involved in that process—far more than you would normally have in a divisional organization headed by a senior vice president. In the environment we were imagining, these people would be playing to one another. They'd be figuring out how what they were doing in marketing, for example, reflected what that person in sales was saying about what the dealers were feeling.

The Circle Organization

As we talked these ideas through, we felt that we had the germ of an idea that might bring about real changes at Harley. And, with further discussion, we came to realize that the way we depicted this structure would be of critical importance. It had to appear to be both *organic*— that is, a natural outgrowth of the realities of the workplace—and *dynamic*.

Our first pass at such a depiction didn't succeed on either count. It was simply a row of unconnected circles:

This depiction didn't capture the shared leadership and cross-functionality that had to be at the heart of the organization we were contemplating. It also failed to convey the permeability of boundaries inherent in natural work groups. We therefore took another pass at depicting what we eventually came to call the "circle organization":

Again, we make a contrast with a traditional, functionally organized divisional structure. In such a traditional structure, individuals and groups charged with marketing (for example) do their jobs with almost no direct contact with their counterparts in manufacturing. Information flows up the organization, reaches the divisional authority figure, leaps across the functional boundary to another divisional authority—assuming, of course, that internal communications are *good*—and then flows back down through the ranks. Information travels slowly. It is distorted through multiple retellings by individuals increasingly far removed from the problem. Overall, the communication process encourages truth stretching and evasion of responsibility. These negative traits are reinforced by organizational structures that denote reporting relationships which have little to do with the way work actually gets done within the organization.

In the circle organization, as we saw it, things would be different. Leadership would be dispersed. Information would flow constantly, cross-functionally, in all helpful directions. The people who understood the problem would be the ones attempting to solve it. Accountability would be clear.

LEE: One metaphor that I sometimes used to describe what we had in mind was the homeroom. In your high school days, you started the day in your homeroom and then went off to six or seven different classes. By analogy, the circle is your homeroom. You go out to where your customers need you to go, in order to do your work.

Jeff Bleustein recalls the first time he encountered the circle diagram.

I remember Rich stood up one day and said, "I think we should be looking at something like this." And he drew these three circles—create demand, produce product, provide service. That's how he thought he wanted the organization to look. And again, this one started out as a kind of fuzzy idea. Traditional organizations were organized into divisions, within which functional heads reported to EVPs, EVPs reported to the president, and so on. Rich thought we ought to be able to do without all that, and thereby improve communication. The point was to get rid of some of the layers and filters.

The circle diagram begged the question of leadership: *Who's in charge here?* (In fact, when we later presented the concept to the organization, this was the single most frequently asked question.) Note that at the core of the overlapping circles lies a zone of intersection. This is where the coordinating function, one of the four core processes of the organization as defined earlier, occurs. Eventually, as we will describe later in this chapter, this zone of overlap was named the "Leadership and Strategy Council," or LSC. Its primary function is to make sure that cross-functional integration occurs with authentic input from informed individuals from each circle.

But this came later. In these early conceptual stages, we focused on the circles, the ways they would organize themselves, and the ways they would overlap. We expected each circle to operate as an empowered work group. Here was a central aspect of what we hoped would be a quiet revolution. We did not expect a single individual to emerge as the leader of a circle. Instead, we anticipated that leadership would be a shared responsibility. At the same time, managers within the circles were expected to operate independently. "Shared leadership, individual management" was a catch phrase that emerged at this time.

RICH: As others have observed before us, leadership is a shared role; management is an individual role. Leadership is thinking about the right things; management is doing things right. This struck us as a powerful set of ideas. We knew that these ideas would not necessarily be popular with managers who were primarily interested in defending their traditional prerogatives.

At the same time, we didn't expect these circles to take effective shape without any assistance. The circles in their infancy would need wise and competent counsel. Tom Gelb, vice president of manufacturing, agreed to coach the "produce product" circle, while marketing vice president Jim Paterson accepted the coaching job for the "create demand" circle. (In effect, they were eliminating executive vice president positions, and serving as coaches and mentors.) Rich, then acting head of the motorcycle company, took responsibility for the "provide support" circle, until a new president was named to head up that company.

Refining the Circles

Between August 1991 and the end of 1992, Rich and his traditionally hierarchical senior colleagues held a series of informal, small-group discussions with Harley's employees. The small groups were gatherings of employees within various traditional functions, or departments when the situation allowed, and the discussions tended to take place in the course of other routine business meetings. Rich and his colleagues described the goals of the new organizational structure, explained why it seemed appropriate for Harley, and asked employees for their input at both the conceptual and the implementation level. They started with people who occupied high-level management posts and extended these conversations out to encompass people at all locations and in most functional areas.

Their message to all audiences consisted of two parts. First, they said, the circle organization was the structure of the future. And, second, now was the time to raise objections, suggest modifications, and otherwise deal with the circle concept.

LEE: Rich was very skilled at making these two points. He'd say, very honestly, that he wanted input and counsel. And he'd also say, "By the way, when the time comes, the concrete is gonna set pretty fast."

RICH: Actually, we put the ideas out there as best we could, and then they just sort of sat there for a while. And some people just ignored the whole initiative as just another flaky idea. That was fine with me, up to a point. I think it's very appropriate to give people time to think about a new idea—and after that time has passed, to get very serious about that idea.

Some members of both management's and labor's ranks assumed that this trial balloon, too, would pass and that they needed only to hunker down and wait out senior management's latest temporary fancy. But no one should have missed the central fact: that Rich and his senior management colleagues were spending time on both picking people's brains and conveying this new "circle concept" to the organization. Certainly some kind of change was imminent. One way or the other, Harley was preparing to embrace a dramatically different organizational structure—one that was based on shared decision making, natural work groups, and flexible leadership.

RICH: I said, "Here's a way of organizing. Let's try it and see what happens." No, we wouldn't have a full-blown natural work group concept within weeks or months, or maybe even years. But we'd be aiming toward that.

The Organizational Embrace

On January 1, 1993, Jeff Bleustein was named the new president and COO of the motorcycle company. Bleustein immediately emphasized that, under his leadership, the Motor Company would commit itself to making the circle organization real and effective.

"In October or November," Bleustein recalls,

Rich and I had a series of discussions. At that time, he said something to the effect that he wanted to name me president in January but that he didn't want the Motor Company to slip back into an old-fashioned command-and-control environment. "I want it to look like this circle stuff," he said. "Are you comfortable with that?"

I said, "Sure. It seems to have merit. But people don't know what a 'circle organization' means. We have to develop it."

And Rich said, "Great. *Do* it!"

In one of his first acts as president, therefore, Bleustein appointed an ad hoc committee to take the broad-brush concept of the circle organization and translate it into a workable plan for organizing and running a large corporation. The ad hoc committee would provide guidance and clarity regarding conflict management, define the different kinds of decisions that would need to be made, and identify who should make those decisions. It would identify potential barriers to the successful implementation of the circle concept, and (conversely) also identify key success factors. What could individuals and groups do to make this new plan work?

"The first I heard of this," recalls Ron Hutchinson, who served on the ad hoc committee,

> was when Rich sat down a bunch of people and said, "OK, we've gotta figure out a way to get empowered teams at the senior level of the company. You guys have to figure out how to make it work." The reaction, by and large, was "Oh . . . *damn*!"
>
> But we sat around and wrestled with the thing. What's this overlapping thing in the middle? Maybe it should be called a "Leadership and Strategy Council." Well, OK, great, but what's its relationship to the president? to the CEO?

The ad hoc committee devoted large amounts of time over the following six months to developing the circle organization in detail. After presenting their report to those who would be affected, the committee assisted the various circles as they implemented this new approach in July and August 1993.

RICH: That ad hoc committee played an absolutely critical role in defining and solidifying the circle organization at Harley. Neither Lee nor I was much involved. Jeff and his colleagues ran with that one.

LEE: Because the people who had to live with the plan designed the plan, that plan had a better than fighting chance of succeeding.

Bleustein and the committee members emphasized that this wasn't "circles for the sake of circles." Each unit would begin with the needs of its customers, internal or external, and reorganize themselves to meet those needs naturally. In other words, there was no logical reason to assume that the "create demand" circle would look or function like the "produce product" group.

By the same token, Bleustein and his colleagues expected these managers to think of themselves as the advance scouts of the natural work group concept. They would serve as role models for the organization. People across the organization would observe how they treated each other—and, if they liked what they saw, they would emulate them. "Remember that we had done a lot of team-based activity on the shop floor and in the offices," recalls Ron Hutchinson. "In fact, there were teams doing everything. But the circle organization forced us to create a situation in which the leaders would model the right behaviors. 'Leaders by their actions are known'—this was one of many times that Rich pulled that expression on us!"

LEE: If we couldn't make this construct work at the top of the organization, why should we expect it to work somewhere else in the organization? If it's not appropriate for managers, why should it be appropriate for the shop floor worker?

The Circle Organization in a Nutshell

The circle organization formally came into being at Harley on July 1, 1993. The company prepared a twelve-page document titled "The Organization," which circulated to all sites. The two-word title straddled three interlocking circles, underscoring the main point of what this new organizational structure was all about. By now, the initiative focused on what were formerly the top three levels of management. The publication clearly implied, however, that this structure eventually would come to bear on all levels and activities in the organization.

The introductory section restated the points that Rich and his colleagues—and subsequently Jeff Bleustein and the ad hoc committee—had been making for many months:

> If we closely examine our current success, there is much waste: functional independence and competition versus interdependence and collaboration; difficult start-ups of most significant projects, be they paint shops, new models, systems/software, capital purchases or merit processes; inability to meet customers' needs in a timely, predictable manner; and a list of others that each of you could quickly add. We have asked ourselves and each other, "If things are going so well, why doesn't it feel better?"
>
> These are critical times. When under stress, individuals and organizations tend to revert to previous comfortable behavior, and for us, that would be back toward a centralized leadership. We cannot return to our former self. We must continue our organizational transition, recognizing that even when someone understands the need for change, it may be an uncomfortable transition when he or she is in the middle of it.
>
> We are putting an organizational structure and process in place that we believe will better support individual growth and excellence, develop interdependence and cross-functional collaboration as a norm, and position this company to continue to meet, head on, whatever is before us in these changing times. This process has already resulted in a flatter organization, replacing a level of hierarchy with groupings of functional leaders who will collaboratively provide senior leadership and direction.

The pamphlet summarized the role of the Functional Leadership Group (FLG), which it defined as "the senior management of the Motor Company with overall responsibility for providing a common leadership direction." Here the rubber would meet the road, and cross-functional leadership would find a home—if, indeed, it found a home anywhere.

The publication also defined the Leadership and Strategy Council (LSC)—the "overlapping thing in the middle," as Ron Hutchinson phrased it. Graphically, it looked as follows:

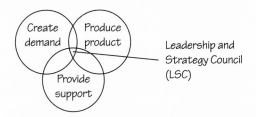

The council would consist of six members of the FLG, nominated by the members of their respective circles, and the president of the Motor Company. The LSC would decide on certain business issues affecting the entire Motor Company, such as budgets, the approval of human resources policies, and the development of other policies as delegated by the president. It would provide "pushback" and counsel to the president on all issues affecting the business. Finally, the LSC was charged with coordinating and facilitating cross-functional interdependent activities.

The document also defined three types of decision making:

1. Type 1, in which an individual decides alone, using available information and without necessarily explaining the rationale for the decision either to superiors or to subordinates
2. Type 2, in which the individual shares the problem with subordinates or peers and seeks their input before deciding
3. Type 3, in which the individual seeks input from subordinates and peers, and these people, working as a group, assist in generating and evaluating alternatives and then decide by consensus

The circle organization comprises much more than we have attempted to capture in this short summary. One of the more exciting innovations in the scheme was the "circle coach," mentioned earlier. The plan defined a coach as someone who would "possess acute communication, listening, and influencing skills, and be highly regarded by Circle Members and the Motor Company president."

"In a typical organization," explains Jeff Bleustein,

you go to the big boss, talk him into your idea, and then count on him to beat your peers into submission. Ultimately, you need their cooperation, but it's easier to get it through the big boss than by talking to them.

The concept of the circle organization takes the big bosses *out* of the circle. You call them "coaches." They're still out there, but now their job is to mentor and help, rather than to make decisions. Coaching could be a temporary post, or it could continue indefinitely. In our case, it went away, although from time to time we've thought about reintroducing it.

The specifics of the circle organization (particularly the roles and responsibilities of the LSC) also changed frequently—twice in 1996, and again in 1997—so the circle organization continues to be a moving target. But by the time this new organizational structure came into being in the summer of 1993, it represented a real, articulated, and substantially new way of doing business.

How were things different? People who historically had taken their ideas, work products, problems, and complaints "up the organization" were now encouraged to work with the right people to get the work done. Decisions began to be made as close to the source of the problem or topic as possible. People who had occupied formally hierarchical command-and-control positions were being transformed from "commanders" into facilitators and coaches.

The complete picture of the circle organization is shown below. Notice that the outward focus on stakeholder is depicted by arrows pointing into the stakeholder area. The arrows that point across circles indicate increased recognition of interdependence.

Jeff Bleustein, for one, recognizes the uniqueness of the circle organization.

Yes, it's *really* different. I've seen nothing like it elsewhere. Sure, there are a lot of companies with self-managing work teams on the factory floor. In fact, that's where a lot of innovation comes in some companies—as far away from the executive offices as you can get it, in fact, because if it blows up, the executives want to be insulated from the explosion!

But we said, "Hey, if it's a good idea for the factory floor, why isn't it a good idea for senior management, too?" So we took the concept of self-managing groups and made that work at the executive level. I

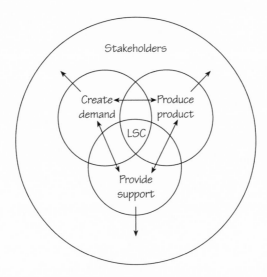

haven't seen another company that's done that. Maybe they're doing it under some other name, but I've never spoken about it without getting a "wow!" kind of reaction. Now, that can be either "wow, great!" or "wow, crazy!" But it's a "wow!" for sure.

Waiting for the Test

The circle organization, as noted, came into being on July 1, 1993. This constituted mostly a symbolic event, because the formal transition mainly ratified the hard work that Harley's leaders already had completed.

Up to that point, implementing the circle organization meant retrofitting existing management structures. That represented a large task, and the people who accomplished it deserve great credit. But the circle organization still faced challenges, beginning with the top of the organization. The Harley board, for example, didn't like the impact of the circle organization on executive succession. Instead of three likely candidates for the top job, for example, now there were none—or else, depending on how one looked at the circles, there were twenty-five.

"That has driven them nuts, at times," Jeff Bleustein confirms.

But the beauty of this concept is that each of those functional leaders sees, at least some part of the time, things that only the executive vice president used to see. On a regular basis, they get to see the other related areas and what their problems and issues are. They get to work on a regular basis on the distribution of resources among competing demands. So, whenever our board has a bad moment on this, I tell them, "We have twenty-five people getting the experience that only three people used to get."

Some senior managers, too, doubted the wisdom of this new organizational structure. "The circle organization has turned out to have a dramatic impact on the company," says Tim Savino. "But in the early days, some members of the senior leadership group were skeptical. They thought of it as some sort of social experiment."

One observer, Don Kieffer, was a manufacturing engineer at the Capitol Drive plant when the circle organization was installed. That plant's capital budgeting process struck Kieffer as strange, almost from his first days at Harley:

When the PPG [Produce Product Group] looked at these different capital budget agendas all at the same time, they said "Oh, *man*! We could have had a V-8!"—meaning that if they had aligned their goals, the same amount of money could have been spent to have a much better effect on the operation.

The action they took as a result was to create a mirror circle of their direct reports. They told this group to think through the capital budget from all three perspectives. This was very different: a group of VPs telling a group of directors, managers, and chief engineers from different functional areas that they had to work together and deliver one budget that was aligned. That was surprising, difficult, and productive.

For an organization unaccustomed to consensus building, the circle organization presented some frustrations. When disagreements arose in the early days of the FLG, some individuals simply "toughed it out," on the theory that the first person to give ground would lose. Other people experienced problems separating *ideas* from *individuals*.

Again, Harley was not an organization that was used to wrestling with ideas. Jim Paterson, circle coach of the "create demand" circle (eventually shortened to CDC) recalls one early episode illustrating this point:

> I was working with the CDC, and at one point, we brought together some people who were not all on the same level—in more ways than one. There was one fellow in particular, from one of the plants, who was as rough around the edges as you could get. Call him "Tom." At one of our meetings, a VP of sales—call him "Dave"—was expounding on some subject. Tom listens to this speech, looks at Dave, and says, "That's the dumbest thing I've ever heard of in my life." He really reamed Dave out pretty good. Dave looked like he'd been shot. Now, remember—this is a vice president, circa 1992.
>
> Later in the meeting, Dave gave his opinion about some other subject, and Tom lights up and says, "Hey, *great* thinking, Dave!" Well, you could see that this completely confused Dave. So I said to Dave, "What are you thinking?" Dave said, in so many words, "Gee, a while ago, I thought he *hated* me. Now I think maybe he thinks I'm okay."
>
> I said, "So which is it, Tom?" And Tom gave us a big grin and said, "Hey, Dave, when we're in a meeting talking about *ideas*, whether I like you or not has absolutely nothing to do with it. My job is to deal with your ideas."

These challenges forced Harley's leaders to articulate the rationale for their new organizational structure. The real tests of the circle organization, though, still lay in the future. What would happen if and when external markets shifted dramatically? Would the circles, and the work groups within them, prove flexible enough to respond to changing circumstances?

When the circle organization was implemented, demand for Harley's products was soaring. All could see that the company soon would need additional manufacturing capacity. What would happen if and when Harley set out to build a new facility from scratch? Could the natural work groups handle that challenge? Would Harley find itself yearning for a return to the command-and-control era, when leaders made decisions centrally and (for better or worse) decisively?

We present one answer to these questions in chapter 11, which describes Harley's effort to build and operate a new manufacturing facility in Kansas City and to change work patterns at all existing plants—significant organizational changes, all based on the principles of the circle organization and natural work groups. We continue that discussion in chapter 12, with several more cases in point.

RICH: Everything we're talking about is a work in process. And it always will be. And if it's working 40 percent of the time, I'm really excited. Because, under the old system, it might have been working 5 percent of the time. Is 40 percent perfection? No, but it's eight times better than 5 percent.

8

The Whole Package

AS WE CONTINUED OUR REVIEW OF ALL THE POLICIES, PROCEDURES, and processes that had to be aligned to make the kind of organization envisioned by Harley's workforce a reality, we soon turned our attention to the issue of *compensation*.

Salaried employees across the company were asserting that Harley's system of compensation prevented certain kinds of positive changes. Employees argued that, at the end of the day, the "real" work of Harley-Davidson was the work that the company recognized in a paycheck. This "touchy-feely" stuff seemed okay, people told us, but the organization would resist the kinds of behaviors that were being proposed until the company recognized and rewarded those behaviors.

This stance came as no surprise, of course. But Rich and his Harley colleagues wanted to state the challenge of compensation in a particular way: How do we motivate people to do what's needed, consistent with the values and principles that we are espousing, and reward them for doing so?

In this chapter, we recount how the people of Harley addressed the challenging issue of compensation, and attempted to link compensation with the larger process of organizational change. The company's leaders on the management side laid out a conscious strategy to achieve two goals. First, the company sought to make a larger portion of the employee's compensation at-risk or variable. Unless hourly employees worked on a piece-rate basis, the only portion of their compensation that varied was the amount of overtime. This, Harley's leaders felt, had to change.

The second goal was to compensate all employees in more or less the same manner. Harley's leaders saw no compelling reason to distinguish one "class" of employees from another class by means of compensation schemes. In fact, Rich and his colleagues saw compelling reasons to move *away* from such a system. The goal was not to pay all employees the same, but to create a set of "pay components" that applied across the company.

> LEE: We pushed on this front to make the point that all Harley people were sailing in the same boat, and that one group wasn't "better" than another. So this initiative felt very congruent with all the other principles we've been describing. And Harley has progressed farther in this direction than any other company I know about.

For simplicity's sake, we'll continue to tell the story from our (Lee's and Rich's) shared perspective. But—as with the organization structure story recounted in the previous chapter—as the changes at Harley gained momentum, they also gained an increasingly broad base of support. The organization, in other words, took more responsibility, and we played less central roles on a day-to-day basis.

What Makes for Happiness?

At the outset of these compensation-related discussions, Lee engaged Harley's executives in a review of the relevant organizational and motivational theorists. For example, the group discussed Abraham Maslow's theories (as they had when Lee was first interviewed by Harley in the fall of 1987). They moved from discussing the "older" theories of Maslow to the current work of Ed Lawler—recognized worldwide as one of the leading theorists in compensation concepts and practices, and the person who had originally steered Lee toward Harley—and his colleagues at the Center for Effective Organizations, who were (and still are) studying and applying leading-edge compensation philosophy.

We concluded that to a great extent, even the most contemporary compensation concepts were rooted not only in the theories of Maslow, but also in the work of Frederick Herzberg, a Case Western Reserve University professor and author of *The Motivation to Work*. Herzberg linked challenge to motivation, arguing that an individual whose job afforded opportunities for growth and development would be more satisfied than an individual whose job "disconnected" effort and achievement.

LEE: Herzberg is a psychologist, and as such, he's not particularly interested in the specific organizational mechanisms that might make his ideas implementable. But his ideas do tend to get people going, in these kinds of discussions.

Herzberg carried his theories to a logical extreme. Compensation, he argued, failed to motivate many people. Under certain conditions, in fact, compensation was actually a "dissatisfier," rather than a "satisfier." Field studies testing Herzberg's work, including a six-year study at Texas Instruments in the 1960s, substantiated many of Herzberg's controversial assertions.

Rich, Lee, and the other participants in these discussions dug deeper into the issue of motivation. Eventually, they reached some conclusions of their own. For example, if one defined "motivation" as *the drive within people that causes them to behave as they do*, then the real challenge before Harley was not to "motivate" people. Our review of the relevant literature and research (as well as our operating experience) confirmed for us that all human behavior is "motivated"—it just may not be motivated in the directions required for organizational effectiveness.

RICH: We were saying that, by definition, Harley's people were already motivated. If that was true—and we believed it was—

then the real challenge was to align people's intrinsic motivation with the needs and priorities of the company.

Harley's leaders brought another data point to these discussions. Through the Joint Vision Process, Harley had learned that on a fundamental level most people wanted the same things from their company. We decided—again, based on a review of current research and literature as well as on our own experiences—that this phenomenon was not unique to Harley. It was true elsewhere, too, although it was seldom effectively acted on in hierarchical, "command-and-control" organizations. This reality of *underlying consensus* implied that if the compensation system focused on the right goals—and, of course, if employees perceived the compensation system as comprehensible and fair—then alignment of motivations would not be all that difficult.

Conversely, if Herzberg and other theorists and practitioners were correct (and our experiences suggested they were), then money alone wouldn't persuade people to give their best efforts to the organization. As Lee commented during one of these discussions, "If you're counting on money to get you there, you'd better have a lot of money!"

Old Theory, New Theory

Somewhere in the course of these discussions, Rich, Lee, and the other participants decided to summarize the real logic behind the existing compensation system. They wanted to capture what was *really* going on—as opposed to what compensation-related policies might claim was going on.

This group arrived at the following set of assertions, all of which seemed to lie behind Harley's then-current approach to compensation:

- People, being extrinsically motivated, only "produce" for money.
- Motivation is always a "good." A motivated employee always advances the company's interest.
- The company must ensure that it provides salary and benefits high enough to attract and retain high-caliber employees.

• Annual salary reviews and performance-based merit increases should reflect measures established by a few key leaders, who have the benefit of the "big picture."

But this summary underscored the obvious flaws in that compensation logic. Based on the Joint Vision Process, Harley's leaders knew that Harley's employees cared about more than money. For example, they cared about the company's products, its reputation, and its heritage. And, although employees had identified many frustrating barriers to the envisioned future, most enjoyed their work. In short, they "gave a damn," and compensation wasn't a serious dissatisfier.

One had only to walk through the plants and offices of Harley to confirm this conviction. People were diligently bent to their work, committed to doing "the right thing" whenever they could, and an ever-increasing number of employees were becoming stockholders of the corporation. It wasn't all that uncommon for someone working in production to scrutinize the part or subassembly that he or she had just completed and say, "Maybe this is okay by the quality standard, but I don't think it's *Harley* quality yet." Or, alternatively, "I know this customer, and he needs this part to be better than it is, so I'm going to make sure it's done *right*." In fact, it was typical for employees to volunteer to work longer hours in all kinds of weather to serve riders at various motorcycle rallies.

In other words, gaps existed between the *theory* behind Harley's compensation practices and the *reality* of the company and its workers. Harley's next task, the leadership group decided, was to come up with a new compensation theory that squared better with reality. After more debate and discussion, it reached four conclusions:

1. People (including Harley's employees) seek opportunities to act on their intrinsic motivation, which exists in everyone and comes to the fore under the right circumstances.
2. Salaries and benefits are only a part of a *totality of rewards and recognition*. This totality—the overall mix—makes an individual want to be a productive contributor to the larger organization.
3. People expect the totality of the rewards and recognition that they receive from their employer to be fair along two dimensions. First, they expect their employer to recognize and reward them fairly in comparison to

workers at other companies where they could reasonably expect to work, and second, they expect fair treatment in comparison to their coworkers.

4. Rewards and recognition must *focus on the right things*. Rewards and recognition that focus on counterproductive behaviors work against the company's best interests.

The leadership group then decided to review all of the existing compensation, benefits, and other recognition and reward systems across the company, to determine which were not compatible with this four-point philosophy of compensation.

They found plenty of examples of bad practices. One of the most obvious was a program called "STIP," or the Short-Term Incentive Plan, which applied to approximately seventy-five relatively senior-level individuals. Success under the STIP formula generated large bonuses for these individuals. Perversely, though, the company calculated STIP bonuses in the late 1980s *purely on the basis of financial performance*, even though the poor quality of the company's products by then was negatively affecting Harley riders—by most accounts, some of the most patient customers in the world!

The irony was hard to miss. Rich and others were struggling to get the company focused on quality, customer service, communications, employee involvement, and open and honest dialogue. Meanwhile, through 1989, the STIP program, which bore the official imprimatur of the company and traded in a very real currency (bonuses!), focused solely on the numbers.

RICH: The "numbers-only" focus of STIP supported conventional wisdom. It was a carryover from the pre-LBO days with AMF, when it would have taken a crystal ball to see where Harley was headed. But STIP was a heck of an illustration of a company working at cross-purposes with itself!

STIP was only one example of the compensation issues that surfaced during this period. Between January 1990 and the end of 1993, Harley's leaders focused on bringing these examples to the surface and on changing practices that did not conform to the new compensation philosophy articulated by the leadership group. Bill Gray, vice president of human resources, and Margaret Crawford, in charge of general compensation planning, led these efforts, assisted by Corty Cammann, one of Lee's ROI colleagues.

Gray, Crawford, and Cammann found their work to be challenging, in part because the standard the company was abandoning—pure financial performance—was so simple and concrete, while the new reward standards were much more complicated. But they also had to resolve the tough issue of *recognition*. Recognition systems often pose an even greater challenge than compensation systems, strictly defined.

For example, one employee might appreciate her merit raise but might *really* value the corporate "seal of approval" that lies behind that raise. Another employee might value and gain recognition from face-to-face discussions with a particular person in the corporate hierarchy. A supervisor might hand out a choice developmental assignment as a form of recognition and reward, even though no one had ever described the assignment that way on a piece of paper. Every day, in countless instances across the organization, individuals and groups awarded "attaboy" and "attagirl" points.

The reward and recognition team had to force to the surface this "shadow system" of rewards and recognition, and reckon with it—at the same time, of course, they were dealing with the company's more visible and traditional compensation structures. Harley's companywide effort, which consisted of literally hundreds of interventions small and large, took the better part of two years.

PEP and Compensation

In chapters 5 and 6, we wrote at length about the Business Process, a key piece of which was the Performance Effectiveness Process (PEP). While Harley's leaders conceived of PEP as a way of aligning the individual's efforts with the values and strategies of the larger organization, they also saw the plan as the foundation for the individual performance review, compensation review, and career development processes.

At Harley, PEP would serve three purposes. First, of course, it would link the individual's objectives tightly with the work unit's plans, which in turn linked to the operating unit's plans and which in turn fit under the corporate Umbrella. As such, PEP played a key role in the larger Business Process.

Second, the review would help the employee understand how her performance squared with the company's expectations of her and with her own "commitments" (jointly developed objectives, agreed to by the individual and her supervisor). This was largely *historical*. "Here's what you and we expected of you," the work unit leader would say in so many words, "and here's what you actually accomplished."

Third, the performance review would help the individual shape his or her own development. "Based on what we've decided about my work objectives," the individual might say, "here are the skills and competencies I need to be more successful at this company in the future."

Ideally, managers would schedule performance appraisal and career development reviews to take place on separate occasions, preferably separated by weeks or months. In Lee's experience, however, most companies cut corners and combined these two functions in one meeting. Individuals learned of their merit raises at the same time that they learned about developmental issues. This, Lee pointed out, almost always proved counterproductive. If the supervisor begins the review session by revealing the amount of the raise, then the employee feels either pleased or displeased. In either case, he or she remains distracted by *that number*. Maybe he dwells on how the extra money will be spent, or he spends the remainder of the session deciding how to demonstrate his unhappiness.

But, if the supervisor withholds the raise information until the end of the developmental phase of the discussion, then the employee tends to be equally distracted. "Why is she holding back? How much did I get? Is it bad news?"

These kinds of problems led eventually to PEP. PEP grew out of the Business Process, which called for the development of plans on four levels: strategic plans, operating plans, work unit plans, and personal plans. Now, for the first time, performance reviews would take place in the context of specific road maps which individuals and their supervisors had devised jointly. This led to significantly more productive reviews.

Concurrently, Harley's human resources managers modified relevant policies and procedures so that the merit increase announcement process was separated, in terms of both time and purpose, from both the performance appraisal feedback and the developmental planning process.

"We separated compensation from the performance review," explains Flip Weber. "On April 1, everybody gets an increase, and that's separate from the review. Of course, you can't *completely* divorce the two, but they're no longer tied together, driving each other."

The change had immediate and positive effects. With the raise issue off the table in one of these two meetings, employee and supervisor could discuss feedback and planning issues cleanly at their other meeting.

From Attitudes to Behaviors

During the early 1990s, Harley began a significant transition in its approach to compensation: away from focusing on an individual's *attitudes*, focusing instead on that person's *behaviors*.

Most companies have what they consider to be "problem employees" (or some other equally damning term). And at most companies, supervisors assume that these problem employees have "attitude problems." The supervisor who reaches this unhappy conclusion really has only two choices: get rid of the problem employee or try to change that person's attitudes. Neither choice has much appeal.

To help Harley begin to address this problem, Lee led the company's senior managers through a series of discussions on why people act the way they do and how those actions should be interpreted. He first likened people to onions—sentient and highly complicated onions, of course, sporting many concentric layers of complexity.

At the core of every person, Lee explained, resides a very private and personal set of *values*. For the most part, these values take shape during early childhood and rarely change in adulthood. They tend to be strongly held and at the same time poorly articulated. They tend to be hidden from others—even those who know us well.

LEE: I've known Rich for twelve years now, for example, and I think I'm beginning to get a good sense of his values. But it's not because of anything he's said about those values. It's because of how he lives them.

The next concentric ring, working outward from the core values, are the individual's *beliefs*. Beliefs represent the person's attempt to articulate core values. When someone declares that he or she "believes in the union movement" or is a "yellow-dog Democrat" or is a "dyed-in-the-wool capitalist," that person indirectly reveals something important about his or her underlying values.

Harley's managers extended the onion metaphor beyond the individual to the organization. When organizations talk about their "values," they are actually talking one level "up" (that is, on the level of a belief structure). Much of the work that Rich and his colleagues had done up to that point, in trying to get the organization to portray its own values, really focused on organizational *beliefs*.

RICH: We continue to talk about "values," however, because that word has the right kind of resonances. That's why, in the new employee orientation manual, we list Harley's values, along with a definition of each one and a corresponding list of indicative behaviors. People understand that and find it useful.

The next two layers outward are *attitudes* and *behaviors* (see figure). *Attitude* generates confusion and even conflict. The confusion results, in part, from the fact that the word itself has multiple meanings, which differ from each other in subtle ways. One sense of the word, usually applied by an individual to himself or herself, is "rationalization," and this sense is usually invoked when the individual knows that his or her behaviors don't fit well with his or her values and beliefs.

For example, an individual may believe that the human body is the temple of the Creator (a belief that speaks to deep religious values). This same individual may smoke little black cigars and understand that inhaling cigar smoke defiles the temple. Beliefs and behaviors come

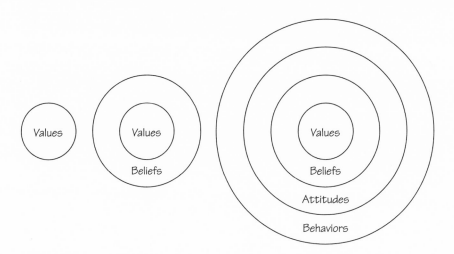

into conflict, and as a result, the individual conjures up an "attitude" to deal with this uncomfortable discrepancy. If I stop smoking, so goes the rationalization, I'll gain 100 pounds and die of a heart attack. So my smoking is "okay." An "attitude" serves as an excuse for a behavior.

People also use the word *attitude* judgmentally. Person A observes the behavior of person B, makes assumptions about person B's values and beliefs (filtered through Person A's own particular lens, of course), and then labels Person B as having a certain bad *attitude*.

Most people have had the experience of being told they "have a bad attitude." This almost always sounds like an accusation and almost always evokes a defensive response. "Oh, yeah?" says the accused. "If you think my attitude is bad, you ought to see so-and-so!" Or, more personally, "If you didn't treat me like dirt, we wouldn't be talking about my attitude!"

Working with Lee, Harley's leaders gradually reached the conclusion that the company should simply sidestep the whole realm of values, beliefs, and (especially!) attitudes. Instead, when it came to compensation, the company should focus strictly on behaviors.

After all, the Joint Vision Process had revealed that Harley's employees held more or less the same beliefs about the company. So, in one important sense, beliefs were not an issue. And, as these experienced managers knew, from a very practical perspective *no one* likes being told what to value or what to believe.

As a result of this emerging consensus, Lee made a series of informal

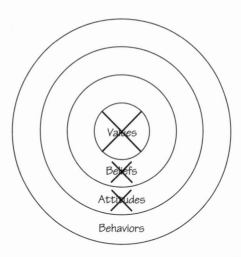

presentations to groups of line managers and supervisors, in which he summarized this way of looking at supervision. Many in these audiences responded positively on a rational level. (Their "heads agreed.") But, on a gut, intuitive level, they wanted to continue their standard ways of doing business, especially in the interpersonal realm. At one of these sessions, for example, a manager challenged Lee.

"I'd *like* to believe what you're saying," he said hesitantly, "but I just see too much evidence against it. For example, right now I've got an employee—call him "Bob"—with what I'd call a real bad attitude problem. He misses at least a day of work a couple of weeks out of each month, and sometimes more. Time and time again, we have to cover for him, and it puts our group in a tough spot. As far as I'm concerned, that's a major attitude problem!"

Lee didn't contradict this manager, who had a difficult problem on his hands. Instead, he suggested that the manager simply *ask* Bob why he was absent so much.

Two weeks later, the manager set up a conversation with Lee to inform him of the results of his conversation with Bob. "I asked him, 'Bob, why is it that, on average, you tend to work only about four days a week?' And he said, 'Well, because I've found I just can't *make* it on three days' pay.'"

Lee and the manager discussed the implications of this exchange. They agreed that the manager didn't really have a problem with Bob's attitude; it was Bob's *behavior* that was problematic. The manager resolved to deal only with the offending behavior— inconsistent attendance—and not with an "attitude."

This approach led to the first constructive and positive conversation that the manager had had with Bob in months. The manager emphasized that Harley expected certain behaviors from its employees and that Bob would have to find a way to meet those expectations. Bob changed his behavior, his work group stopped getting disrupted, and the manager moved on to other pressing issues.

RICH: As far as I'm concerned, you can be a dedicated communist, as long as your behaviors fall into the zone that the company has defined as acceptable. It's only when your beliefs change your behaviors in ways that hurt the company that I start to pay attention. Even then, I don't address the communism. I address the behaviors.

LEE: The classic context is grievances. Typically, the union walks in, throws the grievance on the table, and says, "Everybody in management is a bunch of goddamned liars!" And management responds with "Well, we wish to hell you guys gave a damn about the future of this company, which you obviously don't!" Well, that confrontation is all about values, beliefs, and attitudes. In my experience, it can't go anywhere positive.

Embracing Variable Compensation

Harley began pushing in the late 1980s for variable compensation for *all* of its employees, salaried and union alike.

Regarding the salaried side, Harley's leaders wanted to make sure that the criteria used to determine variable compensation were closely tied, *on an annual basis*, to the evolving goals of the company. The

Salaried Reward Study Group (actually formed as part of the larger Joint Vision Process) outlined a plan for the Motor Company in November 1989 that would achieve a series of broad goals, including:

- not paying bonuses when the company lost money.
- not paying bonuses that would make the company lose money.
- extending variable compensation that was "fiscally responsible, meaningful for participants, and consistent with the Motorcycle Division's strategic direction."

The Short-Term Incentive Plan (STIP), described earlier in this chapter, was the first of Harley's variable compensation plans to be retooled. The human resources group shifted STIP from being based 100 percent on financial performance to being based on one or more of fifteen separate criteria. Financial performance remained the criterion with the heaviest weight—ranging from 30 to 70 percent, from year to year—but other criteria began playing an important role. See table 8-1 for an example of a hypothetical (but realistic) contrast between two years.

TABLE 8-1:   COMPARISON OF WEIGHTING (PERCENTAGES)

1993		1995	
Financial performance	40	Financial performance	50
Quality	30	Quality	20
Delivery	20	Delivery	0
Expense control	10	Expense control	
Working capital	0	Working capital	10
People/PEP process	0	People/PEP process	10
People/Business process		People/Business process	10

Just as significant, the company extended STIP (or programs like STIP) to broader and broader pools of employees. Originally restricted to senior executives, in 1990 STIP was extended to all salaried individuals. In 1992 the company extended a STIP equivalent to Milwaukee-based hourly employees and in 1993 to York's hourly employees.

(The plans at the various plants sported various names but had similar provisions.) Human resources established a schedule of quarterly meetings—now called "Compass" meetings—to update employees on how they were doing, vis à vis their STIP and STIP-like objectives, and to provide an opportunity for a dialogue on other issues of interest.

Slowly, as hoped, the balance shifted—away from a dominant focus on fixed compensation and toward an emphasis on variable compensation. Table 8-2 (again, hypothetical but realistic) is a before-and-after look at this shift, particularly as it pertained to higher-paid executives, who—being paid more—should have more at risk:

TABLE 8-2:   PRE– AND POST–PEP BUSINESS PROCESSES

Pre–PEP/Business Process		Post–PEP/Business Process	
Percentage of compensation		Percentage of compensation	
Fixed	85	Fixed	67
Variable	15	Variable	33
Components of variable		Components of variable	
Financial measures		Financial measures	
		Nonfinancial measures	

Harley's unions embraced this shift only gradually, but they eventually supported it with enthusiasm.[1] In Kansas City, for example, the unions signed a seven-year labor agreement. That agreement specified a base pay and also called for an annual 2 percent wage increase which each year would go into the base rate. In addition, employees could get up to a 3 percent pay raise *only for the ensuing twelve months* if several jointly established goals were met. In other words, if they didn't meet their goals in 1999, they wouldn't get their variable compensation in 2000.

And, finally, beginning in the summer of 1999, as a result of this same collective bargaining process, all employees at the Kansas City plant

---

[1]   When this process of change began, some of Harley's hourly people were still on piece rates. These individuals in particular had to make some large psychological transitions in a relatively short period of time.

became eligible for stock options. The Kansas City employees agreed with management that this important step was in keeping with the company's new compensation philosophy and would serve the interest of employees.

RICH: More than once I tried to persuade our unions that stock options were in the best interest of their members. Way back in the dark days, when we had little else to offer, I suggested stock options as a way for our hourly employees to participate in the successes that we hoped would come. I sincerely wish that they had taken up my offer back then.

Career Banding and Forced Ranking

As noted in chapter 7, the circle organization formally came into being at Harley on July 1, 1993. Among other things, the new organizational structure promoted cross-functional thinking and behaviors.

Harley's leaders had already discovered, however, that the salaried compensation scheme then in place worked actively against this goal. At that time, there were seventeen salaried pay grades across the company, and these grades overlapped only slightly. Increasingly, Harley's HR managers encountered situations in which a salaried individual who wanted to move (with the company's blessing) into a new functional area discovered that such a move would involve a step down in pay grade. Many individuals chose not to make such a move, even though all parties agreed that, from a developmental standpoint, moving made sense long term.

"We spent tons of time," recalls Margaret Crawford,

trying to help people move from one grade to the next. We started to realize that, if we were going to build skills across the organization, the pay grade system would hurt that effort. You wouldn't sign for a job that was an 8 on the other side of the organization if you were already a 9—even though you were qualified and really needed that experience. Because of a hypothetical $12,000 salary difference at the top of the two pay grades, for example, you'd forgo a really important opportunity.

In response, Harley's HR managers came up with a "career banding" scheme. Instead of seventeen pay grades, there would now be six "bands." Since band 1 was reserved for the CEO and band 2 for the vice presidents, this meant that all of the salaried employees at Harley would fall into one of four bands. Substantial overlap existed from band to band. This meant (in theory, at least) that an individual could step sideways in the organization and not take a salary "hit" in the process. And, in theory, individuals would be less inclined to perpetuate the hierarchy and manipulate the system—for example, by changing job descriptions to move people up in grades.

"Career banding," Rich wrote to Vaughn Beals in April 1992, "is the revised compensation and merit review system that will be implemented as PEP becomes fully operational. As you may recall, this system will compensate people not only for their performance, but also on their demonstrated capabilities." In other words, qualifying for a new job meant you could do more; therefore, you should be paid for that capability.

But theory doesn't always translate perfectly into practice. When career banding was put into place in 1995, the salaried ranks at Harley received it with marked hostility. To many, it appeared that the company was taking away opportunities and career paths, rather than making new opportunities more accessible. Through continuing communication efforts, the company has alleviated some (but not all) of these anxieties.

RICH: We need to encourage people to look for their next opportunity within the company. Going from seventeen bands to six opens up opportunities from a compensation point of view. We didn't take the time to explain it properly and make it clear how career banding would introduce more flexibility into the system.

LEE: Most manufacturing companies still struggle with the mechanics of their salaried compensation system. They spend inordinate amounts of time tinkering with those mechanics and wrestling with a huge array of overly specific job descriptions. They finagle titles, rather than promote the creative development of people.

One of the company's biggest mistakes in the compensation area came in April 1993, with the introduction of what was called the "forced distribution component" or, more commonly, "forced ranking." Harley's leaders were concerned that peer reviews tended to degenerate into mutual back-scratching. A suspiciously high percentage of ratings came out as "excellent," year after year—even though it seemed that not everyone being rated was excellent. Drawing on a system developed at pharmaceutical giant Merck, Harley proposed that each department identify a certain number of top performers, a certain number of average performers, and a certain number of poor performers. In theory, the really high performers would receive more pay, and the poor performers would receive extra remedial attention from the company.

Again, reality departed from theory. "Forced ranking qualifies as another big boo-boo," admits Margaret Crawford. "Being perceived as messing with people's pay is not a good thing. Forced ranking was an effort to get the colluding under control, but it had a tremendous impact on the employees, and they were very suspicious about why management was making this change. It translated, in people's minds, into 'more work for less pay.'"

The company abandoned forced ranking within a year. But, in Crawford's mind at least, forced ranking died at birth.

> In truth, we *did* focus more on the poor performers, but we didn't ever say, "Okay, now there has to be a 5 percent contingent identified as poor performers and penalized financially." And meanwhile, of course, we weren't working on really separating the great performers from the inflated-rating performers.
>
> Our biggest mistake was in trying to do everything at once.

RICH: As I see it, in retrospect, our biggest mistake was in not understanding how all these changes fit together and how much of an overall shift this represented. We were putting a lot more responsibility on our supervisors— telling them to stop playing games and compensate people for their performance.

Thinking about the Totality

In retrospect, some of the lessons of our journey together strike us as painfully obvious. But we didn't learn them quickly or easily, and we suspect that other organizations that engage in large-scale change processes will have to learn them again, in their own unique ways.

For us, one such lesson is that "compensation" has to be thought of in the broadest possible way. We spend roughly a third (or more) of our waking hours in the context of a particular human organization. We get paid, at most, once a week. Most of us receive formal reviews only once or twice a year.

All the rest of the time—the huge majority of our working hours—we actively seek rewards and recognition in nonmonetary realms. We seek opportunities to be heard, and we seek evidence that the company values our contributions. We seek genuine involvement in the decision-making and problem-solving processes. We seek to know and understand what is going on. We seek a *positive, total experience* with our organization—and this seems to be a fundamental piece of our human nature.

In one leadership training and development session that Lee conducted for management leaders at the Capitol Drive facility, the participants generated a list of forty-nine steps that could be taken to help create this kind of total experience—specifically, in a union context, in which everyone is paid the same amount for the same work. The list included specifics in two categories:

Things that can be done now

- Keep people informed.
- Be courteous.
- Buy coffee for department.
- Buy lunch for department.
- Improve physical working conditions (e.g., floor mats as requested).
- Provide T-shirts.
- Provide temporary use of company motorcycles.
- Give compliments on good work; say "thank you."
- Delegate extra work to good employees.

- Provide "good" work to good employees.
- Provide challenge or increased responsibility in work content.
- Provide periodic counseling (stressing positive performance).
- Put letter in employee's personnel file.
- Recognize by allowing person to be lead person.
- Select employee to attend training.
- Provide seminars or visits to other HD locations or other companies.
- Give rewards or incentives of nominal value for special effort (e.g., dinner for two).
- Allow compensatory time off (with pay) for extra effort.
- Provide foreman's leave.
- Allow proper grievance adjustment.
- Make invitations to attend staff meetings, opportunities to report on accomplishments/activities.
- Establish quality circles.
- Select employee to blue-ribbon task force.
- Offer profit sharing.
- Get with employees to improve work cells (all subjects).

Things that can be considered in the longer term

- Provide company bike for department use by employees.
- Give front-row parking to top employee in each department.
- Provide flex hours.
- Improve physical working conditions (e.g., offices).
- Provide gain-sharing or profit-sharing programs.
- Offer stock options.
- Modify merit system to provide greater rewards for good performance (and lesser rewards for "average" performance).
- Give bonus for unusual or special accomplishments.
- Provide pay or incentives for completion of cross-training.
- Give promotional opportunities within same job position to recognize performance.
- Provide special training programs outside of plant.
- Throw company-sponsored retirement parties.
- Award attendance bonus at retirement.
- Give company picnic.

- Allow personal leave or time off with pay.
- Provide vacation based on merit or longevity.
- Provide opportunities for high levels of employee involvement.

Clearly, some of these ideas (profit sharing, stock options) were policy-level decisions. But the vast majority were not. Most could be accomplished within existing budgets and needed few or no corporate authorizations.

So why weren't they already being done?

The participants discussed this question seriously. They concluded that they had never before been encouraged to think about this topic in exactly this way. Now that they *were* being encouraged to look at the totality of rewards and recognitions this way, they could easily implement many of these ideas.

RICH: The important thing is that this list came from people thinking about the problem. And, once you start thinking about it, you can't just let it fall off the table and go "plop" on the floor. You have to take the next step and do something about it.

Individual leaders, working with the employees within their area of responsibility, began applying one or more of these forms of recognition. In many cases, the *form* of the recognition was not significantly different from what had been done in the past. The difference was that those affected were asked for *their* thoughts on what actions, behaviors or outcomes should be "recognized," and what form that recognition should take. Now a "pizza party" was well received, whereas in the past, the reason for that same pizza party might not have been well understood and the recognition not appreciated. The Harley ball cap, coffee cup, or T- shirt that may previously have been received with a yawn by the recipient was now perceived as positive recognition, because those involved in the process had participated in the definition of the *criteria for* and *form of* the recognition. And this made all the difference.

Pieces in the Larger Puzzle

Many of these ideas—and others generated subsequently—*were* implemented, and Harley benefited from their positive impact. And, perhaps more importantly, this new way of looking at rewards and recognition, and the attendant new focus on behaviors rather than attitudes, helped in other critical realms, including assessment, education and training, and personal development.

In real life, few (if any) of these changes can go forward in isolation. None is simple. All are pieces of the larger puzzle.

9

Lifelong Learning

BY THE EARLY 1990S, HARLEY'S LEADERS — UNION AND management alike—had committed themselves to encouraging intellectual curiosity across the organization. In fact, during the Business Process, they had put this commitment in writing: "Encourage intellectual curiosity" was one of the stated values of the corporation.

Rich had always enjoyed wrestling with new ideas and indulging his curious streak. As described in chapter 4, he acted on that commitment—and involved others in it—in the context of the first Awareness Expansion session. And, although in Rich's estimation that experience failed on some counts, his own commitment to curiosity and learning remained unshaken. He remained convinced, moreover, that Harley could learn.

RICH: In my experience, Harley had always invested in certain kinds of learning. In 1978, for example, when the company adopted quality circles, it laid out a program specifically for that purpose. When I got to Harley in '81, one of the first things I did was to go through the quality circle instruction. So we always recognized that we had to create the opportunity for people to learn. Beginning in the early 1990s, we started to institutionalize learning and make it a much more important part of the culture. We tried to give people the chance to say what skills and knowledge they needed and get the organization to serve the employees in that way.

LEE: Almost from the time I first met Rich, we tended to get caught up in talking about the latest article, or book, or magazine we had read. We'd compare notes, and push each other with ideas. I can't remember when we first discussed "lifelong learning," but it must have been in the late 1980s. That was something we couldn't have missed. Neither of us would have spent a lot of time with an organization that didn't value continuous learning and growth.

Most companies engage in education and training. Most, too, have structures in which top management defines the hoped-for learning, and that learning is designed, developed, and delivered by trainers and other education specialists. But this model no longer seemed to fit Harley. Rich and others felt strongly that continued success depended on everyone in the company agreeing to be learners throughout their professional lives—and on people agreeing to contribute to the definition and delivery of learning.

After spending some time reviewing adult learning theory and principles, Harley's leadership group decided on a new educational path for the company. That new path incorporated a set of assumptions:

- Adults learn best when they themselves have determined that they need to learn.
- Adults learn best when they determine what they need to learn.
- Individuals must take personal responsibility for their own learning.
- In traditional degree programs (bachelor's, master's, doctorate), educational institutions provide basic technical and conceptual knowledge. The knowledge of particular use to a specific organization is the responsibility of that organization.
- Harley had to encourage and facilitate a lifelong learning environment.

These assumptions led naturally to a number of focused activities—a learning journey, in other words—that eventually led to the creation of new institutions at Harley designed to foster curiosity, teamwork, leadership, and lifelong learning.

More Awareness Expansion

These principles took shape in the second and subsequent Awareness Expansion sessions. The second Awareness Expansion session, held at the Nordic Hills Country Club southwest of Chicago in May 1990, reconvened the same participants from the first Awareness Expansion session (AEI). Like that first session, Awareness Expansion II (AEII) enabled these participants to hear the same subject presented by speakers with very different points of view. However, the AEII approach was entirely different.

In AEI, as described in chapter 4, Lee and his colleagues shared the leadership and program development responsibilities with the Executive Committee, and took sole responsibility for facilitation. Recognized experts presented their views in an effort to challenge the thinking processes of the participants. In AEII, by contrast, internal resources provided the facilitation, and the purpose of the session was to encourage dialogue and debate over *alternative* approaches to the same subject—another step along the leadership journey. (Lee's only role in AEII was as an observer and "backstop" to internal resources; he was available to step in if the situation began to "get out of hand," but this did not occur.)

The AEII session focused on contrasting views of the organization. The first view, presented by organizational theorist Chris Anderson, held that the organization should be driven largely by systems, procedures, plans, and structures. In this type of organization, change comes from revisions to the relevant systems, procedures, plans, or structures.

RICH: I had heard Chris Anderson speak. I knew how strongly he felt about programming people to a desired level of performance. He liked to use the example of maids. According to some studies, the productivity of maids increased dramatically if you gave them a checklist to make sure that everything got done in the room. Well, that seemed like an interesting approach. Is that what we wanted Harley to be like?

The contrasting view, presented by Peter Block (author of *The Empowered Manager*), held that the organization should be driven largely by its *purpose*. Purpose (and, behind purpose, values) should drive all organizational actions and behaviors. In this view, systems, procedures, plans, and structures are simply tools for advancing purpose, and as such, they should be maximally adaptive and responsive.

LEE: The way we presented these contrasting ideas to the participants was that, as far as the Executive Committee was concerned, neither of those two presenters was necessarily the embodiment of what ought to be done at Harley. At the same time, each had something useful to offer. Rich said explicitly, at the opening of the session, that this meeting was about intellectual curiosity. It was about dialogue, argument, and discussion—alternatives to "command and control," where top management would tell employees what was correct.

Participants received the relevant materials in advance—Anderson's audiotapes, Block's *The Empowered Manager*—so they could prepare themselves to engage in the discussions. And, in fact, most came prepared to argue against either Anderson, or Block, or both.

Awareness Expansion II also included a factory simulation exercise. Tom Jacobi of Saginaw Steering Systems, Inc. (who had worked closely with Tom Gelb on quality-in-manufacturing issues) devised the simulation, which aimed to help nonmanufacturing people achieve the following learning goals:

- To better understand material flow as part of a "linked" process
- To learn more about the implications of inventory levels
- To see the impact of varying process yields on the manufacturing operation
- To learn how to improve on manufacturing lead time

This simulation led to several important kinds of learning. First, as intended, participants learned the enormous scope of Harley's real challenges, as the company attempted to become more efficient and effective in its manufacturing operations. Nonmanufacturing managers gained a new appreciation for the difficulties their manufacturing counterparts faced. And, second, participants learned that many of Harley's operations *outside* the manufacturing realm faced similar challenges, which probably entailed other kinds of complexities.

The group's plenary sessions demonstrated that most participants had concluded that Harley did indeed face the challenge of continuous improvement. Continuous improvement was critical not only for price competitiveness, but also for competitiveness in the realms of quality and delivery.

"What I recall most about that session," says Tim Savino,

> is that we heard forceful presentations from both ends of an idea spectrum. Anderson was saying that you needed control, and Block was talking about empowerment. A lot of people found that stimulating, but others felt frustrated. You could hear it around the corners of the room: "Why didn't Rich just tell us what he wants?" And I have to say that those kinds of things kept getting said for a long time. There's a very human tension between wanting to be left enough room to create things for yourself, and wanting to *just be told* what to do, because that's almost always a whole lot easier.

LEE: While there remained some of what we experienced in AEI—the question of why Rich didn't just tell them what he wanted—AEII saw considerably less of that phenomenon. Most of the participants became truly engaged in the learning process and were beginning to get excited about making choices for themselves.

So, although some of the frustrations persisted, by and large the participants generally agreed that Awareness Expansion II surpassed Awareness Expansion I. (Postsession written evaluations went from approximately 50 percent positive to approximately 80 percent positive.) Most participants reported that they had received some useful "take-aways" from the experience, which they planned to apply in their job settings. Most seemed impressed by the magnitude of the challenge facing their company—not only fixing past mistakes and current practices, but also finding avenues for continuous improvement in the future, across a range of functional areas. Helping people start to get out of functional "silos" and figure out how the needs of the larger company had to be defined: this turned out to be an important piece of the learning from Awareness Expansion II.

RICH: That was key. One result of looking at what somebody else does in their work, and why they look at things in the particular way they do, is intellectual curiosity.

LEE: I'd point out how much things had already evolved. In Awareness Expansion I, my ROI colleagues and I facilitated the discussions. In Awareness Expansion II, I was the only one there from my firm, and I only observed and provided some continuity. I didn't do any facilitation; the participants facilitated their own discussions and dialogue. So they were making some progress in these skill areas, and that augured well for the larger process.

RICH: To tell the truth, I still had some problems with the Awareness Expansion experience. And my main problem was that I was still taking personal responsibility for it. What else would I have liked to have happen? I can't say exactly. Maybe some sort of great upwelling of enthusiasm at the end—"Hallelujah, brother! We're going on this journey!" I still had that uncomfortable feeling we could have done better. But I feel that way about a lot of things.

In the fall of 1990, the Awareness Expansion group came together for a third time, although this time the meeting wasn't billed as an "Awareness Expansion" exercise. The venue this time was an unusual facility in Wakarusa, Indiana—near Holiday-Rambler's main manufacturing plant—called the "Port-a-pit," a combination conference center and barbecue restaurant. ("Port-a-pit" was derived from the restaurant's original mobile barbecue units, mounted on trucks.) The purpose of this session was to encourage the participants to review each other's strategic plans and then to break out into functional meetings to discuss how each functional group could help the other.

As it turned out, these goals served other important ends at the same time. By talking through each other's plans, managers practiced thinking and acting as a group, building the kind of trust and skills that would be needed to help Harley get to its newly envisioned future. That future included both individual responsibility and team-based management, and this meant a new kind of culture had to be fostered.

LEE: This felt different. This felt like a group of colleagues trying to make their respective widgets better. They coached each other in trying to improve their product— in this case, their plan. So this represented real progress. Two years earlier, they had never even met each other. Now they were improving each other's strategic plans.

RICH: I would agree that it worked on site. Unfortunately, that kind of cooperation didn't carry forward. Both units—Harley and Holiday-Rambler—were working so hard on their respective problems that they didn't have a chance to really meld. And, in retrospect, I should have taken more responsibility for setting up, say, quarterly integration meetings of manufacturing people companywide. The momentum was there, but we didn't push it.

A culture characterized by intellectual curiosity would render "awareness expansion" sessions unnecessary. In fact, it was accidental that this particular gathering became seen as the third in a series of "awareness expansions." During the afternoon break, one participant rendered a verdict on the experience. "Now, this is *real* 'awareness expansion,'" this participant said. "We're learning from each other, and we're increasing our understanding of our respective businesses."

As a result of comments like this (and other responses from participants who suggested topics and recommended learning processes for such sessions in the future), Lee and the Executive Committee adjusted the design of the next formal Awareness Expansion session, Awareness Expansion IV, held in the summer of 1991. They described Awareness Expansion IV's goal as follows: "These sessions, along with our vision and respective mission statements, have made clear that a critical role of leaders is to teach, counsel, and coach others. With that in mind, Awareness Expansion IV will have as its purpose *learning from each other*."

In retrospect, we (Lee and Rich) read this as being at least a little heavy-handed. But, as noted previously, a central paradox of organizational change is that the formal leaders—even in efforts to replace "command-and-control" forms of leadership—have to nudge the evolution along from time to time.

But how could the company achieve this laudable goal? We decided that we would take this goal statement very literally: Everyone would become a teacher (and, of course, all would become learners). Through an iterative process between the Executive Committee and their respective "reports" at Harley and Holiday-Rambler (in which participants were asked to further refine and identify the learning agenda for the next session), we selected five topics that would serve as the content focus of Awareness Expansion IV:

1. Personal power
2. Time management
3. Leadership
4. Time as a competitive advantage
5. Creating a lifelong learning organization

Several weeks before the session, the Executive Committee assigned each of these subjects to a cross-functional/cross-divisional group of six to eight participants each. We gave each group responsibility for making a presentation to the larger group on its assigned topic. For between sixty and ninety minutes, they would serve as our resident experts on their assigned topics. Within this time period, they would report on their readings and research, and implement a specific learning exercise they had designed. We gave each group a reading list on its assigned topic, and we encouraged them to speak to any consultant or other expert they wanted to in advance of the session. But, when the time came, we told them, they would be entirely on their own—in other words, they couldn't call on any outside consultants during the delivery of the teaching session.

> LEE: I was listed as one of the resources, along with a bunch of other outside authorities. And I got a phone call from a member of every one of those teams. What I got from them was, "Boy, this is really neat. Do you know anybody else who knows more about this?" In a couple of cases, people were nervous and didn't want to make fools of themselves. But, in every case, I got the feeling that people felt this was going to be exciting. This was going to be fun.

Awareness Expansion IV achieved a new level of participation and appeared to generate new levels of satisfaction. Most of the groups made spirited presentations to the larger group, and all seemed to have fun in the process.

The time management group, for example, divided the larger Awareness Expansion group into subgroups whose task it was to develop skits illustrating "time wasters" in a real-life context within the organization. The personal power group, which had read Stephen Covey's *Seven Habits of Highly Successful People*, prepared a video depicting attendance at a very special funeral: *your own.* Each partici-pant was then asked to write his own obituary, focusing on how he would like to be remembered by others.

These creative approaches to the delivery of learning grew out of the interaction between the members of the groups. Working together on this topic was a *real* learning experience for them; the exercise they developed was similarly a learning experience for the other participants.

"When we got together at the Awareness Expansion," recalls Jim Paterson, "we'd put on a skit to summarize the works we had reviewed. And some of the work that came out of those was fantastic."

Awareness Expansion IV was not a complicated event, nor was its design especially elegant. But more than anything else that had pre-ceded it, Awareness Expansion IV successfully demonstrated how

Harley's managers could succeed at both teaching and learning. It showed that individuals could take responsibility for their own learning and also could come together in a process of joint education. These were important lessons for key managers to learn in the evolving Harley culture.

> **LEE:** In terms of my role, Awareness Expansion IV was yet another step along in the evolution of the Awareness Expansion and learning processes. In contrast with other sessions, I wasn't even in attendance at Awareness Expansion IV. Each group discussion was led and facilitated by the group assigned to the topic, not by professionally trained internal resources. This was just one more milestone on the journey.

Exploring the "Fifth Discipline"

Another offshoot of Awareness Expansion IV was a long-term relationship between Harley and the MIT-based Organizational Learning Center (OLC), the research group headed by organizational theorist and consultant Peter Senge.

Senge was the author of *The Fifth Discipline*, a book that both Lee and Rich had already read. Senge argued that successful organizations called upon five key disciplines: personal mastery, mental models, shared vision, team learning, and systems thinking. These disciplines fit together neatly with the initiatives that Harley already had under way (and some, including the Joint Vision Process, that were in a state of suspension or inactivity).

The Executive Committee itself presented *The Fifth Discipline* at Awareness Expansion IV, in advance of which Senge spent a day in Milwaukee as the committee's background resource. Senge evidently enjoyed his interaction with Harley's senior managers and asked if the company would join forces with his then-fledgling OLC.

On Harley's behalf, Rich readily agreed, and Harley soon sent delegations of managers to OLC's initial course offerings. The approach to learning contained in Peter Senge's work was an excellent fit with the approach that was evolving throughout the change process at Harley. Joining forces with OLC would give the organization another potential resource on which it could draw. Senge's original learning design called for a sequence of five two-day courses, but this proved unwieldy over time; eventually, the course evolved into a single five-day "competency" course, which was far more successful from the Harley managers' perspective.

"I was in the service function in 1992," recalls Ron Hutchinson,

> when Teerlink dragooned eight or nine of us into going to Boston for this MIT/organizational learning stuff. The group consisted of three people from human resources, three from other functional areas, and two corporate weenies, including me. We had no idea why we were going there.
>
> But we trucked off to Boston. We did ten days' worth of training over a six-month period—two days of training at either a site in Silicon Valley or at an East Coast site near Boston. Senge himself was involved in the first few sessions. And, to make a long story short, I fell in love with it. Boom! Wonderful. It combined the hard stuff, the discipline of engineering, with the softer stuff.

Tim Savino also became an early convert to Senge and the OLC, and especially to the emphasis on lifelong learning. "The work over the past six or seven years with that group has been really powerful," he says. "Many senior leaders have involved themselves directly, helping to form the core learning labs that they do today. We began to do a lot of experiments here—piloting learning labs, learning maps, systems labs, computer simulations, and so on. We'd introduce these tools, and different people would get excited about different aspects of them."

LEE: From my perspective, this represents one more major vehicle that Harley has embraced for the purpose of organizational and individual learning. It's a rich menu, in a sense. People find what moves them, and they take responsibility for their own learning.

RICH: Things take time to gestate when they're really different. And Senge's work with the OLC was really different. It took time for those ideas to put down roots around the organization. But as long as you have a few zealots running around promoting this kind of idea, the idea doesn't go away. And sooner or later, it comes to full flower.

Harley had a history of zealots in the ranks, although, traditionally, they had turned up in the product and design realms. Now a growing number of "zealots" emerged who strongly supported the newly envisioned organization and culture (as well as the "continuous learning" concept). In part because of its prior experiences with zealots, Harley accepted its newest ones with relative good will and grace. The innovative thinking and creativity exhibited in the product design and manufacturing history of Harley was now finding a form on the "softer" side of the business.

Learning Leadership

Each Awareness Expansion session helped its participants graduate to a new level of understanding and learning. We knew, though, that this approach was limited, in part because it simply couldn't reach enough people. Learning opportunities like the Awareness Expansion sessions had to affect many more people, and on a more frequent basis.

LEE: We were also beginning to get some pushback from the unions by this point. People were beginning to ask, "Well, if this stuff is so great, why aren't those responsible for this process at these meetings?" I won't say it was overwhelming, but word was seeping out, and more people wanted in. I took that as an indicator of success.

To accomplish this end, Harley in 1991 created the "Harley-Davidson Leadership Institute." The institute would formalize and centralize all the various learning, training, and development initiatives and activities then going on across the company. In the design stage, we debated for some time about the name of the proposed institute. In some ways, "leadership" seemed too narrow, given that the institute would focus on a broad range of topics in addition to leadership. But, from another perspective, "leadership" seemed exactly right. Harley was asking all of its employees to be leaders in everything they did. An institute explicitly focused on that challenge seemed like a clear and appropriate symbol.

"When we first established the Leadership Institute," recalls Margaret Crawford, "we tried to identify the behaviors that would help people assume leadership even if they didn't have formal 'leadership' responsibility. We wanted to help build the leadership competencies that were needed to create the kind of environment in which empowerment flourishes across functional lines, and in which people have the necessary skills to communicate effectively."

In August 1991, as a first step toward creating specific course offerings for the Leadership Institute, Jim Paterson and human resources leader Bill Gray interviewed a number of outside experts who had excellent reputations for designing and implementing leadership programs in other organizations. Harley retained two of these experts—David Ulrich and Ray Reilly, then faculty members at the University of Michigan's School of Business—and, after a series of discussions, agreed that a two-week program in leadership should be the institute's first offering.

At the outset, Ulrich and Reilly believed that Harley and its leadership had already achieved a reasonable level of sophistication. What else, they asked rhetorically, would explain Harley's remarkable success in the marketplace? Jim, Bill, and Rich suggested the existence of a gap between Harley's public image and the reality, and implied that the consultants might need to climb a few rungs down the sophistication ladder.

LEE: It's interesting to note that, once again, the external world thought Harley was doing superbly in product quality, financial performance, and, implicitly, managerial competence. The folks inside Harley, however, had "signed on" to a process of continuous improvement and learning: the journey. The image and the reality were not one and the same, but, fortunately, the Harley people usually weren't seduced into resting on their public laurels.

RICH: Dave and Ray started talking about course design. Dave had done a lot of very interesting work with GE and suggested that some of that learning might apply to Harley. We said, in effect, "That may be a little advanced. Why don't you go around the company and interview people, and then come back and tell us what you want to do?"

These interviews led to a substantial shift in direction. The consultants reported that what Harley really needed was a more basic course in management skills, probably of a week's duration. Longer and more sophisticated courses might follow later, but for now, the company's managers needed fundamentals.

LEE: During this same period, the Joint Vision Process was identifying barriers, and it turned out that people regularly cited inadequate supervision as a barrier. This, combined with the consultants' findings through the interview process, led to the one-week supervisor training program, which we first offered at Capitol Drive.

The human resources group introduced two initial five-day courses—Leadership Fundamentals and Functional Excellence—in the early months of 1993. They enrolled 436 "students" in the former, and 349 in the latter. Participants provided almost uniformly positive feedback, emphasizing in particular the benefits of meeting and studying with employees from other functional areas in the company. Based in part on this positive response, Harley has continued to offer these courses periodically since 1993.

"Of all the assignments I've had at Harley," says Margaret Crawford, working on this project was one of the most rewarding. First, it was fun working with Rich, who had a real clear vision of how he wanted this thing to go. And, second, it was fun to be involved in something that had such an enduring impact. People still cite examples from the first runs of those courses around here. When I was working on a revised mission statement a few years back, for example, I kept hearing about Domino's Pizza and their succinct, right-to-the-point mission statement: "a fresh, hot, tasty pizza." Well, I knew that they knew that story because they had gone through a course at the Leadership Institute.

Since 1993, employee enrollment in Leadership Institute–sponsored courses has increased dramatically. In 1994, for example, more than 2,000 of the company's 5,800 employees took courses sponsored by the institute. "This improves our competitiveness in the marketplace," noted the 1994 annual report, "while giving our employees the skills and encouragement needed for personal growth and development."

The number and scope of programs provided by the Leadership Institute also have expanded dramatically, principally because the institute brought the most popular and valued programs under its wing. Today, the Leadership Institute's "Training and Development Catalog" runs more than 140 pages. It includes courses in these twelve general subject areas:

1. Harley-Davidson: About the business
2. Employee development
3. Leadership
4. Interpersonal communications skills
5. Planning and organizational skills
6. Quality and continuous improvement
7. Teamwork and group development
8. Computer training
9. Service (product training)
10. Safety and wellness training
11. Personal enrichment (including training in motorcycle riding and stress management)
12. Technical training/engineering

It also organizes these courses in a "Competency Matrix" (described in chapter 6), which correlates particular courses to one or more of ten skills. These include:

- Personal example
- Communication
- Teamwork
- Conflict resolution
- Stakeholder focus
- Problem solving/decision making
- Planning
- Performance management
- Continuous improvement
- Technical excellence

Futurist Alvin Toffler once remarked that the illiterate of the twenty-first century will not be those who cannot read or write, but, those who cannot learn, unlearn, and relearn. Through the many programs now being offered under the large umbrella of the Leadership Institute—as well as through tuition-reimbursement programs at the undergraduate and graduate levels, and an on-site degree program offered in conjunction with Marquette University—Harley is equipping its employees to learn, unlearn, and learn again.

The Business Process Modules

In October 1993, as part of the larger Business Process (see chapter 5), the Functional Leadership Group agreed to develop a series of modules that reinforced the elements of that process. This represented an important step forward both for the Business Process and for Harley's overall lifelong learning effort.

The first course modules designed to disseminate the Business Process dealt with *values*. To get the full attention of the senior managers who would present these modules to their respective employees, Rich and Jeff Bleustein asked that the modules first be presented to *them*. The presenters put their best efforts into a module that they knew would be "test-marketed" on the chairman/CEO and the chief operating officer of the company.

RICH: We got the senior leadership group together and we asked, "Okay, who's going to take responsibility for designing the values module?" Three or four people volunteered, and that went forward.

These sessions were good practice for the more difficult sessions that were to follow: the sessions involving the *real* audience, the employees. Senior managers assembled ten or twelve people in a room and led them through a discussion of, for example, "telling the truth." Does telling the truth mean "the whole truth and nothing but the truth" (the legal standard)? Or does telling the truth mean "the truth as seen through your personal screens (to the extent that you understand those screens)"? What is an "objective" perspective? What should you do when the truth might hurt you, a coworker, or the company?

During 1994, in addition to the values modules, the following elements were covered:

- Issues
- Stakeholders
- Empowerment
- Value added

Additional modules provided during 1995 and 1996 were:

- Planning
- Continuous improvement
- Leadership
- Diversity
- Employment development
- Learning organization concepts

After these modules completed their "journey" of all the functional areas, they were presented to groups of new employees on a periodic basis.

In-House Learning Centers

Beginning in the early 1980s, when Bob Bartelme (current Executive Board member of PACE Local 7209) was a union job analyst, he saw the need to provide union members with opportunities for learning. He felt even more strongly about this as new computerized machinery proliferated on the shop floor. Finally, in 1988, Bob and Ron Lewandowski created the Capitol Drive Learning Center in a small room within that plant's offices. The center was sparsely equipped: four hand-me-down computers from the accounting department, a VCR, and an obsolete laser disc player with a geometric tolerancing program and a machine-tool programming exercise. Because Harley couldn't find anyone internal who was qualified to direct this learning effort, the company arranged to partner with Milwaukee Area Technical College (MATC). MATC provided a part-time instructional staff, and this impromptu arrangement continued for several years.

In 1991 the state of Wisconsin began encouraging the establishment of in-house corporate learning centers. Due in large part to the energy and persistence of Peggy Patterson, now manager of labor relations at Capitol Drive, Harley received a grant to create such a center. Harley expanded the partnership with MATC and at this point was able to hire a full-time adult education instructor.

Since then, Harley has added two new facilities in the Milwaukee area and has created "Lifelong Learning Centers" at each of these new locations. Eight employees—four management, four union—oversee the activities at each of the three centers. In 1992 10 percent of the employees in these three facilities used their respective learning centers; that number had increased to 60 percent by 1998.

The Tomahawk, York, and Kansas City plants, as well as the corporate offices in Milwaukee, also have learning centers and/or multimedia computer classrooms. All seven centers are open seven days a week, twenty-four hours a day. Depending on the availability of space, family members are also invited to attend specific class offerings.

Harley's human resources managers have taken many creative steps to involve larger numbers of Harley employees in lifelong learning. One was the creation of Harley's "Peer Network." This is a group of fifty specially trained employees who encourage their peers to enroll in the courses offered by their center. Members of the Peer Network wear special T-shirts every Thursday, thereby reminding other employees of the network and making it easy for those peers to seek out educational opportunities.

This work carries with it special kinds of rewards. Recently, one employee originally "recruited" by the Peer Network received his graduate equivalent degree (GED). Originally, this employee was too embarrassed to admit that he didn't have a high school diploma; now he proudly boasts of his GED.

Learning Maps

As a result of Harley's partnering approach with its bargaining units (see chapter 11), Rich and his colleagues decided that the company needed to embark on an enhanced level of specific training and education for all employees. As a result of some freewheeling discussions, management and labor jointly decided to adopt an approach called Learning Maps®, developed by the Perrysburg, Ohio–based Root Learning, Inc.

Root Learning's concept is built on the premise of the old Chinese proverb:

Tell me, I'll forget
Show me and I may remember
But involve me, and I'll understand.

Their process (according to their literature) has the following attributes:

- A large, visually rich "mental map visual" (40" x 60") is placed on a table and explored by a group of between five and seven people.
- The session includes no teachers or trainers; instead, a guide or coach is chosen. This person can be a supervisor, manager, or hourly employee.

- No one provides "answers." Instead, the process forces to the surface some targeted and provocative questions that focus on core business issues. These questions challenge everyone to think and in many cases to address unpleasant (but nonetheless vital) business and market realities.

At Harley-Davidson, groups of hourly and salaried employees from all locations have developed four such large maps. The maps address the following four topics:

1. *Our market:* Analysis of Harley's customers, dealers, and competition, and how their needs influence the direction the company takes
2. *The Business Process:* A full review of Harley's decision-making process, including the Business Process Umbrella and supporting principles
3. *Our processes:* The methods Harley uses to design and build its products, including how cost, time, and quality factor into the continuous improvement process
4. *The money cycle:* How Harley generates and spends money, and how six key financial measures influence the money flow

As with many of the initiatives at Harley, this one had what many people might consider to be a long gestation period. By the end of 1995, Harley and its unions had defined the Partnership philosophy, and saw the need to develop new and compelling ways to help *every single employee* understand the company's critical business issues *in the same way.* The Training Best Practices Circle had talked to several traditional vendors, but couldn't agree on a single format.

Consequently, the training (or HR) manager from each site was asked to identify a "joint pair" (union member and manager) to investigate whether Root Learning might be helpful. On August 8, 1996, about fifteen people traveled to Ohio to evaluate the company and its techniques.

One of these evaluators, Darlene Rindo, recalls that the group got the opportunity to "try out the learning process, and we were duly impressed with the interest and enthusiasm that it could generate even for dry statistical data." But there was a stumbling block: The Root Learning consultants had not had much success with joint approaches.

Harley's representatives made it clear—and Root Learning agreed—that if the two organizations decided to work together, the work would grow out of a joint (that is, union and management) process.

Harley's representatives went home to their respective sites, and—as so often happens—the pressure of the day-to-day distracted them. The initiative was put on a back burner until January 1997, when it was picked up again in earnest. Over the next three months, the participants built support for the concept. In April, a contract was signed to develop fully the four custom Learning Maps identified above.

The development process continued until March 1998, when fifty facilitators from all the sites started to guide their coworkers through the maps. By mid 1999, *all* Harley emloyees had been through this process.

Motorcycle U

Space constraints keep this book focused largely on the employees of Harley. Reluctantly, we give short shrift to the company's other key stakeholders, one of the most important of whom is Harley's direct customer: the dealer. And although we can't escape our space constraints entirely, neither can we write a chapter about lifelong learning at Harley-Davidson and not touch upon the story of Harley-Davidson University (HDU).

Harley depends on the skills of its dealers to build and sustain the overall market for Harley products. Customer satisfaction, competency in store layout, excellence in merchandising—all must be developed at the local level. Harley therefore must invest in the skills of its dealers.

Like the Leadership Institute, HDU was formally founded in 1992. In HDU's first run, the sales and marketing group sponsored it, and it was aimed at increasing competency levels at the dealer level. First, though, Harley had to improve its own skills. Ron Hutchinson, who refers to HDU as his "love," tells the story:

> A training outfit out of Michigan actually put together the first run of HDU. That group took four existing automotive-industry

courses—F&I (Finance and Insurance), Dealership Management, and so on—stuck them between two covers, and offered them in February in a hotel somewhere west of Milwaukee. The courses were terrible, it snowed like a bastard, and the hotel ran out of beer.

Maybe even worse, we gave that course away. We gave the dealers the course, gave them the airfare to get there, and, I'm told, gave them each a *really nice* leather jacket.

Okay. The following year, Harley took a different tack. They turned to the service function, and said, "Hutch, we want *you* to run HDU. And, by the way, you won't have half the budget that they had in Marketing, so you have to find a way to get the dealers to pay for part of it."

Tall order! But a group of us got together and cooked up a new approach. We put together a much more aggressive program, with better courses and wonderful keynoters. Basically we interviewed the dealers and found out what they really wanted, and built an educational seminar around that. And then we went out and *sold* the bugger. Very successfully, I think.

Some 750 people attended the first three-day run of the revamped HDU. The following year, that number increased to almost 1,000, representing more than 650 dealerships worldwide. Gradually, as with the Leadership Institute, the number of participants and the number of course offerings increased. By 2000, HDU could boast 1,800 paying participants enrolled in twenty-three courses. Today, dealer tuitions and fees cover approximately 60 percent of the cost of HDU, while the company picks up the rest of the tab.

We designed both the internal and the external training programs to do the same thing. We designed them to put leadership at the lowest possible level in the organization and thereby turn the bureaucratic triangle upside down. This was good for the organization, and also good for its traditional "leaders." We freed ourselves to change our roles—from providing purely directive leadership to providing supportive, creative, even visionary leadership. That's what giving people skills is all about.

Building Skills, Cherishing Ideas

In this chapter, we've omitted a whole other strain of learning and skill building—that which took place in Harley's engineering and manufacturing realms. We tell that story in a more extended way in chapter 12.

Part of the challenge Rich and Lee faced at the first Awareness Expansion, which all of Harley's leaders subsequently faced, was persuading their colleagues to embrace ideas. In business, the "hard" tends to drive out the "soft." Especially in bad economic times, numbers tend to overwhelm ideas. Things that have nonquantifiable value—and this is usually the case for ideas—get undervalued.

But when a corporation adopts "encourage intellectual curiosity" as one of its core values, ideas get a toehold. They get a fighting chance to prove their immense value to that corporation over the long run.

RICH: It's always a struggle. I remember one point when some employees tried to organize a book group at lunchtime. It didn't get to where they wanted it to, and it dissolved itself. People told me that they enjoyed those lunchtime discussions, but that they really couldn't spare the time. My response was, "Well, okay, but how will you find the time to do the things that are important?" How do you make ideas important enough so that, sometimes at least, you're willing to play with ideas rather than do "real work"? Lee and I always put "real work" in quotes, but I'm not sure people always hear those quotes.

LEE: I agree with Rich's main point. But, at the same time, I have to say that I've seen real and positive changes. When I first started working with Harley, I was struck by all the groups of two that would head off to lunch at the nearby sandwich shops. Harley had a very specific kind of collegiality.

Today, I see larger groups coming together. You find people saying, "Let's reserve a conference room for tomorrow and get the six of us together, so we can pick each other's brains about so-and-so." They haven't exactly gotten off the work train, but they're definitely worrying about ideas. To me, that's a real affirmation of progress.

10

Determined to Communicate

THROUGHOUT THE TWELVE-YEAR JOURNEY DETAILED IN THIS book, one of the most difficult challenges Harley faced as a company was the thorny issue of *communications*.

Like most of the companies that Lee and Rich had worked with, Harley spends a lot of time, money, and energy on the task of communicating with its employees. And, despite this substantial investment, communications problems—in other words, failing to convey the right information to the right people, at the right time—remain one of the biggest bones of contention at Harley.

"What we have here," said Paul Newman's jailer in *Cool Hand Luke*, "is a failure to communicate." Perhaps the human need to communicate can never be perfectly satisfied in the context of an imperfect organization. But we still have to try as hard as possible to promote effective communications in our organizations. In other words, we need to get the *right* information to the *right* people at the *right* time by the *right* medium.

In this chapter, we recount Harley's efforts to make communications among its people mean more and work better. To a large extent, leaders at the company's individual plant locations drove these efforts.

To Dictate or to Influence?

Back in the good old days (which continue to this day in many corporations), the senior managers in the corporation determined what everyone needed to know, when they needed to hear it, and the best method for delivering the message. By design, they owned the big picture. They therefore took responsibility for figuring out which piece of that big picture they would communicate, to whom, and in what form.

When this top-down approach to communications proved ineffective—as it usually did, and does—senior managers tended to blame their audiences. "They don't care about the company and its needs," they would grumble among themselves. Or, worse, "Obviously, these people can't *understand* such complexities!" A logical next step in these circumstances was to cut back on the information flow. Why share the big picture with people who can't appreciate it?

RICH: In a very, very strong command-and-control atmosphere, employees may not feel that they need much information. They've opted into that situation for one reason or another—perhaps the pay scales, or the benefits packages. But, once you start getting away from command and control, the demand for information starts to go way up, and that's a good thing for the organization, as I see it.

LEE: A company pays a steep price for having a bunch of highly paid automatons doing its work. They don't think for themselves, and they don't make that company any better. Harley didn't want that.

We recognized many of these same symptoms and tendencies as information flowed, or failed to flow, across Harley. In one of our discussions on the subject, one manager made a powerful observation. "It's interesting," he said. "We want all of our people to be 'on the same page,' but we don't necessarily want them to read the book."

What explains this reluctance among managers to share information? We've already introduced several of the managerial assumptions behind this reluctance:

- Employees don't care enough about the company's fate to be trusted with sensitive data.
- Employees can't understand complex issues.
- Employees really don't *want* to know what's going on.

As we talked about these issues, we added a fourth explanation: managers who are stuck in a command-and-control mind-set see information as power. Information, in this mind-set, is a finite commodity, and transactions involving information are zero-sum games. If you acquire some of my information, you acquire some of my power.

The information-as-finite-commodity perspective represents a larger view of management's power and prerogatives. Let's call this kind of authority *dictate power*. Dictate power is measured by one's ability to dictate actions and outcomes. Almost by definition, dictate power is finite. (If you and I issue contradictory orders, only one of us can prevail.) Dictate power must be reinforced constantly, in part through the *relentless acquisition* and *limited dissemination* of information.

We decided early that attempts to control people through dictate power are almost always (1) wrong and (2) wrong-headed. Aside from the ethical issues, information is available to almost anyone—not only courtesy of the Internet, but also from other sources, such as investment advisers, rumor mills, and the news media. In many cases, the information is already out there, usually sooner and in a far more complete form than most organizations even imagine.

We'll call the other kind of power *influence power*. In this view, the true measure of a manager's power is his or her ability to *influence* actions and outcomes. But, to achieve influence power, the leader must share information as broadly as possible. The believer in influence power seeks to maximize the knowledge and information that others possess and thereby to extend his or her influence across the organization.

Rich and his colleagues were not interested in dictate power. Indeed, they found it hard to imagine any circumstance in which the effective communication of information would hurt the company or diminish the authority of its leaders.

But this still left open some extremely important questions. Should everybody get exactly the same information? In what depth? No one wants to have a fire hose turned on them. If Harley disseminated *all* information to *everyone*, it would be the information equivalent of turning on a very large fire hose. Could Harley's leaders develop an approach to customizing and conveying information selectively, an approach that wasn't at its heart a disguised form of dictate power?

A New Approach

Our emerging sense that Harley had to find a new path was strongly reinforced by several complementary sets of data: the results of the barrier identification and communications committee discussions that grew out of the Joint Vision Process and several surveys conducted among all Harley employees in 1991 and 1993.

These different streams of information highlighted some consistent views among the people who worked for Harley (management and union alike). In general, people were very positive about

- the company in general.
- Harley's products and services.
- Harley's "close-to-the-customer" philosophy.
- the work that people did in the course of their jobs.
- the company's pay and benefit programs (considered as a whole).

Just as consistently, though, employees were far less positive about

- communications.
- relationships with their supervisors.

These latter findings concerned us. Discussions with key union and management leaders (as well as with the communications committee established during the Joint Vision Process) did nothing to allay our concerns. First-, second-, and middle-level supervisors and managers felt that they communicated diligently to employees in their respective areas of responsibilities—*to the extent that they had the information and the time to do so.*

Many of these key supervisory leaders saw themselves as "good soldiers" caught in a tough process. They dutifully passed along corporate information to the employees in their area of responsibility, without modifying (or seeking reactions to) that information. Few of these "good soldiers" were happy with the quality of the information they were passing along. In fact, some of them told us, the information sent down the chain of command rarely spoke to the needs of the employees. Meanwhile, things that employees *did* want to know about weren't discussed.

A smaller (but significant) number of this same group confessed that they did the minimum amount of communications-related work possible—usually just enough to avoid problems with their immediate supervisors. The reason? They already felt overwhelmed by the "real work" of the corporation. Anything that wasn't urgent—including most forms of top-down communications—wasn't viewed as real work, and therefore the task of communicating didn't get done.

Of course, this realization in and of itself wouldn't surprise anyone who was familiar with corporate life. What *was* different was the way Harley ultimately went about addressing these concerns. We decided to apply the principles of the larger change process at Harley to the communications challenge. Harley's only sustainable advantage (we believed) was its people. Harley therefore should stop "taking solutions to the people." Every employee should take personal responsibility and be accountable for the success of the company. Sticking with the old patterns of communication therefore made no sense. Harley's senior leadership couldn't unilaterally determine what the company's employees wanted and needed to know, nor could they be the sole repository of wisdom concerning the form and timing of communications.

Instead, Harley's leaders should ask those employees what they needed and wanted to know, and then give them that information. This we were philosophically inclined to do, and we also recognized that this was a practical and realistic approach. Why hide information that people already had access to, in one form or another?

LEE: Let's imagine, for example, that Harley's managers in the mid-1990s had gone to the bargaining table pleading poverty.

Well, who's sitting across the table from them? Smart people who ride bikes themselves, who go to the dealerships as customers, who know the dealers are telling people there's a two-year wait for a new bike, and who know—based on published information, as well as these kinds of first-person discoveries—that Harley's making a ton of money. Is it smart to come into the first negotiating session dressed in rags? Of course not. You destroy your own credibility.

Concurrently, if we succeeded in making information more valuable to people, we also had to ensure that this information flowed successfully. And, finally, we had to ensure that people understood effective communications to be an essential part of the "real work" of the company. Harley's reward and recognition system had to place a real and visible value on effective communications.

RICH: When I first became a supervisor, my dad took me aside and told me something. "Your whole life just changed," he said. "You've just become the most important person in the world to the people who work for you. You are responsible for what they're paid, when they take vacations, and to some extent even what they know. You are their line of communication."

Asking What People Want

These discussions took place in the early 1990s, at roughly the same time that Rich and his Harley colleagues were focusing on the changes that collectively took the name of the "Business Process" (see chapter 5). Lee, Rich, and others saw that the Business Process would fail without effective communications up, down, and across the organization.

Lee and Jim Paterson worked simultaneously on several fronts, which they conceived as complementary and mutually reinforcing.

First, they developed a simple data collection worksheet, which included the following questions:

1. What information/communications do you now receive that you do not need or want? *(Be specific.)*
2. What information/communications do you now receive that would be more effective and/or helpful if delivered in a different way and or a different time? *(Be specific, and include suggestions for improvement.)*
3. What information are you NOT now getting that you would like to get? *(Be specific, and include suggestions re/ what, when, how.)*
4. Other suggestions that you may have to help HD better meet your communications and information needs? *(Be specific.)*

All employees at Harley's manufacturing facilities in Wisconsin filled out this worksheet, and an outside agency compiled the results. Concurrently, Lee and Jim initiated a series of focus group discussions (not involving worksheets) at Harley's Milwaukee headquarters.

Lee cautioned the Harley leaders involved in the communications review to expect the unexpected. This heads-up proved to be a relevant one. The surveys and focus groups strongly suggested that much of the information that the company was then providing to its employees—in an earnest, reasonably thorough, and expensive effort to keep people informed—was perceived by employees as neither *necessary* nor *valuable*.

Many respondents felt that Harley disseminated far too much "global" information, which most perceived as unrelated to the realities of their own responsibilities. Others felt that the content of Harley's communications took too academic or complex a form. Still others felt that company information tended to be delivered from "on high," in too formal a manner, or in ways that limited employees' opportunities to ask questions and engage with the content of the message. A number of respondents objected to the fact that the company disseminated information to them only *after* the same message had appeared in local newspapers or on the evening news.

The results generated by question 3 on the data collection form ("What information are you NOT now getting that you would like to get?") were particularly enlightening. Responses to the previous two questions clearly indicated that many people felt they were suffering from the fire hose syndrome: too much information coming too fast. But responses to question 3 indicated that people had an active interest in how companywide data might help them in their own jobs and areas of responsibility.

In other words, these employees *were* interested in the affairs and fate of the company. (In fact, Harley's leaders were surprised to learn the depth of interest in strategic issues that faced the company: new products and services, long-range marketing strategies, diversification plans, and so on.) But this kind of information remained inaccessible and useless to individual employees until it was translated into the terms of their particular work area.

One step Harley's leaders took to effect this translation involved reinvigorating the company's tradition of "Town Hall" meetings at the plant level (a process kicked off by the Joint Vision Process described in chapter 3). Senior corporate leaders personally held sessions with employees at all of Harley's facilities.

"We ran quarterly meetings with every employee in the organization," recalls Jim Paterson. "I'd go out to York for two days every quarter and hit all three shifts. I'd do a day every quarter at Tomahawk and another day at Capitol Drive, with one colleague or another. We tried to be thorough and frank. We took notes, did follow-up, and tried to get back to people on their issues. Sometimes people raised issues that we couldn't address, but we made an honest effort."

In addition, plant leaders at each site translated the corporate macrodata in a way that had meaning for that particular plant. Then the next management level "down" in the plant, working with their union counterparts, shaped and detailed the data for the needs of particular departments. The numbers themselves didn't change from plant to plant, of course, and different departments within plants wouldn't get contradictory information. But data became increasingly focused on each unit of the organization, as information flowed "downward." There was less companywide information and much more information of specific departmental interest.

For example, in past communications efforts, "warranty costs"—the costs incurred by Harley for repairs and/or upgrades accomplished by dealers under the factory warranty on the motorcycles—were reported corporatewide. In the new approach, the reporting of these data was broken down into the models and types of motorcycles, so that employees learned the warranty costs for the motorcycles *they produced*. Similarly, cost-of-manufacturing reports were broken down by plant, department, and even shift, so that employees could get the data reflecting activities that could be affected by *their own actions*.

On a third front, Rich and his colleagues held discussions with every individual then in a management leadership position. The discussions aimed at helping to make communications an essential part of the "real work" of the organization.

Some contextual details and chronology might be helpful at this point. We were just getting under way with the work described in chapter 8 (aimed at retooling the company's recognition and rewards systems). The company had not yet made the transition from rewarding general traits and characteristics to rewarding specific, observable behaviors. So although "good communications" were supposed to be a management goal, people had few clues as to what that meant in terms of concrete and observable behaviors, or how a manager might communicate more effectively.

A second problem also emerged at this point. At Harley, as at other corporations, the "hard" tends to drive out the "soft," unless there are strong countervailing pressures in place. Production tends to overwhelm "people issues." Why? In part because it's far easier to measure objectively "hard" areas (units produced, defect rates, absenteeism) than soft areas.

We didn't expect to find easy answers to these questions. But key leaders, in their meetings with Harley's middle-level managers, hammered away at a central theme: that creating and maintaining an atmosphere of open and honest dialogue was an *essential task* of any manager in a leadership position at Harley. They translated the lessons learned in the context of this communications initiative into the emerging language of the recognition-and-rewards initiative.

At the same time, the human resources group developed training programs to help managers demonstrate the behaviors that would encourage open and honest dialogue—for example, two-way versus one-way communications, active listening, encouraging dialogue, and so on. Human resources personnel delivered these training programs to small groups of managers beginning in the summer of 1993. (They continue, to this day.) Many of the tools, techniques, and internal resources developed during the Joint Vision Process (see chapter 3) also helped managers and employees engage in more effective dialogues. As noted above, Town Hall meetings occurred more frequently, and plant managers and other leaders revised their format in response to suggestions by employees. Managers made themselves much more visible to their employees and learned to depend more on face-to-face communications and somewhat less on written communications.

As the Business Process described in chapter 5 unfolded, it provided an even more structured and "real work"–like communications vehicle. The Business Process began primarily as a vehicle for improving a two-way dialogue. It evolved into the primary mechanism for personal and unit goal-setting and performance review, which in turn enhanced the kinds of communications described in this chapter. Once again, independent initiatives converged to help the company.

LEE: Each hand washed the other. It's difficult today to imagine how one would work without the other.

The Other Survey

The survey administered by Lee and Jim in 1991 was only one of two large-scale communications audits conducted in that year. The other— a survey in which Lee and his colleagues were not involved—was conceived by the human resources group as the first in a series of biennial audits. These surveys would track employee attitudes over time, and this first effort would serve as a baseline.

Rich and his colleagues hoped for relatively good news from this baseline audit. After all, Harley had spent more than three years on a large-scale effort to improve relationships and communications across the organization. Its leadership (management and union) hoped to receive high marks for those efforts. As it turned out, they did not.

"The results were abysmal," recalls Ron Hutchinson. "People told us in what looked like large numbers that we weren't walking the talk. People told us that they never saw senior management. In short, the numbers were terrible."

"I remember when that first survey came back," adds Jim Paterson, who at that time was spending one week out of every twelve full time on his Town Hall meetings at various plants. "That was devastating to me, as well as to Rich."

In the immediate aftermath of that survey, people pointed fingers in many directions. Most people in leadership positions assumed that the criticisms implied by the survey were directed at *other* people, not themselves. Rich, upset by the results, made his unhappiness known.

"Oh, yeah," Ron Hutchinson says,

Rich got angry—as angry as I've seen him, I think. "It's your fault, you guys! You go fix this!" But we all knew on some level that we couldn't just "go fix it." Because we were dealing with a huge change. We were forcing more responsibility down into the organization, and what people needed was lots more reassurance that they were doing the right thing. They needed more visibility from their boss's boss, or from the functional leader. We were doing a lot, and it simply wasn't enough, in light of the scale and the pace of the changes.

"Rich drove himself *nuts* with those surveys," Jeff Bleustein added.

He was very, very hard on himself. Results like that devastated him. And in a bad moment, he'd blame the Functional Leadership Group: "You guys are too busy 'doing things!' You don't care about the important stuff!"

Frankly, that drove a bit of a wedge at times, because people really *were* trying to succeed at all this stuff. Maybe they didn't have all the necessary tools, but they believed, and they were trying. But coming up short was very, very frustrating to Rich. Sometimes he thought he was out there all alone, when in fact he wasn't, at all. He had a lot of committed people behind him, changing their own behavior and trying to drive this change throughout the whole organization. They weren't perfect, and their efforts weren't flawless. But they—we—were *pioneering*. We were venturing out into unknown territory, and it wasn't easy.

As the dust settled, Harley's leaders began thinking more rationally about what the survey "meant." They realized, for example, that these results (and the results of any successor surveys) would always have to be interpreted in a vacuum. There were no global norms against which they could be compared. If, for example, "only" 27 percent of employees endorsed Harley's communications efforts as "adequate," was Harley doing better or worse than other companies? No one knew.

The 1991 survey seemed to portray an unhappy group of employees. And yet the same survey revealed that almost everyone would recommend that a friend seek employment at Harley. In addition, few employees were *leaving*. True, the company paid its hourly people well and its salaried people relatively well, but would this keep people on the job if they were truly unhappy? This didn't fit together with what Rich, Lee, and others had already concluded about compensation and recognition (see chapter 8).

LEE: Not unlike the other organizations with which I have worked, the initial reaction of Harley's leaders was defensive: "It's their fault, not mine," or "These people are never happy, no matter what we do!" But they got beyond that defensive posture— something that too many other organizations don't do, by the way —took the data seriously, and folded these data into all of the other change efforts under way. In other words, these data reinforced and instructed all the other actions being taken to move the culture of the organization.

Kathleen "Kal" Demitros provides one perspective on polls and their interpretation. Demitros is currently Harley's vice president for communications, but in 1991 she was on assignment in Europe.

"There's a tendency to confuse the effectiveness of communications with how employees feel about their employers," she explains. "And these are two distinct animals.

> The 1991 survey was very much an employee relations survey, in my opinion. It uncovered lots of emotion. It got at issues like trust. It tried to reveal whether employees felt they were being treated as competent human beings. But it didn't really uncover a lot about the levels of understanding as to where the company was going, and how well the formal communications channels worked to raise levels of understanding.
>
> In the frustration of the moment, it seems, my colleagues also overlooked the fact that the more you communicate, the more people will want. It turns out to be difficult to get to the point where people feel they have enough information. But layering on more newsletters won't necessarily make the difference.

Fixing Communications

In the wake of the 1991 survey—and again, after a 1993 survey generated only slightly better results—Rich and Jeff had a series of discussions on the general subject of communications. Perhaps Harley needed new ways to deploy existing resources, rather than vastly bigger budgets and new legions of people devoted to the communications function.

At that time, employee-related communications came out of HR. Marketing handled public relations and media communications related to products. Financial people ran investor communications. Web-based communications, still a novelty at that time, were nobody's responsibility. Buell, the new Harley-owned sports motorcycle manufacturer, had no formal communications functions. Surveying this landscape, Rich and Jeff reasoned that perhaps a lack of integration and coordination contributed to the frustration of employees.

To a limited extent, the circle organization (see chapter 7) began to overcome some of these difficulties. Functional leaders came together, in many cases for the first time, and began to improvise ad hoc responses to pressing communications problems. Meanwhile, individual plants took steps to improve their own communications flows. Several sites launched plant-based newsletters, which in some cases hadn't existed before.

But a more formal step forward came in 1996, with the creation of a formal communications department. It was headed by Kal Demitros, who returned from Europe to lead the new group.

RICH: There had been communications committees at several of the plants, but in 1996 there was a need to "capture" the dollars that previously were used in scattershot ways. The risk there, of course, is that a centralized communications program will start thinking that it knows what people need to know—and then you're back where you started.

LEE: The centralized communications function should do three basic things. First, it should provide a "global" view—the view from 50,000 feet. Second, it should provide some general guidelines about what official corporate publications should and shouldn't talk about. And, finally, it should provide specialized resources to help the local units do what they want to do.

Demitros and her new colleagues first focused on ensuring consistency of communication. The circle organization provided early access to her colleagues' functional decisions and strategies. Demitros herself is based in the provide support circle, but estimates that she spends half of her time in the create demand circle. "The information sharing that goes on in those circles is absolutely vital to my being able to do my job," she says.

One of our goals as a group when we got together two and a half years ago was to deal with the sense of urgency that employees feel about getting information before, or at least concurrently with, the media or dealers, for example. We now have the mechanisms in place to do that. We have a number of channels, including a magazine, *Harley-Davidson World*, which is published twice a month. It's pretty fresh news, written in *USA Today* style, with site inserts. We also have electronic bulletin boards. There's probably an announcement on there right now about yesterday's dividend announcement. And we've just launched an employee intranet we call RIDE, which stands for Rapid Information Delivery and Exchange.

To feed the magazine, electronic bulletin boards, intranets, and other communications channels, Demitros and her colleagues assembled a network of employee communicators at each site. They participate in teleconferences to establish the content of and review articles for each issue of *Harley-Davidson World* and also provide input for RIDE. The goal is for all plant groups to have computer terminals, which will provide every employee with access to RIDE.

Meanwhile, Demitros relies on a "waterfall" system to push breaking news out into the employee system. In theory, supervisors and managers learn in advance of an important development through e-mail and have the responsibility to "waterfall" that information throughout their organizations. The communicator role intimidates some people, so all Harley supervisors and managers are being taught communications skills to help them in their leadership roles.

Demitros inherited a tool called the "Eagle News Network," a continuous video feed of Harley-related information which can be seen in lunchrooms and break rooms across the company. "It popped up at York," she explains, "and the other plant managers picked up on it. It is effective for communicating production status to employees, and they can strive to hit the daily goals. Because it came out of a relatively noisy plant environment, audio didn't make any sense. So it's Harley's version of the silent movies. But it also has the capability for live satellite broadcasts, which is something that we'll probably call upon in the future."

These "silent movies" include all kinds of data: information aimed at welcoming new employees; production, cost, and quality data for the location; news about visitors to the plant; snippets of economic news and Wall Street results from the previous day (including the closing price of Harley's stock); training schedules; and more. Employees within each location coordinate with central employee communications to determine what will be broadcast, and—in many cases—in helping to collect and post their site-specific information.

Circles have begun to emerge at the director level—not formal, she explains, but designed to encourage cross-functional communications within the subfunctions of her circle.

Demitros sees evidence that circle philosophy is "moving down" through the organization. To her, this is a very positive sign for the company's future. "Rich was always incredibly impatient," she adds. "He had, and has, wonderful ideas about how to create teamwork. And, up until recently, he's complained about how it hasn't taken hold. And my answer to that is that he's *wrong*—it *has* taken hold. No, it's not perfect, and never will be. But we've made tremendous progress."

Eyes on the Prize

The formal biennial surveys stopped after the 1993 effort, mainly because it wasn't clear what the company could learn from them. The preponderantly negative findings, too, discouraged the proponents of these audits.

Briefly, Harley's leaders took some encouragement from a 1997 *Fortune* magazine article on the 100 best companies to work for in America. The article (an annual event, looked forward to by some companies and dreaded by others) was based on in-company employee surveys conducted by *Fortune*. Overall, Harley ranked seventeenth, a more than respectable showing. And on the communications effectiveness front, Harley outperformed even this distinguished peer group. In response to the statement that "management keeps me informed about issues and changes," an average of 72 percent of all surveyed employees at the 100 best companies agreed. At Harley, the number was 84 percent.

Because these rankings grew out of employee surveys, and because the 100 best constituted an illustrious peer group, maybe Harley could conclude that the communications challenge had been effectively addressed. But in the following year, Harley slipped to seventy-seventh.

More discouraging still, Harley's communications effectiveness rating sank from 84 to 58 percent positive.

Perhaps the most important lesson we take away from these experiences is that Harley can't afford to stop worrying about communications and, at the same time, can't flog itself for not meeting its high standards.

"Harley is its own biggest critic," says Jeff Bleustein. "We're *very* hard on ourselves. And while that's sometimes a burden, it's also a great strength. The Business Process has succeeded in getting commitment. Harley people now have very high expectations of themselves, and the company, and everybody around them. So, when things aren't going the way they'd like, they are very, very vocal about it."

LEE: I don't hear today the complaints about communication that I used to hear. I tend to hear things like, "Hey, they're finally doing some good work; they're almost there; why don't they try this one more thing?"

But I don't want to let them off the hook, either. Some companies rank high in these kinds of ratings year after year. Companies that never get those kinds of ratings—or companies that bounce around a bit, like Harley has done in recent years—have to ask themselves what they ought to be doing differently.

Communication is not an end in itself, but a tool for making other critical changes possible. In the next chapter, we give one example of a highly favorable outcome for Harley that could not have happened without good communications.

11

Partnering
A Case in Point

THE VISION OF HARLEY-DAVIDSON DESCRIBED IN CHAPTER 5 TODAY includes the statement that Harley exists, in part, to "continuously improve the quality of mutually beneficial relationships with all stakeholders." This statement implicitly comprises the concept of *partnership*—an overworked word, but one that captures several ideas that have become increasingly important to Harley in the 1990s and beyond.

First, a definition. At Harley, "partnering" means that

- the relationship is an interdependent one.
- the interests of both parties in the relationship are valid.
- neither party can succeed alone.
- the parties to the relationship are responsible not only for the results each party achieves, but also for the relationship itself.

Who might join the company in such a relationship? When Harley's Executive Committee first drew up a list of the company's key stakeholders in 1988, they settled on the following:

- Customers (dealers and riders)
- Employees
- Suppliers

- Shareholders[1]
- Government
- Society

In the ensuing decade-plus, Harley has tried to work in a partnering relationship with groups in all six of these categories. The company's efforts in *each* area—some successful, others less successful—could fill a book.

Consider, for example, Harley's relationship with its dealer organization. In 1993, for the first time in the history of the company, the sales service agreement that governs the relationship between Harley and its dealers was developed jointly by the company and the Dealer Advisory Council.

RICH: It's hard to convey how big a change this really was. In most cases, contracts are written by the party that holds the power, and it's a zero-sum game: I win, you lose. It's highly unusual for a manufacturer to go to its first-line customers—its dealers—and say, "Hey, let's get together and work out the right kind of contract for our relationship."

Suppliers, too, build partnering relationships with Harley. For example, the company has created a "Top 70" program. Harley's senior managers spend a day each year at each of the company's seventy most important suppliers, explaining what's going on in the business and learning what's going on from the suppliers' perspectives. At the same time, these suppliers (and others not in the Top 70) work with Harley's purchasing department to define how they will jointly build a mutually beneficial relationship.

Each of these stakeholder relationships warrants attention. In this chapter, however, we focus specifically on Harley's partnering efforts

---

[1] In 1994, as noted in previous chapters, "investors" replaced "shareholders" on this list, because "investors" was a more comprehensive and accurate description of this stakeholder group.

with two particular subgroups of its employees, as a means of illustrating the philosophy and significance of the partnering concept.
Those subgroups are the two international unions that together represent a large percentage of Harley's employees: the International Association of Machinists (IAM) and the United Paper Workers International Union (PACE).

We will also present this partnering effort as the first of a number
of cases in point, intended to demonstrate how the initiatives described
in previous chapters can converge to bring about positive changes.
Without those prior investments in people and ideas, partnering would
not have been possible.

The Roots of Partnering

Harley's partnership with IAM and PACE traces its roots back to the
crisis faced by the company in the late 1970s and early 1980s. This
was when *survival* was everyone's shared goal. Union leaders and members recognized the deadly seriousness of the company's situation and
worked collaboratively with Harley's management to save the company.

Once the crisis passed and Harley began its financial recovery and
market rebound, the motivation for working together collaboratively
began to fade. All parties—including management, union leaders and
members, and nonunion employees—began reverting to their former
habits. The old patterns of behaving and interacting had "worked well
enough" before the crisis—although a few people, union and management
alike, wondered if the old behaviors had contributed to the company's
near-death experience. But nobody knew of any *other* way to behave.

Beginning in late 1986, Harley's management became convinced
that the "old ways" wouldn't meet the company's needs in the coming
years. This realization led to the series of steps described in chapters 2
and 3: the retaining of Lee and his ROI colleagues, the cooperative
Joint Vision Process, and the whole range of related activities detailed
in this book. As related in chapter 3, the Joint Vision Process took
place between mid-1988 and early 1990. Then, in February 1990,
PACE Local Union 7209 requested a suspension of the process.

Suspension, as noted earlier, was a setback but not a deadly blow to cooperative activities. Harley's two other, smaller unions continued with the Joint Vision Process. And joint action continued on a number of fronts in all locations, including equipment purchases, customer visits, safety and health committees, and others. But Harley's senior managers in late 1993 and early 1994 again began worrying that these activities would not provide the kinds of continuous improvement that the company had to achieve.

What evidence could they point to? Market demand was exploding. This might have seemed like good news, rather than bad, but Harley had no way to meet this growing demand. Dealers were clamoring for bikes. Customers were furious at having to wait eighteen months or more for a Harley. The integrity of the suggested-retail price structure was at risk. Price gouging was starting to take place, which led to more complaints from angry customers.

One risk inherent in all of Harley's highly visible success—high margins (at least by motorcycle industry standards), customers standing in line for product, attention in the business press—was that Harley would strengthen its own competition. Current competitors could further undercut the Milwaukee-based manufacturer's prices, and new competitors might be tempted to jump into the fray. Meanwhile, of course, Wall Street made it clear that it intended to hold Harley to the company's own high performance standards. Present successes led to expectations of even greater growth in the future. But Harley, with its factories already running at full bore, had literally no room for growth.

Expanding manufacturing capacity seemed like an obvious first step. But without some kind of radical departure from past practice, expansion would have to happen at existing facilities dominated by PACE and IAM. What role, if any, should union members in existing Harley locations play in capacity expansion planning?

Not surprisingly, some executives and managers argued in favor of a radical departure. The time had come, they said, for Harley to build a new plant far from its existing unionized facilities. By following this strategy, they argued, Harley could operate "union free," with all of the advantages thought to be associated with that way of doing business. And, as an added bonus, by building an entirely new facility, Harley could avoid all of the turf wars and similar struggles that would result from expanding one existing location rather than another.

During the later months of 1994, Rich, Jeff Bleustein, and their colleagues gave this "clean break" proposal a fair hearing. After much debate, they decided that, although a new facility made sense, Harley should *not* use the circumstances of the moment as an excuse for disrupting the company's long-standing relationship with its unions.

Having reached a consensus against a new union-free facility, Rich and Jeff Bleustein asked for a meeting in December 1994 with George Kourpias (international president of IAM) and Wayne Glenn (international president of PACE), to begin talking about how Harley could solve its capacity problems. Rich and Jeff emphasized that Harley wanted to explore the possibility of entering into a true partnership with its unions.

The meeting succeeded beyond expectations. The top leadership of three institutions—Harley, PACE, and IAM—agreed that a full-fledged partnership would serve the interests of all three parties. They agreed that their joint goals should include (1) continuing improvement in existing facilities and (2) *dramatic* improvement in the new facility. (The unions would not expect, and the company would not agree, simply to carry forward an existing contract into the new plant.) Finally, they also agreed on a structure and procedure for moving the partnership discussions forward. Jeff, Rich, and the two international union presidents would be called "principals" in the process, but these principals would intervene only when absolutely necessary. They described themselves as policy makers, and arbiters in the court of last resort.

The JPIC at Work

The principals assigned the hard work of building the partnership to a group that eventually came to be called the "Joint Partnership Implementation Committee" (JPIC). It consisted of two senior representatives from the IAM (Jim Pinto and Lou Kiefer), two from PACE (Keith Kirchner and Gordon Brehm), two from Harley's management (Tom Gelb and Vice President of Human Resources Bill Gray), and John Ciparro, a liaison representative from the Industrial Union Department of the AFL-CIO. John had previously assisted in labor-management situations involving both unions.

The JPIC began meeting in early January 1995. It quickly decided that it needed the help of an experienced and impartial third-party facilitator. At the first session, management representatives arrived with Lee in tow and suggested that he be retained as the facilitator. The union representatives criticized management for attempting to impose a solution on the nascent JPIC process. But, to their credit, the JPIC got past this procedural error, interviewed Lee for the job, and—based on his prior experience with both of Harley's international unions and at other companies—retained him as facilitator.

LEE: This episode was a case of missed communications. I thought everyone already knew about my proposed role and was on board. Well, obviously, they weren't. I offered to bow out immediately, but the parties came together and worked things out. Management had made a mistake, but not one that would "kill" the partnership effort.

The JPIC first tackled the task of defining the phrase "true partnership." What were the goals of such a partnership? What principles would guide its creation and evolution? This was a formidable task. The JPIC engaged in more than 120 hours of intense, candid, and increasingly productive dialogue between January and March. Toward the end of March, the JPIC sent the first draft of its statement to the principals for a formal consideration. It read, in part,

> This partnership is based on a commitment to create a new era in labor-management relations. The key goals of the partnership are to improve quality, productivity, participation, flexibility, and the financial performance (issues of the Business Process Umbrella) of the Company while enhancing earning opportunities, long-term employment, job satisfaction, and safety for employees.
>
> The parties recognize that achieving this partnership will involve people in all parts of the organization in the information exchange, problem-solving, and decision-making processes to a far greater extent than in the past. The IAM, PACE, and Harley-

Davidson recognize their collective responsibility to gain commitment from all employees, hourly and salaried, to contribute to the success of the Company and the establishment of a positive work environment which is beneficial to all.

We will develop, through shared decision-making, approaches to work focused on the development, production, and timely distribution of products and services, including administrative support systems required to meet the current and future needs of our customers. These approaches to work will maximize the contribution of skills, knowledge, and information through the ongoing efforts and commitment of people to seek out, learn, and apply competence in diverse disciplines.

Overcoming Skepticism

The principals soon made it clear that they had mixed reactions to this initial draft. From the management perspective, the draft statement provided clear and welcome evidence that PACE and IAM were prepared to take a large measure of responsibility for continuous improvement in all locations. The unions understood and were committed to the goals and objectives of the company.

On the other hand, the draft agreement called for substantially more union input into activities that were traditionally the sole domain of management. Gradually, through a series of conversations (facilitated by Lee), Bill and Tom helped Rich and Jeff become more comfortable with the document *in its entirety*. Rich and Jeff continued to have reservations about specific parts of the draft, however. They also felt that, even where they agreed wholeheartedly with the document's underlying principles, a great deal of hard work still lay ahead. For example, aligning the behavior of leaders across the company (union and management alike) with a new and very different way of doing business seemed fraught with difficulties and perils.

Harley's board, too, was very skeptical about the plan when management first presented it to the board in February 1996. As some board members saw it, the company had a rare opening. It had the chance to set up its first new factory in years, far away from the history and "baggage" of Milwaukee, and now management proposed to bring the unions along. Did this make sense?

RICH: There isn't a lot of drama in the kinds of changes we're talking about, but this was a dramatic episode. Several board members went after us pretty aggressively, and several people on the management side began to waver.

I took Jeff Bleustein aside after dinner and said, "Hey— tonight's the night that you decide whether or not you want partnering, because tomorrow, it's likely to be on the block." So Jeff, Jim McCaslin, and their colleagues stayed up until 2:00 in the morning putting together a presentation for the board, which they delivered at the formal meeting eight hours or so later.

It was a case in which the board did its job well, forcing management to think through what it was getting into. And Harley's managers responded in kind. Their presentation was very powerful and won the day. I was very pleased about that. Things had taken root.

The union leaders, too, expressed mixed reactions to the draft. Yes, they liked the provisions that called for increased union input into key decisions, and the unions' leaders were happy with the statement's written commitments to (1) grow the business and (2) expand the unions' membership. They were less happy about other commitments in the statement; for example, the commitment on the unions' part to take joint responsibility with management for results. Historically, unions have taken a reactive posture in traditional labor-management relations. Management acts, and the unions react; management makes a decision, and the unions either agree with it or fight against it.

Agreeing to take joint responsibility meant working with management to reach decisions together. This would be a venture into unknown territory, and the union leaders weren't entirely sure that their members would approve of this new "proactive" role for their union.

Meanwhile, the principals thought through their respective responses to the draft proposal, and the JPIC forged ahead with the next phase of its work. They had produced their initial draft, as noted above, on the level of general principle. But these principles had little real meaning until translated into practical terms. For example, the initial draft committed all parties to the principle of "shared decision making." But what, exactly, did that mean?

To answer that question, Lee suggested a framework for a JPIC brainstorming session. Together, the JPIC's members identified all the kinds of decisions that an organization like Harley would make in the normal course of business. The resulting list comprised some thirty kinds of decisions, including (for example) the content of training and education programs, staffing and sourcing decisions, and decisions related to mergers and acquisitions. The JPIC then sorted these decisions into three broad categories:

1. *Unilateral decisions without input,* to be made unilaterally by one institution or the other (that is, management or unions), without prior input from the other institution
2. *Unilateral decisions with input,* to be made unilaterally by one institution after seeking and considering the input of the other
3. *Decisions of consensus,* which required participation in the decision-making process of all institutions affected by such decisions.[2]

The JPIC's definition of "consensus" was specific and somewhat unusual. Included as an appendix to the final partnership agreement, it read as follows:

> As partners in running the business, we use consensus as our preferred mode of group decision-making. . . .
>
> Consensus will have been achieved in the group setting when:
>
> • Alternatives have been identified.
> • All legitimate concerns of individuals have been addressed to the satisfaction of the group, and

---

[2] Note how similar these definitions were to the decision-making processes defined in the Joint Vision Process and also in the circle organization blueprint. Although participants weren't always aware of it, they drew on and benefited from work performed months or years earlier.

• The group decides it will choose and support one such alternative.

In its purest sense, consensus means the group has reached a decision which will be supported by the actions of every member of such group. The decision need not be the primary choice of every group member, but support of the decision once consensus has been reached is key.

Our success as partners lies in our ability to process information quickly, and make decisions which allow the organization to move forward at the pace required.

In the event that a group is divided as to which decisions they can support, the group must continue to work through the issue, relying on data and facts as the basis for such consensus decision-making. In the event that a portion of the group is unable to indicate support for a decision that the balance of the group supports, those person(s) must either withdraw their objection or offer alternatives and convince the group of the merits of this alternative position, in effect allowing the group to reach consensus on the alternate idea. Simply saying "no" is never an acceptable option.

Again the principals reviewed the work of the JPIC, and again they expressed both satisfaction and reservations. As the fine-grained details of a shared decision-making process began to be filled in, it was becoming clear how dramatically different the roles of all parties would be, if and when the parties adopted this new approach. Management would involve union representatives much earlier and much more broadly in the decision-making process than ever before. Union leaders would be responsible not only for representing the interests of their membership in the wake of a real or proposed change, as had traditionally been the case, but also for convincing their members of the *rightness* of a tough decision.

Despite the risks inherent in these proposed changes, all four principals supported the JPIC's proposals. The process was about to enter a new phase. A small group of dedicated individuals had worked together intensively for several months to reach an agreement, and they had succeeded in getting four individuals higher up on their respective institutional ladders to bless this agreement. Now came the hard part: getting support for the agreement from local leaders—union and management alike—at each existing Harley location.

From the 35 to the 100

The large-scale consensus-building process actually started in the prior year. The JPIC in the summer of 1995 convened the first in a series of meetings with what it informally called "The 35." These were the thirty-five key management and union leaders at Harley's York, Milwaukee, and Tomahawk facilities. The ground rules governing these meetings surprised some members of The 35. The JPIC stated candidly that the essential principles and goals of the proposed partnership, as well as the concept of shared leadership and decision making, could *not* be changed radically. (These goals and methods had been decided upon through a consensual process supported and sustained by key institutional leaders.) But the JPIC encouraged The 35 to suggest better ways to *state* the principles and goals in the proposed agreement; it also encouraged the larger group to look for omissions in the agreement and suggest ways of dealing with such omissions.

The 35 responded constructively and with a kind of guarded optimism. Publicly, they expressed their determination to help make these principles a reality and suggested a number of ways in which the JPIC could improve the existing document. (For example, they suggested a way to reduce the original list of "decision types" from more than thirty to twenty-three.) Privately, with varying levels of anxiety, they expressed two concerns: first, that their counterparts on the other side of the union-management "divide" might not be able to deliver on their promises; and, second, that they *themselves* might not be able to deliver on the commitments inherent in the proposed agreement.

The 35 also identified two major issues that, if left unresolved, could block a successful implementation of the agreement. The first was employment security: a volatile issue of increasing importance in an era when many U.S. companies were downsizing or moving manufacturing jobs offshore in order to stay competitive. The second issue was more parochial. What impact would this proposed partnership have on the contracts that were already in place at all locations, which were significantly different from site to site?

The JPIC incorporated all of The 35's wording changes and other suggested clarifications into the document. Between August and November of 1995, the committee also tackled the two potential "deal breakers" identified by the local site leaders. The problem of potential

conflicts between the partnership agreement and existing collective bargaining agreements proved remarkably easy to resolve. The respective
local contracts were where the "rubber met the road" and (by law and
by past practice) would stay in force until changed at the local level.
With this guideline in mind, the JPIC drew up a memorandum of
agreement for review and approval by local leaders.

The second issue, employment security, proved far more difficult
to resolve. This surprised no one on the JPIC. Its members recalled all
too clearly what had happened in 1982, when Harley had laid off 40
percent of its workforce. The rationale for these massive cuts, understood and accepted by all parties at the time, was that large-scale layoffs were the only way to keep the company alive. Couldn't equally
hard times return, at some point in the future?

As the committee debated this contentious issue, management's
representatives on the JPIC asked some very pointed questions. "It's all
well and good to sing the praises of employment security and to argue
for some kind of guaranteed-employment provision," they argued.
"But does that really balance the interests of our stakeholders? And
what happens if Harley *does* get back into desperate circumstances?
Do we let the company go under in order to honor a commitment to
employment security?"

But labor's representatives made their own strong arguments. The
proposed partnership aimed to promote continuous improvement and
increases in productivity. If the plan succeeded, it might make some
workers unnecessary. This led the union representatives to ask their
own pointed questions: "Why should we agree to work ourselves out
of our jobs?"

These internal JPIC debates were passionate and, in the memo-
ries of several participants, sometimes very *loud*. But two factors kept
traditional role-based passions (union versus management) more or
less in check. First, the members of the JPIC had enormous respect for
each other as people (in accordance with Harley's values). And, second,
the members of the committee realized that they were already embody-
ing the fundamental principles contained in the proposed agreement.
All had committed themselves to the long-term health and viability of
the company. In that context, no one would seriously entertain a proposal that would serve the interests of one constituency but threaten

the larger company. As a result, the JPIC's debates were almost always civil and substantive, and ultimately generated results.

LEE: I told the JPIC that in my thirty years of professional experience, I had never seen such difficult issues debated at such a level of excellence. The members listened to and respected each other's viewpoints. Each side proved that it understood the valid concerns of the other side—sometimes even sharpening the other side's arguments. Most important, they stayed focused on goals and principles, and didn't get bogged down in the kinds of details that can kill an agreement.

The enormity and intensity of the JPIC's work during this period would be difficult to overstate. The committee logged scores of hours of face-to-face discussions over the course of three months. In between these periodic group sessions, individuals and subgroups spent uncounted numbers of hours researching specific policy proposals, attempting to figure out how the company might implement such policies and what their impacts might be.

This phase flowed into another round of consultations with the principals, which led to more requests for changes and in turn to more debate by the JPIC. The JPIC was proposing very real changes in the way the company organized and managed itself, and getting "buy-in" from the principals was extremely difficult.

Based on these iterative rounds of discussions, the JPIC ultimately produced a set of documents containing much-amended versions of the proposed partnership's goals and principles, a memorandum of agreement covering conflicts between the partnership agreement and local collective bargaining agreements, and—most elusive of all!—an agreement governing employment security. That agreement read, in part, as follows:

Our partnership is based on all employees being fully committed to accept their obligation to actively participate in efforts to address capacity needs, while continuously improving productivity, quality, flexibility, and financial performance.

As a result of this active participation, jobs and job require-ments will change. When changes occur, employees will be pro-vided training and be reassigned in accordance with applicable collective bargaining agreements.

To actively participate in this partnership environment, employee concerns regarding loss of employment are legitimate; therefore, the Partners agree that there will be no loss of employ-ment of "employment security eligible" employees as a result of their participation in the partnership, including subcontracting and expansion in new and existing plants and/or products. "Employment security eligible" employees are defined as:

A. all regular, full-time employees employed on the effective date of this agreement, or,

B. any employee hired as a regular full-time employee follow-ing the effective date of this agreement who has achieved two years of Company service.

This agreement is based upon the principle that each employee demonstrates a willingness to continuously improve their skills and learn new skills and competencies. The Partners have the obligation to provide education and training on Company time and to provide additional work which continues to utilize the tal-ent of all employees.

In the event of severe economic hardship, the Partners will explore alternative courses of action before considering the neces-sity for employment reduction.

With this set of agreements in hand, the JPIC went back to The 35 to get a new round of reactions and to discuss possible next steps in the larger process. To everyone's relief—especially the JPIC's!—the thirty-five local union and management leaders announced that they were pleased with the JPIC's work. The 35 also suggested that, at this point, the process demanded broader involvement on the part of both union and management. This suggestion resulted in the expansion of The 35 into "The 100." The addition of sixty-five more members enabled each location to bring in broader representation and ensured that many more leaders could "spread the word" at each site.

RICH: I recall a meeting on October 19, 1997, at which Jeff and I took the gist of the JPIC message to York. Our point at that meeting was that the JPIC had built its work on the foundation of the Business Process. We wanted to make sure people saw these connections.

The products developed by the JPIC, and improved on by The 35, were discussed at length with The 100. As the dialogue progressed in a second meeting, and then a third, an ever-growing number of local union and management leaders took the opportunity to learn more about the "why" behind the partnership. They gained a better understanding of the comprehensive work being done to ensure that the goals and principles of the partnership took into account the legitimate needs, interests, and realities of each location. As a result, a broader segment of the union and management leadership began to feel more comfortable with the envisioned relationship. Comments during these meetings of The 100 were initially positive yet skeptical ("sounds good, but it will never work"); the commentary evolved as the participants began to take heart ("sounds good, and maybe it *could* work") and began to be supportive ("sounds good, and I see how it *can* work"). During these meetings, the magnitude of the changes that individual leaders—union and management alike—would have to implement to "make it happen" also became more clear. Most of the leaders were apprehensive, of course, but most realized that a great deal of groundwork had been accomplished, and this gave them greater confidence that something called "partnership" really could be achieved.

The discussions between the JPIC and The 100 led quickly to a first product: a partnership orientation and training program. Representatives of all three institutions jointly developed the program, which was subsequently delivered by internal resources at all Harley locations in the latter half of 1997. The program aimed to orient, educate, and train all Harley employees in the partnership—in its rationale, principles, and expectations (implicit and explicit).

The journey of change initiated by Rich and his colleagues in the latter half of 1987, and joined by Lee shortly thereafter, had now been under way for a decade. Rich and Lee noted with satisfaction that many people at Harley, in both the management and union ranks, connected the partnering initiative to all that had gone before. One PACE member from the Tomahawk plant, for example, expressed his appreciation directly to Rich, in more or less the following words: "I hope that everybody who took the lead in the Joint Vision Process understands how important that process was in preparing us all for this partnership."

LEE: This PACE member was one of many who made similar statements, and we expected and welcomed such statements. Given the history of Harley-Davidson, the Joint Vision Process (when it began) was a major departure from the past. Management and union leaders alike were simply unprepared to jump right in and implement such a different way of working and behaving. The "plant the seeds and nurture them" approach was nothing like "command and control," and often gave us a "two steps forward, one step backward" reality. People came to see the benefits, but it took time.

A leader from the IAM local lodge in Milwaukee was equally enthusiastic. "This is great," he told Lee in the course of a one-on-one discussion of the partnering initiative. "It's an extension of all the work we did in the Joint Vision Process." Another union leader (representing the membership of the PACE local in Milwaukee, which had requested the suspension of the Joint Vision Process) confessed his long-standing puzzlement about where Harley's leaders had been trying to go with the Joint Vision Process. "It makes sense to me now," he said. "I can see how tough the next phase of the partnership is going to be, and I think we've all been well prepared for that phase."

Back to the Tough Question: New Capacity

While the JPIC brought the invention, consensus-building, and implementation phases of its work to an end, it also explored the issue of additional capacity. The resolution of this difficult issue had been delayed, but not deferred, by the partnering initiative; meanwhile, the demand for Harley motorcycles continued to increase.

Early in 1996, Harley had announced that it would obtain the additional capacity it needed by building a brand-new facility. Representatives of Harley's management, the IAM, and the PACE would jointly locate and design the new plant. If and when the local employees took a vote designating the IAM and PACE as their formal bargaining units, the company would recognize the unions' status at the new plant.

This was the first major decision reached in the new partnership mode, and it illustrated both the benefits and the perils of the new approach. By agreeing to union participation in key aspects of the decision, management avoided all of the labor relations problems it had been envisioning since 1994. Harley also stood to gain from the input of a broader spectrum of unionized employees regarding the work methods, systems design, and start-up of the new plant. The price, of course, was that management would lose unilateral control over the outcomes.

The international unions got clear benefits—especially Harley's neutrality toward their efforts to organize and represent the new facility—but also experienced precisely the kind of backlash that union leaders had been worrying about since the partnership plan was first broached. For obvious reasons, the local rank and file (as well as some managers) felt strongly that the company could and *should* expand capacity by expanding one or more of the existing locations. Many expressed the strong opinion that no new facility was needed, and that the existing plants should get the opportunity to put together their *own* plans for a partnering process that would increase productivity and expand capacity.

In short order, the local unions representing the existing plants formally asked for the opportunity to make formal proposals to the company—proposals which, if accepted, might eliminate the need for a new plant. Wisconsin presented Rich with a written request at the end of a labor-management meeting. York representatives presented their proposal to management during the Annual Dealer Meeting in San Diego.

These challenges put the JPIC's creativity, credibility, and nerve to the test. Of course, the JPIC's members had anticipated these kinds of reactions since the earliest days of the committee's work. Sooner or later, the committee knew, a decision reached consensually at the JPIC's level would create unhappiness at the "local" level. Now the fat was on the fire. What could the JPIC do to put the fire out?

"When we agreed to do this partnership with the internationals," recalls Jeff Bleustein,

> the locals looked at this and said, "Hey—great for the internationals, but what does this mean for *us*?" They were concerned that this would be the first step away from existing locations. So the two local unions from York and Milwaukee came to us. They said, "Hey, you said you wanted to work in a new way. Well, we're prepared to work with you in that new way. You don't need a new factory to demonstrate that. Give us a chance to prove that we can work with you in that new way. If we do, will you change your mind about the new factory?"
>
> We said, "We've already made a commitment to our board that we're going to have a new factory in which we'll make a whole motorcycle, from stem to stern. And there are a number of other things we'll be getting from that new factory in addition to a new relationship. So we can't promise you anything, but we'll give you the chance to make your pitch."

This request and response led to another intensive round of discussions and, ultimately, to an amended plan from the JPIC. A skeptical Harley board agreed to a six-month delay, allowing the JPIC to buy time for this new process of invention. The JPIC encouraged existing locations to develop specific capacity expansion plans for their respective facilities, but this encouragement came with a number of preconditions. First, labor and management had to develop any such plans *jointly*. Second, these plans had to be developed within the specified six months. And, third, any such plans had to meet at least the following minimum standards:

- Full commitment to the partnership. This meant that each location had to first ratify, by a *two-thirds vote of all eligible voters*, their commitment to engaging in the partnering process. (Two-thirds represented a high level of commitment, which the JPIC demanded from the unions.)

- Full commitment to the elements of shared decision making
- A "world-class" operation (including the ability to compete internationally)
- Meaningful employment security
- Substantial and increasing employee training and development
- A shared concern for the business and its people on the part of all leaders and employees
- Continuous improvement, including a work organization based on natural work groups
- Full commitment to Harley's values and Business Process, as well as the values of the two unions
- Nontraditional labor agreements, *again ratified by at least two-thirds of all eligible members*:
  - Long term
  - Based on full recognition of seniority

The JPIC didn't establish these standards to frustrate or hurt the chances of existing facilities. Rather, as the JPIC saw it, existing facilities had to match the standards to which the new facility would be held, because only by hitting these kinds of high standards could Harley compete more effectively in the future.

Ultimately, the Wisconsin-based facilities *did* develop major capacity expansion programs and did secure two two-thirds votes in favor of those plans. (York's union and management leadership decided not to meet the agreed-upon timetable, although they did produce a plan that met the standards.) All of the Wisconsin-based plans met the stated criteria—although timetables for implementation varied significantly—and the JPIC approved all of them. As a result, the JPIC scaled back the proposed capacity of the new plant accordingly.

Going to Kansas City

While negotiations proceeded with existing locations, a subgroup of the JPIC—including management representative Karl Eberle and union representatives Jim Pinto and Keith Kirchner (IAM's and PACE's representatives, respectively)—searched for a site for the new facility and worked through what particular functions that facility might perform.

This proved to be a moving target. As the JPIC approved existing locations' expansion plans, the size and scope of the proposed new facility shrank dramatically.

But the need for a new facility did not go away entirely. So the three-person subgroup spent many hours thinking through the challenges and opportunities of a new site.

They visited potential locations. They worked with internal resources, resources within the two international unions, as well as a jointly selected specialist in site locations, to develop innovative new designs for the facility, comprising plant layout, equipment, "human systems," and other critical features.

For this trio, a collaborative approach to decision making and problem solving became standard operating procedure. Occasionally, however, an outside-world contact underscored just how unusual the new Harley approach actually was. Most cities that vied for new plants had well-established techniques for wooing corporations, usually through community or economic development groups that were accustomed to working only with management representatives. None was prepared to deal effectively with a *joint* decision-making process in which union leaders had as much say as management. Historically, some communities had pushed their sites with the argument that there was a low probability of union organizing efforts. Obviously, this approach was inappropriate for a presentation to a joint decision-making body!

To make this pitch, the communities had to bring in data about the state of positive labor-management relations in the area. This was information that they didn't usually include, but which was of considerable interest to the HD/IAM/PACE leaders. Some cities even came up with their own version of "union and management collaboration" as they retailored their presentations, putting together teams of presenters to make their pitches to Harley. The subcommittee's members enjoyed watching various city fathers scramble to change their pitches. "This was something," recalls Pinto, "that they had never seen before."

The JPIC's three-person subcommittee narrowed the list of suitable locations to three cities. Their recommended choice, which soon was approved by the principals, was Kansas City, Missouri. Harley's board of directors subsequently approved the decision.

The reader will recall that two of the three members of this advance team were union members. Given that fact, we (Rich and Lee) found it amazing that the subcommittee's second-choice city was in a right-to-work state. Under normal circumstances—that is, outside of the JPIC process—this would have been anathema to union members.

RICH: Early in the process, before the JPIC began its work, the unions had said to us, "Wherever this new plant goes, it can't be in a right-to-work state." That was a nonnegotiable. The JPIC process transformed that stance into a shared position: "All other things being equal, we will not go to a right-to-work state." That's a very different stance, and it illustrates the kinds of contributions that the JPIC can make.

Breaking New Ground

Harley broke ground for its new Kansas City plant on August 24, 1996. The new Kansas City facility celebrated the production of its first motorcycle at ceremonies in Kansas City in January 1998.

Four years had passed since Harley's leadership first contemplated its capacity expansion options, and only two years since Kansas City was selected as the site for the new facility. In only two years, in other words, Harley had constructed the physical plant and equipment, created and installed innovative production and human work systems, and completed its first products. Meanwhile, profound changes had also taken place across the company, as existing plants added new capacity in conformance with their approved plans. Harley had accomplished much during a short span of time.

The scope and pace of those changes proved most dramatic at the new Kansas City facility. Jointly led and managed by Harley management personnel and representatives of the IAM and PACE, the new facility ran on the principles of *partnership* and *shared decision making*. The "natural work group" concept, built into the plant from day one, has helped the Kansas City facility go more quickly down the road toward continuous improvement.

A lack of history and precedent also helps. In most circumstances, Kansas City has found new answers to both new and recurring questions, drawing on the goals and principles of partnership articulated by the JPIC. We should note, though, that *all* of Harley's facilities have made significant strides toward achieving the true partnership originally defined and advocated by the JPIC.

At this point, many of the JPIC's goals (stated earlier in the chapter) were becoming realities. Harley's effort to build a true partnership has resulted, among other things, in

- A companywide commitment to joint leadership and shared decision making
- Long-term, nontraditional labor agreements across the company
- Employment security for all
- Joint commitment from all three institutions (Harley and its two international unions) to continue to improve on the partnership

"We've come to a great place," concludes Jeff Bleustein.

We can't take it for granted. We have to keep working on it. Partnering is like values—people are always ready to hold it hostage. People seize on whatever goes wrong, and say, "You guys aren't living the values, because of x, y, and z." Same thing with partnering. A supervisor looks cross-eyed at an employee, or some decision-making process leaves somebody out, and it's, "Aha! I *knew* it! You guys don't believe in partnering. It's all *words*!"

So we always have to keep working on it, evolving it, protecting it. But it's very strong, and it's done remarkable things for the company.

Giving up traditional powers and taking on new responsibilities has challenged all members of the partnership. Members of each group have felt ambivalence—even hostility—toward the partnership. No group has avoided all the potholes that the partnership road has presented.

Nor has any single site, group, or function at Harley yet realized the full potential of the true partnership envisioned by the JPIC. But the very premise of the partnership—continuous improvement—argues that the partnership will always have more potential. "Success," in other words, is measured one improvement at a time.

12

Signposts of the Journey

THE PRECEDING CHAPTER RECOUNTED HOW ALL THE VARIOUS
streams of activity that we (Rich, Lee, and many others) set in
motion—efforts to help Harley evolve away from a top-down, hierarchical, command-and-control structure—came together in one very
complex arena: labor-management relations. These complementary
activities not only contributed to a new kind of partnership, but also
helped Harley expand capacity dramatically and at the same time foster continuous improvement at all existing locations.

We believe that these changes would not have been possible without the investments made by many, many people—in union and management, hourly and salaried ranks alike—over the previous decade
or so. And other Harley people, including some who had been skeptical of our efforts, began telling us that, in retrospect, all those investments, as confusing and frustrating as they sometimes were to the individuals involved, appeared to have been worthwhile.

In this chapter, we present four more cases in point (three short,
one somewhat longer) that we think support our argument that Harley
has benefited directly and materially from the changes described in this
book. We view them as welcome signposts—indicators that, although
Harley is (and always will be) far from perfect, its journey toward a
new way of doing business is well under way.

Retooling Information Systems

In November 1992, Dave Storm arrived at Harley as director of operations strategy and systems. To this position Dave brought the significant experience that he had gained as a partner in a prestigious worldwide consulting organization. In May 1994 Harley named him a vice president and added logistics and information services to his responsibilities.

As he contemplated the array of tasks that now lay before him, Dave began to wonder if the job of chief information officer (CIO) was too complex for any one person. By his own estimate, the half-life of a CIO was approximately three years. By the time one factors in the required learning curve and the normal company orientation needed to reach any level of effectiveness, it becomes clear that the average CIO doesn't have a great deal of time within which to lead a major change effort. (Indeed, he or she is in some cases lucky to have any impact beyond simply holding a fast-moving organization together.) Dave therefore decided to use the circle organization/natural work group concept to restructure the leadership of his IS function.

These concepts fit well with Dave's well-established management philosophy. (Back when he was a shop supervisor, he posted a sign prominently on his office wall: "None of us is as smart as all of us.") In addition, Dave became convinced shortly after arriving at Harley that the company's organizational structure was having a positive impact on senior management. Why not "download" the corporate philosophy into his own functional area?

He established the Information Services Leadership Circle (ISLC). The circle, he told his colleagues, would include three IS directors in addition to himself. Within the existing structure, there was a single director, Rich Kolbe, who up to this point had assumed total responsibility for IS. This was an unrealistic burden, as Dave saw it, and the structure unnecessarily isolated the IS function from the rest of the company. Dave had already identified another Harley manager, Laurel Tschurwald, whom he intended to promote to a director's position, but first he wanted to recruit externally to fill the third director's position.

Recruiting for this slot proved to be an interesting experience. Most of the people Dave interviewed really wanted to be CIO, and the ISLC structure clearly didn't hold out much hope for that position.

Dave soon settled on a favorite candidate—Cory Mason, who had fifteen years of relevant experience—and Dave's challenge became convincing Cory to make what most of the corporate world would interpret as a lateral move. Persuading Cory that shared leadership made sense wasn't a simple task, especially because (as far as Dave knew) there was no similar model operating anywhere in the world of corporate IS. Eventually, though, Dave made the sale and persuaded Cory to sign on. The fact that Cory's father recently had retired from Harley after more than fiteen years with the company may have helped Dave's sales pitch.

With Cory on board, Dave promptly promoted Laurel Tschurwald to the third IS director position. Now he had a four-person circle consisting of three directors (Kolbe, who left in 1998 and was replaced by Reid Engstrom; Mason; and Tschurwald) and himself. After some sustained discussions, the three directors distributed the responsibilities of the IS function among themselves so that each had

- *Specific management responsibility for the interface with one of the three leadership circles: create demand, produce product, and provide support.* In order to understand the future strategic direction required by each leadership circle, and to translate direction into action, the IS directors established "Information Technology Councils" (ITCs). The ITCs' purpose is threefold:

  - To be steward on behalf of the business circle on the information (IT) initiatives, including setting priorities, review and approval of business cases, monitoring milestones, and postimplementation review.
  - To partner in discussing strategy and direction for IT capabilities and emphasis as it affects the circle.
  - To communicate back to the home organization on IT issues and changes that affect each circle.

  Between late 1995 and mid-1996, ITCs were established for each business circle. The ITC consists of the ISLC member responsible for the specific circle, plus representatives from each function within that leadership circle. This group discusses the expectations of the leadership circle and the capabilities of IS to deliver against those expectations.

This is unlike most organizations, where top-level "steering committees" are established to allocate the organization's resources in a top-down manner. Instead, Harley asks the individuals "on the firing line" to allocate the available people and financial resources. Or, as one of the directors says, "They are empowered by the business circle leaders to do the right thing on their behalf."

- *Specific technical responsibility for an aspect of the IS function.* Each of the directors brought specific strengths to their new assignments. Laurel, for example, had significant Harley experience, having started with the company in 1977. She therefore accepted responsibility for the business history, heritage, and culture. Kolbe (and later Reid) had significant experience in the IS architecture, so he took on that responsibility. Cory, for his part, had significant experience in leading various IS functions, so he became responsible for the people issues.
- *Shared leadership responsibility for strategic decision making.* This began with the development of an IS strategic plan which, in addition to providing the future road map, provided the direction to deal with issues such as recruiting/retention, staff competency development, communication, and so on.

Whatever concerns the IS directors had as they adopted the Information Services Leadership Circle (ISLC) structure were soon overcome by the clear advantages that the ISLC presented. The directors have made the following observations regarding this approach to shared leadership:

"While having autonomy in decision making may appear to be able to deliver quick action, the shared leadership model, with its diversity of viewpoint, develops better decisions, which provides better results."

"Command and control creates cohesion through dictate, whereas an approach that creates strong relationships creates cohesion through personal commitment to do the thing right."

"In this environment, I'm energized to grow and make a difference, and to give others that same opportunity."

In fact, the three directors elected to take shared leadership an important step further. In late 1995, they decided to establish an Information

Services Managers Circle (ISMC), comprising the direct reports of the three directors. In total, there are twelve members in this "minicircle," and most in the IS function would quickly acknowledge that this is where most of the day-to-day work gets done. These individuals include five site managers, four applications managers, and three other IS managers.

Every month, the ISMC meets to compare notes and determine what actions are required to accomplish their respective and shared tasks. Specifically, they address four areas for which they are directly responsible: day-to-day work group activities, active projects, standing councils, and decision-making groups. Toward the end of the meeting, the ISLC members are invited to join in a general discussion regarding the points above and to hear any requests for director-level actions that the ISMC feels are needed.

The IS group holds an annual meeting in January to ensure that all employees have the opportunity to influence their own work unit plans and develop their own PEP commitments and career development plans. The agenda covers

- a presentation and discussion regarding all elements of the Business Process, from the Umbrella to strategies.
- a review of the past year's activities.
- specific IS strategies for the next year.

With this information in hand, the work units and individual employees are armed to complete their PEP commitments and carry out their career development plans.

In short, the IS group has invented a pair of tiered and interlocking circles, which together put shared decision-making authority in the hands of those closest to the action and also provide those individuals with a meaningful opportunity for personal development.

Recently, Harley's IS group was honored for the third consecutive year as one of the 100 best such organizations in the country in which to work. (Only twenty other companies have received the honor as many times.) And since these innovations took hold, turnover within the IS group ran at only around 4 to 5 percent through 1998. Compared to norms at other companies, this is a remarkably low turnover rate in an area increasingly characterized by staff volatility.

"I think it's fair to say that our turnover is far lower than in most corporate IS areas," says Dave,

> and it's also fair to credit that situation to the changes that have taken place at this company. There's no doubt in my mind that the circle organization, the respect for intellectual curiosity, and all the other stuff that make Harley what it is today are the reasons why we have been able to accomplish so much in this very complex piece of the larger organization and at the same time to retain the very talented people we have. I think people stay with Harley, and with this particular part of Harley, because they are "turned on," they're treated with respect, and they love the way they are able to work.

Learning from Experience

One of the most frustrating experiences for people in an organization is to work hard to fix a problem, only to have it reappear in a similar form at later date. (In the corporate setting, as on the battlefield, replaying past mistakes can have dire consequences.) One of the benefits that Harley received from its work with the Organizational Learning Center described in chapter 9 was that the company had the opportunity to learn from others and therefore avoid the trap of repeating mistakes.

This particular type of learning was reinforced and extended as a result of a visit to the War College at Carlyle, Pennsylvania, in 1997. There, a senior army officer described a team learning process called "After Action Reviews," or AARs. The goal of AARs is to change the organizational focus from quickly fixing something after the fact to understanding the root causes of a problem. This requires that an organization consider reflection as a legitimate use of one's time. As Harley's leaders knew well from personal experience, the process of reflection is often undervalued. Most organizations put their primary (or even their exclusive) emphasis on *fixing*, rather than on understanding.

Harley-Davidson has adopted and adapted the army's "learn-from-experience" techniques. Tim Savino, director of development and training, summarizes the basics of the approach as follows:

- Simple to learn but challenging to practice
- Based on the premise that the best way to learn is while the experience is fresh
- Learning requires the perspective of all who participated (in other words, it is a team responsibility)

The steps in the AAR process, as it is employed at Harley, are fairly straightforward:

- Review the *intent* of the recent action.
- Reconstruct key events: *What happened?*
- Discuss the *lessons learned* from that action.
- Define the action *implications*.
- Take *action* based on the implications.
- Share lessons with others.

In other words, the report provides a high-level snapshot of what went right and what went wrong. It deepens an understanding of the underlying systems and culture through the use of causal loops. As shown below, it identifies potential "high-leverage" points by combining interview data and current product development metrics. And, finally, it outlines an action plan whereby responsible parties will commit to change and metrics will be established to track results.

AARs have been used successfully in many areas at Harley. In the wake of a recent product launch, for example, they provided a corporatewide perspective regarding the current state of product development. Although they were a formal report, their real purpose was to be used as a tool for improvement.

How was this report developed? The AAR leaders made visits to seven locations and conducted thirty-eight interviews (individual and group) which included more than 150 participants involved in sixteen different activities across the company.

So what changed as a result? Three comprehensive initiatives are being implemented—not short-term fixes, but reasoned approaches to help the company become predictable, improve quality, and develop problem-free launches in the future. And, more generally, Harley was reminded again that a situation that may at first be perceived as a single-plant problem frequently can develop into a problem that affects many other areas of the organization. Allowing the single plant to focus on its problem in an isolated way can put larger, shared activities at risk. Through the AAR process, there is now a real recognition that a plant is not an island and that each plant has a responsibility to communicate to and receive input from all of its affected stakeholders.

As is true of many of the lessons that Harley has learned in recent years, improvements can grow out of simple and seemingly obvious changes in the way that information is gathered, analyzed, and disseminated. Yes, AARs sound simple, but the fact remains that few organizations have a formal procedure for reviewing what goes right and what goes wrong, *promptly*, after an important effort. When things go wrong, most organizations (1) allocate blame and (2) vow to try harder next time.

And, again, AARs can't happen in an organizational vacuum. The ground for this kind of exchange and this level of honesty must be prepared in advance. "It's the ongoing effort to develop a more involved and participatory work environment," says Don Kieffer, general manager of Capitol Drive operations, "that makes this approach possible."

Recruiting and Retaining

As noted in previous chapters, Harley in the 1980s became an insular and thinly populated company. Large-scale layoffs in management ranks had taken their toll on Harley's management. So, too, had salary freezes and the general uncertainty of working for a company that was clearly on the ropes.

The recovery effected by Vaughn Beals and his colleagues solved the company's most pressing problems but left many others unresolved. As the company continued to progress, and as laid-off employees who wanted to return rejoined the ranks, the need for new skills and capabilities became apparent. The new challenges posed by continued growth and progress naturally called for periodic infusions of talented people from outside the company. At the same time, however, people within Harley seemed to "repel" outsiders—people who hadn't "been there" in the bad times. In fact, it was very difficult for anyone from the outside to break into the Harley organization.

Margaret Crawford, at that time heavily involved in recruiting new talent for the organization, recalls the challenges she faced.

> In the late eighties, many of the candidates who were interested in joining the Harley family were attracted by the brand. Others wanted the employee discount. Still others had heard about the turnaround or were intrigued by our rapid growth. These were good selling points for us, but frankly, they didn't appeal to all of the people we wanted. In many cases, it was difficult to attract the very high caliber of talented people we needed.

By the mid-1990s, however, things were changing. Comprehensive education and training programs, rewards and recognition systems focused on the individual's contribution as part of a group, improved communications, the circle organization, and the Business Process were all falling into place. Margaret Crawford, for one, detected a real change in the way her company was perceived in the outside world. "Today," she explains,

> Harley still attracts some candidates who are enthusiasts, and others who would like to benefit from our financial performance. But what's changed is that the company now appeals to a much larger group—including highly talented individuals who are aggressively pursued by other companies—who want to join Harley because they are excited by the way Harley operates and by what we're trying to do with the culture.

According to Margaret, new employees frequently cite the company's values, and its open and participatory environment, as key reasons why they joined the company. One candidate for a vice president's post, for example, said that she wanted to join Harley because she believed it would offer her deeper personal meaning and a closer "connection" than her then-current job. She was impressed by the company's "soul," she said, in addition to the enthusiasm that employees demonstrated for their coworkers, their company, and its products.

Harley, of course, is still a proud and tradition-rich company, which means that it is still a difficult place to earn acceptance. It appears, however, that the Business Process—and the many other changes described in preceding chapters—help create a common view of the company's purpose, its code of ethics, and its *direction*: where it is headed and how it's going to get there.

Changing How Products Happen

During the mid-1980s, Harley brought to market some desperately needed new products: the Evolution engine, five-speed transmissions, belt drives, two new motorcycles, different finishes, better brakes, sound systems, cruise control, and a host of other changes.

But these product introductions, welcome as they were, tended to be both overdue and imperfect. They taxed the company's technical resources and often proved difficult to accomplish. And, when things went wrong, engineering and manufacturing had to fix those mistakes on an ad hoc basis with a shoestring budget.

By the early 1990s, Harley's leaders knew that the company had to get away from its traditional sequential process of product design and development: the engineers first doing their thing, then manufacturing and purchasing (suppliers) doing their thing, while sales and marketing pleaded for attention from the sidelines. In 1991 the word came down: *We have to fix product development.*

At this same point in time, Awareness Expansion IV was having an impact on managers across the organization. As explained in chapter 9, one outgrowth of the Awareness Expansion experience was that ten senior Harley executives enrolled in the "core course" offered by organizational theorist Peter Senge through MIT's Organizational Learning Center (OLC). Among many other observations, Senge made the case that the life span of most companies is surprisingly brief: start-up to bankruptcy, he noted, seldom takes more than about fifty years. Why? Because, despite their enormous assets, these companies forget how to learn.

One of the remedies that Senge prescribed to break this cycle of nonlearning was the "causal loop diagram," a visual representation

of a particular work process emphasizing "feedback"; that is, recipro-
cal flows of influence. "Nothing is ever influenced in just one direction," as Senge explains in his book, *The Fifth Discipline*. A causal
loop diagram emphasizes causes and effects, and casts a bright light
on the strengths and weaknesses of the process being studied. Most
importantly, it promotes systems thinking by stressing that "every
influence is both a cause and effect."

These ideas, too, influenced Harley's leaders enormously, including the leaders of the product development group. In the fall of 1991,
Ron Hutchinson (then vice president for quality) drew up a causal loop
diagram representing the product development and introduction
process at Harley. He and his colleagues discussed it and, declining to
pull any punches, labeled this diagram "LEW"—*late, expensive,* and
wrong. It showed a variety of managerial goals converging on resource
allocation, overlapping initiatives, "knee-jerk" and counterproductive
reactions to problems, and unhappy stakeholders. Eloquently, it
graphed organizational frustration (see the diagram following).

Although the LEW diagram captured the frustrations of the moment,
it also began creating consensus on what was wrong with the then-current
processes of product design and development. These included

- a desire to please and a cultural propensity to manage by crisis.
- the lack of a shared vision regarding expectations and strategy.
- the inability to say no (or to say no and be believed).
- fear of failure and fear of change.
- a lack of knowledge about creating a better process.
- a lack of time to make change.[1]

The Harley engineers and managers shared the LEW diagram with
their Senge/OLC counterparts in January 1992. Building on this foundation, the two groups agreed to work together for the bulk of 1992.
Harley's "core learning team" would draw on the outside organization's resources to plan for an event called a "learning lab," scheduled
for October. This session would last several days and would focus on
ways to improve product development at Harley. Meanwhile, the core

---

[1] Much of this discussion, including these points, comes from the Harley "learning history,"
described later in this chapter.

Causal Loop Diagram of "LEW"

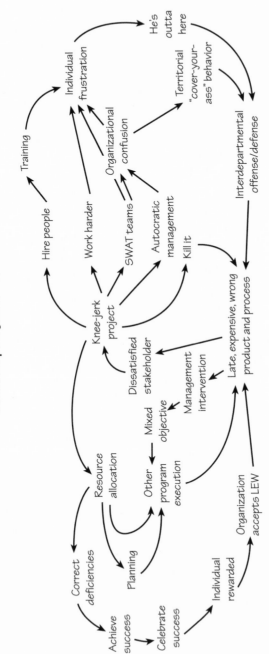

For more on causal loop diagrams, and the related topics of systems thinking and systems archetypes, see Peter Senge, *The Fifth Discipline* (Doubleday, 1990), pp. 93–113 and 378–390; Daniel H. Kim, *Systems Archetypes: Diagnosing Systemic Issues and Designing High-Leverage Interventions* (Pegasus Communications, 1993); and Senge et al., *The Fifth Discipline Fieldbook* (Doubleday, 1994), pp. 121–150.

learning team would hone its ability to apply systems thinking to the resolution of practical business problems.

This process, too, created frustrations. By coincidence, OLC was then working on a similar project with an automaker, which had enough depth in its technical ranks to "spare" engineers and designers for large stretches of time over the course of many months. Harley had no such depth, and, as a result, the technical side often lacked representation on the core learning team. For their part, the members of the core learning team often found the vagueness of what they were trying to do frustrating. What, exactly, was a "learning lab," and what was it supposed to accomplish?

Even some of the valuable learning that occurred was irritating, threatening, or both. "For many people at Harley," one participant later observed, "thinking about what they were doing—rather than just *doing* it—was a foreign concept. Having to reflect on the past made it seem to some of our task-driven engineers and managers that there was an 'alien force' present [at Harley]."

The Learning Lab

According to the systems experts at OLC, a learning laboratory is a workshop (sometimes referred to by the OLC as a "managerial practice field") at which people develop new skills by cycling back and forth between study and practice. Participants "train" less and "practice" more. "Real" business situations are simulated, and participants get the chance to make "real" mistakes (without the penalties associated with real-world snafus). They learn new tools and apply them in a setting that is as similar as possible to the day-to-day workplace.

As they prepared for Harley's Learning Lab, the core learning team explored a number of Senge's business "archetypes" and discovered that several of these common business practices and systems applied to Harley. They recognized, for example, the "tragedy of the commons," in which multiple entities had the right to call on a limited central resource—in this case, product design and engineering skills—with no effective constraints on those demands.

The OLC refused to tell the Harley team exactly what Harley's Learning Lab should look like. (Although the OLC shared the form and content of labs run by other companies, it discouraged Harley from simply mimicking those efforts.) In October 1992, some two dozen Harley people attended a two-day Learning Lab in Milwaukee. There they explored a number of OLC-developed learning tools, including Senge's five disciplines, archetypal behaviors, computer simulations, the "ladder of inference" (developed by MIT researcher Chris Argyris), the "left-hand-column" exercise (developed by Argyris and his colleague Don Schon), and other resources.

Again, the process generated more questions than answers. Participants created their own causal loop diagram of product development at Harley, and no one was happy with the resulting depictions. "A mess," one person called it. "An ugly picture," said another. Some participants found this causal loop exercise a stimulating challenge and wanted to move forward to find ways to break and change the bad loops. But others, conditioned by past command-and-control experiences at Harley to expect a "silver-bullet" solution, emerged from the lab frustrated. What was it all about? Where was the *prescription?*

By most accounts, nothing concrete came out of the Learning Lab effort. "Meanwhile," project manager and twenty-year Harley veteran Hugh Vallely recalls, "people were so busy getting products launched that they stopped coming to meetings." The Learning Lab had come and gone, but people in both the divisional management and senior management ranks remained puzzled. "We still don't know how to *fix* it," many complained. Engineering suspended its relationship with Senge and the OLC for more than a year. Fixing product development, it seemed, no longer commanded leadership's attention.

RICH: But this stuff never really dies, if it's any good. It simply goes underground for a while. It steeps and percolates. In the wake of the Learning Lab, you'd hear people using phrases in their conversations like "ladders of inference" or "left-hand/right-hand column situations." To me, these signs indicate real progress, even when things seem to be dead in the water.

First Steps toward a Shared Vision

In the spring of 1993, Harley hired Earl K. Werner, a General Motors engineer, to work under Vice President of Engineering Mark Tuttle. Werner accepted the post on the understanding that he eventually would succeed Tuttle.

Werner quickly discovered that his new organization had some limitations. Its technical resources were limited, especially in contrast to GM's. Harley's "new" products represented mostly variations on products that had existed for decades. Meanwhile, competitors were applying technology to their replicas of Harley's products and trying to beat Harley at its own game: adding performance and other innovations that Harley couldn't match because of its technical limitations.

RICH: Werner, of course, arrived with two strikes against him: he came from outside, and he came from the automotive field. Then he started asking questions that had implied criticisms in them. Strike three! Fortunately, he got another chance at the plate.

Werner decided that Harley needed a shared image of product development—one that could serve as a technical road map and would be the common property of everybody in the Harley technical community. By this time, Werner had absorbed the lessons of OLC, the early "core competency" courses, the causal loop diagrams, and the Learning Lab. He believed that these new ways of thinking were valuable to Harley in general, and to the product development function in particular.

As a result, Werner created for his colleagues a new forum for learning (who began reporting to him when Mark Tuttle retired). Werner's team renewed its relationship with the OLC. Werner, meanwhile, set up a schedule of monthly meetings, which started as half-day sessions. The product development group sequestered itself in a conference room and, with time out only for lunch, wrestled to come up with a joint description of a desired future state. In a sense, Werner's group was replaying aspects of both Awareness Expansion and the Joint Vision Process, all within its own functional area.

"Getting commitment to this process was a tough job," Werner recalls. "Harley is a very 'tasky' company. Task orientation is very, very strong here, and not many people saw intellectual exercising, as I'll call it, as productive. In spite of this, I started to have half-day meetings. And occasionally I had to take an autocratic approach. For example, one time when the validity of these meetings was challenged by a very busy engineer, I replied, 'This is our *work*. You *will* spend this time—it is a requirement of employment.'"

> LEE: As we've said many times, this is the paradox inherent in the transition from compliance to commitment. You need a dose of command and control to start the evolution away from command and control.

A full six months elapsed before Werner's group committed itself to the process, and this was only the beginning. Over the ensuing year, the once-a-month sessions continued. Half-day sessions evolved into full-day meetings, and the group acquired an informal label: the "Leadership Team."

"At times," recalls Hugh Vallely, "these meetings became very reflective and personal. We started to show openness and trust as we discussed the undiscussables. We kept talking about the vision, trying to make it *our* vision, as opposed to Earl's alone."

"We began to make progress," Werner says. "We had developed a whole new mind-set. We had developed enthusiasm for, and commitment to, what was now a shared vision."

The Vision

That vision, committed to paper in April of 1994, comprised a dozen pages. The first page consisted of three "vision objectives":

> Fundamentally, as an organization, we need to shift from our current product development model to a new one that achieves the following objectives:
>
> • Become predictable.

- Reduce product development cycle time.
- Demonstrate product and process feasibility and establish confidence that [our] targets are achievable, prior to production implementation.

Next came a one-page schematic that represented a cross between the charts Lee had drawn in his first meeting (in the fall of 1987) with Harley's senior managers and the ideas that people had taken away from Senge's OLC. The left-hand side of the schematic, a flowchart, depicted the "current reality" of product development, with text annotations at the bottom. "Knowledge is 'tribal,' and difficult to retrieve/share," read one. The right-hand side of the schematic depicted the envisioned reality. "Captured learning adds to knowledge base, forming higher-level starting point for next design," read one of the text annotations below this column.

Notably, the envisioned future state of product development at Harley began with the *customer* ("determine the voice of the customer"), with the *competition*, and with a *continuously improving knowledge base*. (The voice of the customer did not appear in the "current reality" column.) The envisioned future state delayed prototyping, designing, and tooling until much later in the process, allowing for *analysis, simulation, optimization,* and *visualization* in the meantime. And, rather than being a linear process, the envisioned future of product development involved a circular, *learning* process, in which continuous improvement would concentrate on the knowledge base, rather than on the manufacturing process.

The document then detailed fifteen "key attributes of the envisioned state" and a series of strategies and initiatives intended to move the product development function toward that state. Two themes predominated throughout these sections: *collect wisdom* and *keep separate activities separate*. "Keep the persons assigned to new product and process development from becoming involved with day-to-day problem solving or crisis management responsibility for current products," read one strategy statement. The document also emphasized visualization, modeling, and graphic representation. "Meet around the hardware," read another strategy statement. "Continually ask the question, 'Can this idea, change, etc. be visualized?'"

The vision statement concluded by summarizing the challenges the company faced in the realms of government regulation, competition, product liability, and cost. It restated Harley's five core values—tell the truth, be fair, keep your promises, respect the individual, and encourage intellectual curiosity—and extended those values into a set of operating philosophies for the product development group. "A thirst for learning from all available sources moves the organization to the next plateau of achievement," read one philosophy statement. "Failure to build upon the existing pool of knowledge wastes intellectual resources while we relearn what is already known."

RICH: I see two critical pieces in that statement. One is the "thirst for learning," and the other is a commitment to retain what has been learned. It's a great illustration of how a functional area injects what's important to them—not making the same mistake twice—and improves on the learning mandate for the larger organization.

LEE: It was really great to observe this process as it unfolded. It contained the same principles and concepts that underlay all the other efforts—vision, now, plan—plant seeds, involve people, create consensus and commitment.

Adds Werner, "We arrived at a common methodology for developing new products. We agreed on a way to design motorcycles that was predictable, sequenced in time, produced results that were logical, and could be counted on by the organization. For the first time, we found a way to leave behind LEW—late, expensive, and wrong—and move to something much better."

The PDL2T

We should remind the reader that this functionally based visioning initiative took place in a changing organizational context. The circle organization, described in chapter 7, was born in July 1993 and evolved rapidly during the period when the product development group was developing its new vision. Werner and his colleagues belonged to the produce product group, or PPG.[2] But the visioning process demonstrated convincingly that product design and development couldn't remain the sole province of the PPG. If Harley considered the customer's perspective to be a vital input, for example, didn't the create demand circle have to play a part?

Organizational acceptance of this idea came hard. As Hugh Vallely recalls, "Earl and the rest of us were having lots of trouble getting the PPG to understand that we were all responsible for product development—that product development belonged not only to engineering, but also purchasing, manufacturing, styling, and so on."

Late in 1995, therefore, Werner's group came up with a new invention. They called it the "Product Development Leadership and Learning Team," soon shortened to "PDL2T."

LEE: Our premise all along was that Harley had to get the right people doing the right work at the right time in the right way. What this group had to do was define all four of those parameters. That's not an easy assignment!

The premise of the PDL2T was that product development consisted of more than just engineering. In the old model, the engineering group saw itself as (and was seen as) solely responsible for the development and delivery of new products. But, with help from the OLC researchers and through hard work on their own, Harley's product developers now saw their job as part of an "enterprise activity," involving manufacturing, purchasing, marketing, finance, and so on. Technical content still dominated, of course, but it could not claim a monopoly. "Engineering, by itself, can't deliver a new product," Werner says flatly.

---

[2] Unfortunately for organizational consistency, the acronym PPC—the logical acronym for what should have been dubbed the "produce product circle," comparable to the create demand circle (CDC)—was already in use by an existing group. So the produce product circle became the PPG.

The PDL2T therefore sought to involve a much larger group of people. Members of other relevant functions, both within and outside the PPG circle, were invited to participate in the visioning process. Soon, purchasing, service, manufacturing, and a host of other functional areas took their place at the PDL2T table. This led to a "good news/bad news" situation. The good news was that assembling this larger group ensured that the new vision eventually would enjoy a broader base of ownership across the organization. The bad news was that, at least to some extent, the envisioning process had to start all over again.

"Ultimately," Werner recalls, "we succeeded in expanding the group cross-functionally, across the enterprise, and getting the vision going among all these other people. Now we had a powerful leadership group, which sat just 'below' the Functional Leadership Group executive level. These were the heirs apparent, if you will. That group soon became very influential—close enough to both the VPs and also the day-to-day activities that they could effectively push the organization toward change."

LEE: Again, the resemblance to the original partnering process—in which the Group of 35 became the Group of 100—was strong. The process of building concentric circles of involvement, commitment, and ownership was also similar and illustrates an underlying dynamic: You can't start big, but you can't stay small.

RICH: The PDL2T captures the essence of the work that Lee and I did during all those years. They worked through the circle organization to draw in their colleagues in different functional areas and eventually caught the eye of the higher-ups across the organization. Energy concentrated itself in the middle of the organization, and, in good time, all that energy dragged along the organization's so-called leaders.

One diagram inserted in the middle of the original vision statement struck an enduring chord. It depicted an "engineering factory," complete with a stylized smokestack. The "raw materials" going into the factory bore labels that read "detailed product plans," and the "finished products" leaving the factory were "quality designs on time."

Existing facilities had manifest problems. "In the Juneau Avenue facility," recalls Hugh Vallely, "there was literally no place to put a motorcycle where the engineers could stand around and talk about it." Worse still, Harley's critical engineering resources were dispersed across the company's manufacturing landscape. Some were at Juneau Avenue, others were at the Capitol Drive facility, and still others were elsewhere in the state or at the York, Pennsylvania, factory. And now, with the expansion of the PDL2T, new groups needed the chance to "meet around the hardware." Was purchasing really going to participate in product design and development, from now on? If so, then Harley couldn't leave its buyers in relative isolation at the individual plants.

The PDL2T began designing a facility to make the envisioned future possible. It did not set out to design a "technical facility" per se. Instead, it sought to create a space that would facilitate cross-functional work and support Harley's new product development process.

At the end of the PDL2T's design process, it found it had come up with a large box with a minimum of interior walls, which created large amounts of open space. Test labs, prototype-building areas, and a variety of specialized labs—emissions, acoustics, dyno, and others—sat in close proximity to the design teams. When a designer ran a test in a lab, therefore, he or she would have immediate access to the results. The design also included a large "mock-up" area, where new designs and products would be displayed and discussed. This area embodied a key component of the original product development vision: The mock-ups would develop as the designs developed.

Harley broke ground on its new 213,000-square-foot Product Development Center in 1995. "Approximately 400 people, dedicated to the collaborative development of new products and manufacturing processes, are slated to relocate here when the facility is completed by year-end 1996," according to the 1995 annual report. "The new facility will allow us to further assimilate state-of-the-art technologies—and the employee training required to take full advantage of them—to support our growth." The company officially dedicated the PDC in 1997 and renamed it the "Willie G. Davidson Product Development Center," honoring the company's beloved vice president for styling (and founding-family member).

Welcome Evidence

Although we've presented a sustained look at how the product development process at Harley has changed, we don't mean to imply that either this process or the new facility within which it is now being carried out is perfect. "Perfect" isn't in our organizational vocabulary. Continuous improvement means that nothing is ever perfect, or, if magically it became so, it wouldn't stay so for long. Earl Werner and other key leaders within the product development function drew on the work of Peter Senge and other outside experts to achieve results that were highly positive, but still imperfect.

Similarly, the IS function, the After Action Review (AAR) technique, and the management recruiting process described earlier in the chapter are far from perfect. But, again in these instances, we see evidence that good and creative processes came into play. Through the careful collection, analysis, and dissemination of information in the AAR process, plants learn (again) that they don't exist in a vacuum. Margaret Crawford—on the front lines of the management recruitment challenge for more than a decade—is particularly well situated to gauge whether the recent changes at Harley appeal to smart and demanding managers in the "outside world." Like Earl and his colleagues, Dave Storm found ways to "download" elements of the circle organization to make his own functional area far more productive and responsive to the needs of the larger organization.

To us, these are highly positive trends. They don't lend themselves particularly well to quantification—*How many dollars has Harley saved or earned as a result of steps X, Y, or Z?*—but they are valid measures of an organization's flexibility and vitality.

In our estimation at least, they make a key point: *This stuff works.* This is a subject to which we'll return in our final chapter.

13

Reflections on a Journey

A SENIOR MANAGER AT HARLEY RECENTLY MADE A TELLING analogy. The sequence of experiences that we had shared with the organization in the preceding decade or so, he said, had been something like taking a ride on a Harley. "It's the journey," he explained, echoing the theme of a long-ago Harley ad campaign. "The fun is not in the destination; the fun is in the journey."

Most of the previous chapters of this book document a process of change at one American manufacturing company between roughly the late 1980s and the late 1990s. We noted in our Introduction that Harley's history and circumstances in some ways were unique and that offering a universal prescription based on the company's recent experiences would be a bad idea, at best. But we also suggested that there were some general themes and lessons in the Harley experience that might have broad applicability to business, and that's the substance of this chapter.

First, a few words about success and how we think about "success." Throughout this book, we have mainly avoided using statistics to support our contentions. Why? Because most of the efforts we've described didn't lend themselves to a quantitative assessment. Did we consider Awareness Expansion II a "success"? Well, the postevent evaluations indicated that participants felt Awareness Expansion II was more successful than Awareness Expansion I. But *far more important* things didn't and don't lend themselves to quantification.

For example, five years after these Awareness Expansions came and went, were the members of Harley's leadership group more open to new ideas and more interested in bringing new ideas to their jobs? We are absolutely convinced that they were, and are. Was Margaret Crawford's job of recruiting and retaining talented managers, as described in the previous chapter, made easier? We believe so. But neither contention can be proven, at least to the scientist's satisfaction.

Are the members of Harley's unions more committed to continuous improvement, to taking personal responsibility for making the company more effective and efficient, to working across functional lines, and to *leading the company* in a thousand other ways? Yes, they are—and, again, we can't point to simple measures that make our case conclusively.

But let's update a chart that we introduced in chapter 1. In 1982, you will recall, Harley was at death's door—losing money and losing market share. In that grim year, 40 percent of the company's employees lost their jobs.

Four years later, in 1986, the company's vital signs looked substantially better, due to the leadership of Vaughn Beals and his associates on the management side, and also to the magnificent "all hands to the pumps" effort made by Harley's employees.

The following year, the journey described in this book began. Rich began assuming more responsibility for the company's affairs. He also began his search for the leadership model that would succeed the command-and-control model that had seen Harley through its years of crisis.

By 1999, the company's vital signs looked even better (see table 13-1). How much of this improvement resulted from the efforts

TABLE 13-1: HARLEY: THEN AND NOW

	1982	1986	1999
U.S. market share (651+ cc)	15.2%	19.4%	49.5%
Units shipped	32,400	36,700	177,187
Revenue ($millions)	210	295	2,453
Operating profit (loss) ($millions)	(15.5)	7.3	415.9
Employees*	2,289	2,211	7,200

*Estimate (includes employees of Eaglemark Financial Services, Inc., a Harley subsidiary).

described in this book? We believe that the answer is: A great deal. But ultimately that is a question for the reader to answer.

Another initial observation, before we move on to the specifics of this chapter: The reader may have noticed that, over the course of this book, our own roles have changed considerably. At the outset, we (Lee and Rich) were among a small group of isolated leaders pushing for and initiating change we weren't yet able to define. Later, we served more as resources than as guides, and our roles became less central.

This, we think, is another way of measuring success. If the changes at Harley over the last decade or so have lasting significance, it will be because they have become ingrained and embedded in the very fabric of the organization. They can't depend on Rich (now retired) making an inspirational speech, or Lee (as of this writing, still consulting to Harley) suggesting yet another organizational innovation. But we believe that the partnering, recruitment, information systems, and product development stories related in chapters 11 and 12—and dozens of others like them which we could have cited—*do* suggest that our efforts to teach others to teach have been successful.

In the rest of this chapter, we'll examine how the specifics of our efforts, beginning back before 1987 and carrying through up to the present, may be helpful to other leaders who seek to upend the pyramid, delegate authority, and inspire others to lead.

Living Your Values

The best starting point is recognizing that *values count*. Here, we're talking about the personal values of people in leadership positions. Leaders have to live the right message, day in and day out. When an organization picks up signals of ambivalence—or, worse, a gap between asserted belief and behavior—there is little chance of sustainable progress.

Second, values have to be *shared* values, across the leadership of the organization. Values must be congruent to get the leaders over the inevitable bumps in the road. They must also be congruent to ensure that the efforts of employees won't be tugged and pulled in contradictory directions.

As noted in chapter 2, we came to our shared journey with remarkably congruent value systems. Both of us, for example, believed in the overriding importance of ethical behavior. (Neither of us reacts well to being called a "liar" or a "cheat.") We believed in the importance of being genuine and doing what you say you're going to do.

As the sons of extremely hard-working parents, we believed that earning your keep is critically important, and that earning your keep almost always involves long hours and the occasional sleepless night. Both sets of parents hammered hard on the golden rule—that treating people as you'd have them treat you is essential to a successful and happy life.

As former plant managers, we both believed that people almost always overrate the contributions of senior management and almost always underrate the contributions of the people who actually do the hard work of designing, making, marketing, and moving things.

Although we traveled very different paths before coming together in the context of Harley, each of us had been exposed to a wide variety of businesses. Each of us felt confident that he could handle whatever tomorrow might throw at him, and both of us were at least smart enough to realize that other people were more experienced and more competent than we were, so we had better listen hard to their ideas.

Experience had taught each of us that dialogue can resolve most problems in the workplace. Many problems in the workplace grow directly out of a lack of effective communication.

We both believed that people are people and generally want the same things from life, including their organizational life. We believed that the process of leadership must provide people with the right tools and then more or less get out of the way.

And, although the phrase is Rich's, both of us believed firmly that *people are the organization's only sustainable competitive advantage.*

Betting on People

Perhaps this last point needs a little elaboration. Peter Senge makes the point that, on average, organizations die sooner than people. Fifty years is an unusually long life span for a company. There is relatively little overlap between the Fortune 500 of fifty (or even twenty-five) years ago and that of today.

Why? In part, it's because of what economist Joseph Schumpeter called the "creative destruction" inherent in capitalism. New ideas drive out old ones; new ways of deploying resources displace traditional ones.

But we think this high corporate mortality rate also arises because companies place long-term bets on the wrong assets. Some (like Wang Laboratories and Digital Equipment Corporation) bet on technologies that they believe will be sustainable over the long run. This strategy never pans out over the long run. Patents expire; technology marches on.

Other companies place bets on their organizational structure. Alfred Sloan's invention of the multidivisional organization—as embodied in General Motors—spelled serious trouble for Henry Ford's vision of the world. And most observers would agree that General Motors only got "better" at being hierarchical over subsequent decades. And yet betting on hierarchy has proven disastrous for the giants of Motor City. Ford began to heal itself when it abandoned Henry Ford's vision of a totally integrated car company—from rubber plantations to showrooms—and General Motors got into deeper and deeper trouble as it ossified into vertical integration.

Some organizations bet on elaborate, rigorous, and highly refined procedures, systems, processes, or plans. Sometimes these "tilt" toward a particular functional area: marketing methods, cash management, and so on. To invoke a racing analogy, this puts more value on the car than on the driver. We believe that organizations should bet on the values, judgment, and skills of people. We believe that leadership means providing employees with the freedom and abilities, including decision-making parameters, to use those values, judgment, and skills.

Leaving Command and Control Behind

So people are what counts. But what's the best way to structure a company (or other organization) to ensure that people can do their best work?

Both of us had experienced command-and-control organizations, and Rich had personally led organizations (or pieces of organizations) structured in this way. Both of us understood that command and control works in certain situations—and in fact is the *only* thing that works when circumstances are desperate enough. When the ox is in the ditch, get it out of the ditch. When the barn's on fire, don't organize a committee—put the fire out!

Based on our shared and separate experiences, though, we know that great hierarchies don't make great organizations. In particular, top-down, command-and-control organizations are fatally flawed in the long run. Their flaws include

- a lack of acceptance of personal responsibility.
- a widespread "not my job" syndrome.
- a focus on narrow tasks and duties.
- limited or narrow input into problem solving and decision making.
- frustration.
- compliance, rather than commitment.

Unilateral decision making at the top, a clear chain of command, and foot soldiers who take orders and execute someone else's plans meticulously—all of these serve well in the crisis mode but don't help the organization months or years after the fire is extinguished.

RICH: I also argue that command-and-control organizations render themselves vulnerable to subtle shifts in the external environment and that most organization-threatening changes begin as small and subtle shifts that hierarchies tend to miss.

LEE: And organizations react unpredictably to the crises identified by command-and-control leaders. Look at the challenges faced by the U.S. military, for example. What were the respective levels of rank-and-file commitment engendered by World War I, World War II, the Korean War, the Vietnam War, and Desert Storm? Very different, to say the least.

Seen from the top of the pyramid, command-and-control leadership is both limiting and lonely. The leader needs to have all the answers and must maintain an aura of infallibility. In our experience, *no one* has all the answers. No one is that good. When a company's fortunes hinge on the vision and experience of one person (or, more likely, only a few people), that company will fail over the long run.

Another flaw in the command-and-control approach lies on the level of individual motivation. Money is certainly one kind of motivator. Mercenaries join causes based on the lure of financial reward. But history tells us that mercenaries—even overpaid mercenaries—tend to be undermotivated. The Hessians whom the British hired to roust out George Washington's ragtag Continental Army were well equipped, well fed, and well paid—and lost.

The analogy to corporate life is obvious. You can always buy someone's time, and you may even get the best person, but with money alone you won't get the best person's *heart*. Why does a great software engineer leave a high-paying job to make a lateral move to a cutting-edge software shop? To find the most exciting professional challenges, and to find the joy of intrinsic motivation. Being paid top dollar may well be a secondary consideration.

"You are advocating that the inmates take over the asylum," a fellow CEO once said to Rich, only half in jest. Not exactly. We certainly believe that corporations need structures, procedures, and processes. (We're both former plant managers, after all, and plant managers love predictability.) But our experiences have taught us that leaders are *far better off* when they devise structures, procedures, and processes in collaboration with the people who have to make them work. This increases the breadth of the ideas and builds a broader base of ownership. It creates both the *freedoms* and the *fences* that are necessary for flexibility and creativity. In many cases, the inmates are the only resource that can save the asylum.

Creating the Environment

If people are the organization's only sustainable competitive advantage, and if a command-and-control model fails to tap the intrinsic motivation of people over the long term, then the leader must create and maintain a different kind of environment—one in which people can thrive.

The overriding challenge in creating that environment is to *enlist a lot of co-inventors*. This approach permeated all of the initiatives described in the prior chapters. No one person can create the environment alone. The change must engage as many coinventors as possible.

Maybe that prescription seems self-evident. But, in our experience, this is true for most successful organizational change efforts. The leadership challenge does not take rocket science, just a little common sense. Common sense permeates all of the principles that guided our own actions. For example,

- Understand what the organization is trying to accomplish.
- Provide everyone with the opportunity to participate in his or her performance evaluations and career development.
- Structure the organization in a manner that truly encourages all the people to participate.
- Create an environment that values lifelong learning.
- Find effective approaches to communication.

Taking these principles point by point: Everybody in the organization has to know what the company is trying to accomplish. Some might relegate that task to a communication effort, but it's more than that—it's an attempt to give everybody a stake in its success. We developed a simple process that starts with values and ends with the individual, as described in chapters 5 and 8.

Most of us want to make a difference in what we do every day. Given how much time we spend at work, we naturally want to have an opportunity to influence how we can make that difference. We want effective assessment of our performance, and we want meaningful recognition and compensation. We described Harley's efforts in this realm in chapters 6 and 8.

The structure of an organization has a significant influence on how people behave. In a strict hierarchy, people generally have very specific limits on their responsibility and authority. One of the ways we tried to provide people with greater responsibility and authority was to reduce the hierarchy through the establishment of natural work groups. This is detailed in chapter 7.

As human beings, we all like to feel appreciated. Many companies feel that appreciation is best expressed through compensation and benefits. But we knew that something more was needed. We decided to find additional ways to say thank you. These are covered in chapter 8.

People who want or have increased levels of accountability and responsibility need opportunities to develop the new competencies necessary to operate at this new level. This we described in chapter 9.

Without effective communication at all levels of the organization, nothing will work. The organization will fail to be connected and focused. We have described our communications-related initiatives in chapter 10.

Chapters 11 and 12 give examples of how the principles listed above, when acted on, can make a real difference in the life of a company. As an alternative to these kinds of anecdotal accounts, we could have looked at more quantitative measures, such as the table included at the beginning of this chapter. Market share, profitability, or market capitalization: By any of these measures—and, for that matter, by all other standard measures of which we're aware—Harley has performed extraordinarily well in recent years. But some of the most important changes, as we've explained, lie outside the realm of the quantifiable.

Some Personal Observations

We would like to end this book, and symbolically close this phase of our journey together, by offering some sustained personal observations about what we've learned on that journey.

LEE: I saw our challenge from the outset as this: to lead without leading. How could we help foster an organization in which the people, not the bosses, would shape and grow the organization, without being told to do so or how to do so?

Was this difficult? Absolutely. Complex? Much more so than most treatises on organizational change imply. Humbling? Always. Frightening? Not really. After all, as noted, Rich and I worked from a base of remarkably similar values and beliefs. Each knew the other wouldn't abandon ship. Frustrating? Absolutely. But mostly we were frustrated with ourselves, individually, rather than with each other or with the people of Harley.

In retrospect, what would we do differently? I think we could have been more patient with ourselves, individually. But asking Rich Teerlink to cut himself some more slack is a waste of breath, and I suspect he might say the same thing about me.

I have confidence that Harley's journey will continue, well after Rich and I have left the scene. On January 13, 1999, at a session of Harley-Davidson University at which some 300 dealers and a smattering of employees were present, Rich was honored on the occasion of his impending retirement. The comments of one attendee affected me powerfully. "Don't worry, Rich," this dealer said. "We can't and don't want to go back to where we were before. We are on our way, and nothing will stop us from continuing the journey we've begun."

Again on a personal level, I viewed my journey with Rich less as a CEO/consultant relationship and more as a relationship between colleagues, equals, and mutual advisers. We respected each other's prerogatives and had confidence that the other would act skillfully, based on a firm foundation of values. We didn't keep score, because that's not what either of us was about.

I approached the Harley engagement (as I approach my other professional engagements) with five basic guiding principles:

1. At the outset, the consultant should help identify the problem and help the prospective client find the right resource to address that problem. Very often, this means that someone else is more appropriate for the job at hand.

2. The consultant must take responsibility for managing the relationship and making sure that the client uses the consultant's services in a cost-effective way.

3. The consultant should do for the client only what it cannot or will not do for itself. My most successful engagements have been those in which the client over time has built an internal capability to identify and solve problems on its own.

4. For practical reasons, the consultant should find the in-house people who already know the "right" answers—and

there are almost always at least of few of these people—make them allies, and give them due credit for their wisdom.

5. Together, the consultant and client must develop a very explicit "contract," which I put in quotes because I mean much more than a legal document. I mean clear agreement about roles, responsibilities, and accountabilities for both the internal and external resources involved in an initiative. Throughout my twelve-year relationship with Harley described in this book, continuous contracting and recontracting took place, comprising all the people involved in and personally affected by the relationship.

I should note that Rich, Tom Gelb, John Campbell, and others took care (along with me) to communicate both the specifics of the contract and the philosophy that lay behind it. Collectively, we made it clear what I would and would not do, and what the organization would and would not do. For example, we all agreed that I and my ROI colleagues would never violate internal confidences, nor allow ourselves to be used as message carriers. Harley people tested these commitments frequently in the early days of the relationship. Eventually, people decided that we meant what we said.

The two of us—Rich and Lee—regularly sat down to assess our evolving relationship. We talked explicitly about whether Harley was getting good value. Among other things, this modeled appropriate behaviors for the organization's benefit. As stated regularly in the preceding chapters, leaders must behave in congruence with their stated values.

Let me finish by saying that it has been my privilege to get to know and work closely with more than two dozen chief executive officers. I respected and admired them all. But I have never met and worked with a person, CEO or otherwise, whom I respect, admire, or like as much as I do Rich.

In many ways, Rich doesn't conform to Hollywood's stereotype of a CEO. He's not tall enough, his hair isn't silver, and he prefers leather riding gear to pinstripes. He is blunt, rather than political. He is as smart as they come, but one of the first things you notice about Rich is how hard he listens. He is determined to learn from you, whoever and wherever you are.

We have had, and still have, a relationship that is unique. We've worked closely together for twelve years. He has served me in many of the same ways I've served him—as coach and consultant to my own organization. In many cases, he's given me the best kind of advice: unwelcome advice.

For all of that, I thank him. And I congratulate him on initiating and fostering one of the most successful transformations of a human organization that I have ever encountered.

RICH: It's been nearly forty years since I graduated from college. In that time, I have worked for seven companies. These companies were large and small, public and private, and I had assignments at both the corporate and the divisional level. Over time, the scale and scope of my responsibilities expanded: junior auditor, accounting supervisor, internal auditor/tax manager, plant manager, corporate planning director, chief financial officer, president, chief executive officer, and chairman of the board.

At each of these companies, I got both "how to" and "how not to" lessons. I received wise counsel from many coaches and mentors. A gentleman named Earl Fester, for example, tried to teach me how to be a plant manager and stressed the importance of strong manufacturing processes and operational flexibility. Another quiet leader, Rollie Nelson, demonstrated the importance of being in touch with all of the people in the organization. Herman Miller's Max DePree helped me understand the job of a leader, distilled in a quote that I often cited in my years at Harley: "Leaders by their actions, not by their words, establish the sense of justice within the organization."

In addition to those in the companies I have worked for, there are many others who wrote books, or presented seminars, or in other ways influenced my personal growth. Two of the most significant of these are Michael Kami and Peter Senge. In the late 1970s, Mike wrote a book entitled *Management in Crisis, or Why the Mighty Fail.* This book came to mind in 1982 when we at Harley were seeking a consultant to help us sort out our future. Ultimately, Mike became an adviser to Harley and then a member of the board of directors. Although he was required to retire from the board at age seventy, he is still an active adviser to the company. There is no doubt in my mind that he helped save Harley-Davidson.

Peter Senge wrote *The Fifth Discipline* in 1990. For me, that book brought together many of the concepts I'd been struggling with for years. It talked about the interrelationships among systems. Peter clearly demonstrated that, if you examine phenomena in isolation from each other, you can't understand all the possible causes of a problem, and therefore you can't solve that problem effectively. He provided readers with tools to use to improve their ability to analyze and communicate. I consider Mike and Peter not only great thinkers, but also, more importantly, good friends, who have opened my eyes to new and usable concepts.

So far, I've identified five people who influenced my career. There are hundreds of others who helped along the way, as I tried to work with them and for them. They listened to my ideas and came back at me with better ideas. In the best circumstances, we drew on collective wisdom and jointly developed effective actions. These individuals might have been viewed by outsiders as shop people, office people, hourly employees, salaried employees, but I saw them, and still see them today, as partners, teachers, coaches, and mentors. Many of them became lifelong friends. I often fell short of their expectations, but they always let me try again. I'm especially grateful to all those in the Harley family who played such an important role in creating that environment in which everybody has an opportunity to make a difference and grow. Without them, this book would not have been written.

Let me depart from discussing those to whom I'm indebted for my success and talk about some of the learning I've taken away from the experience of being a CEO. These lessons may or may not be of value to other CEOs, and I offer them simply as food for thought, not as prescriptions.

CEOs are human beings who, by some mysterious set of happenings, have ascended to the ultimate position of power in corporate life. By force of circumstance, they are encouraged to think that they are the only ones who can lead their respective organizations. All of the trappings of CEO-dom reinforce this conclusion on a daily basis. But I suggest that CEOs keep in mind the fact that there are many who could do what they have done, and would do so if they had the opportunity. You are only as "special" as your actions. Ultimately, you have only the authority you earn.

As CEOs, we are vested with enormous power. How we exercise that power has a significant impact on lots of people. We can act as tyrants, benevolent dictators, or enablers. Good CEOs are rarely (if ever) tyrants, are occasionally benevolent dictators, and very frequently are enablers. As enablers, we have the opportunity to foster and participate in the success of others.

Personally, I have developed a high level of passion for Harley-Davidson as a proud, skilled, and principled institution. It is all of those things. But my greater passion is for the thousands of people who, every day, maintain the heritage of Harley. Some earn their livelihood as employees, dealers, or suppliers; others are customers who buy and use our products. Without these people, who in reality are all volunteers, we would not have the success we have experienced. I consider them family—not just numbers that get reflected in the various external and internal reports. I earnestly hope that they know how valuable they are to Harley's success. I tell them so every chance I get.

CEOs are the "keepers of the values" of their organization, at least until those values become a real, engrained, embedded part of the organization's members. With or without a context of change, but especially in a context of change, the CEO must act as the organizational role model. A single beacon alone is not sufficient illumination, of course, but the absence of this one beacon can undercut all others.

When necessary, a CEO must serve as an initiator of change but must make the transition quickly to the role of enabler, facilitator, supporter, nurturer.

A CEO must help other leaders to understand their primary role: as enablers and supporters of the efforts of others.

A CEO must be vulnerable. This makes it possible for the CEO to learn and for others to learn as well.

CEOs must make themselves visible and available to the organization. The larger, more complex, or more geographically dispersed the organization, the more difficult that task becomes. Although technology can be an effective aid, CEOs must learn to depend on other leaders at all levels to carry the ongoing message to all of the organization's people.

CEOs need a source of ongoing counsel. Max DePree called for a "secretariat": a group of individuals who aren't afraid to tell the emperor that he has no clothes. For twelve years, I've had a one-man secretariat: Lee Ozley. As you read this book, you've learned how he brought years of experience in dealing with organizational change to Harley-Davidson. He has helped us grow in knowledge and wisdom. He has challenged our thinking without making us feel condescended to or inferior. His counsel is actively sought after by employees throughout the Harley organization. He is viewed as a partner.

For me personally, he arrived as a consultant, but a different kind of consultant. He is a generalist, and therefore perhaps a member of an endangered species in this world of high tech and specialization. He never pushed the latest fad on Harley. His company never renamed a tool or approach for marketing purposes. Instead, Lee and his colleagues always sought to understand what we thought we wanted. When Lee felt we hadn't identified the real concern, he led us through a learning process. This was refreshing, and his generalist's approach enabled him to provide us with a broad base of consulting services which touched all the functional areas of the company.

Lee first stood out in our eyes as a kindred spirit, and then emerged as a coach, mentor, and colleague. He forced me to rethink subjects about which I thought I had sufficient and clear understanding. He mentored me through very difficult and stressful times during our change process. He learned about my life experiences and built them into his repertoire of tools for helping Harley and me. And he paid me the great compliment of accepting my coaching and mentoring as his own career evolved, and as he changed his own work focus.

The relationship Lee and I had, as CEO and consultant, was a unique one—one that I think allowed for the changes at Harley to evolve. Individually, we weren't interested in being identified as the owner of an idea, but were more interested in moving an idea to the implementation stage through the efforts of others. This approach allowed for the development of the real and enduring personal benefit of the journey Lee and I have shared. I have gained a friend.

We both hope (and believe, passionately) that Harley has benefited from the changes described in this book. We hope that other organizations can build on our experiences and make themselves better in their own creative ways. "History doesn't repeat itself," Mark Twain once wrote, "but sometimes it rhymes." This book can't serve as a cookbook—but maybe our thoughts can serve as a source of good rhymes.

We look forward to continuing our dialogue—with each other, and with others who seek to build and improve effective human organizations. If you wish to continue the dialogue with us, you can reach us at http://www.richleebooks.com.

Index

AARs (After Action Reviews), 238–240
accountability center analysis, 129–130
Allied Industrial Workers. *See* unions
AMF
    acquisition of Harley, 6–8
Anderson, Chris, 169, 171
Argyris, Chris, 246
attitudes
    assessing, 154
    attitudes toward, 155
    versus behaviors, 153–155
Awareness Expansion
    background of, 69–72
    evaluation of, 255–256
    first session of, 75–82
    fourth session of, 174–178, 242
    Port-a-pit session, 172–173
    second session of, 169–176
    Tinker Toy exercise, 73–74
Axelrod, Dick, 72

Bangor Punta, 5
Bartelme, Bob, 184
Beals, Vaughn, 8–11, 15, 16, 161, 240,
    256
Beckhard, Richard, 35
Beer, Michael, 35

behaviors
    versus attitudes, 153–155
    focusing on, 153–157
beliefs, 154
Berra, Yogi, 29
Bleustein, Jeff, 58, 70, 86, 93, 99,
    105, 110, 112, 132, 135–137,
    139–141, 182, 201, 213, 215,
    226
Block, Peter, 170, 171
Brehm, Gordon, 213
Business Process, 83–85
    assessment of, 104–106
    communication and, 196
    development of, 86–99
    importance of, 86–88
    integrative aspect of, 92–99, 104–105
    learning modules, 182–183
    structure of, 100–103

Cammann, Corty, 151
Campbell, John, 19, 20, 21, 24, 25, 29,
    36, 38, 43, 46, 70, 93, 265
Capitol Drive Learning Center, 184
career banding, 160–161
career development, competencies and,
    116–118

causal loop diagram, 242–243
CEO
    aspects of job, 267–268
    assistants to, 269
    tasks of, 268–269
chain of command, advantages and disadvantages of, 260
change
    beginnings of, 39–41
    factors in, 35–37
    road map for, 43–68
Ciparro, John, 213
circle organization, 131–133
    challenges of, 141–144
    implementation of, 135–137
    refinements to, 133–135
    structure of, 137–141
Citicorp, 9
command-and-control organization, 15–16
    communication and, 192–194
    flaws of, 260–261
    transcending, 259–261
communication
    assessment of, 197–203
    in command-and-control atmosphere, 192–194
    fixing problems in, 203–207
    importance of, 102
    issues regarding, 191–194
    optimizing, 194–207
compensation
    broad view of, 163–166
    emotional issues regarding, 145, 146–148
    evolution of system of, 146
    theories of, 148–151
    variable, 157–160
consultancy, principles of, 264–265
Covey, Stephen, 175
Crawford, Margaret, 66, 86, 108, 119, 151, 160, 162, 179, 180, 240, 254

create demand circle (CDC), 143
customers
    core processes related to, 128–129
    needs of, 126, 249
    organization based on, 128

Dahl, Wayne, 70, 93
Davidson brothers, 5
Demitros, Kathleen ("Kal"), 202–203, 204–205
DePree, Max, 31, 266, 269

Eberle, Karl, 227
education. See learning
employee involvement (EI), 11
employment security, 219–220
Empowered Manager, The, 170
engagement, 36
Engstrom, Reid, 235
environment, creation of, 261–263
evaluation, criteria for, 110–113. See also Performance Effectiveness Process (PEP)

Fester, Earl, 13, 266
Fifth Discipline, The, 165, 243, 267
forced ranking, 160, 162
Ford, Henry, 259
Functional Leadership Group (FLG), 138, 139, 142, 182

gain sharing, 20–26, 28–29
gap analysis, 35
Gelb, Tom, 11, 15, 19, 20, 21, 24, 25, 27, 29, 31, 36, 38, 39, 43, 45, 46, 48, 53, 54–55, 58, 70, 93, 133, 170, 213, 215, 265
Glenn, Wayne, 213
Gray, Bill, 151, 179, 213, 215

happiness, compensation and, 146–148
Harley, William, 5
Harley-Davidson
  AARs at, 238–240
  and AMF, 6–8
  Beals regime of, 8–11, 256
  capacity issues, 212, 224–227
  chronology of events at, x–xiii
  compensation system of, 145–166
  corporate umbrella of, 97–99, 100
  dealer organization of, 210
  economic health of, 256–257
  facility expansion of, 227–230
  focus of, 94–95
  information systems at, 234–238
  in-house communications organs
    of, 204–206
  initial public offering of, 12, 27–28
  innovation at, 19–41, 242
  Joint Vision for, 43–68
  learning at, 167–169, 178–190
  learning goals at, 170–171
  Learning Lab at, 245–246
  mission of, 88–90
  ninety-fifth anniversary of, 1–2
  objectives of, 90–91
  peer network at, 184–185
  pitfalls of success, 212
  product development at, 242–253
  Product Development Center of, 253
  proposal for nonunion factory,
    212–213
  public image of, 179–180
  recruiting and retaining at, 240–242
  relationship with unions, 43–46,
    57–58, 63, 256
  stakeholders of, 95–96, 209–210
  strategies of, 91–92
  strike of 1974, 7
  strike at York plant, 122
  structure of, 121–144, 262
  suppliers of, 210
  turmoil of 1980s, 2

  turnaround of, 13–17
  values of, 93–94
  vision of, 96–99
  worker satisfaction at, 202
  workplace innovation at, 11
Harley-Davidson Dealer Alliance, 10
Harley-Davidson Leadership Institute,
    178–179
  courses of, 180–182
  establishment of, 179–180
Harley-Davidson University (HDU),
    187–188
Harley Owners Group (H.O.G.), 11
Herzberg, Frederick, 147, 148
hierarchy of needs (Maslow), 26
Holiday-Rambler, 17
  and Joint Vision Process, 70–76
Horniman, Alex, 93–94
Hutchinson, Ron, 136, 137, 138, 177,
    187, 201, 243

Information Services Leadership Circle
    (ISLC), 236
Information Services Managers Circle
    (ISMC), 236–237
information systems
  ITCs and, 235–237
  policy issues, 236
  retooling, 234–238
  technical issues, 236
Information Technology Councils
    (ITCs), 235–237
International Association of Machinists
    (IAM), 6

Jacobi, Tom, 170
Joint Leadership Group (JLG), 53, 57
Joint Vision Process, 43–68, 211–212
  barriers to, 55–58
  commitment to, 69–82
  early impact of, 67–68

Joint Vision Process (*continued*)
　groundwork for, 55–62
　guidelines for, 53
　Holiday-Rambler and, 70–76
　organization of, 49–55
　process of, 47–49
　structure of, 46–47
　suspension of, 63–67
　upper management and, 69–82
JPIC (Joint Partnership Implementation
　　Committee)
　accomplishments of, 229–231
　consensus building at, 219,
　　220–222, 225–227
　expansion of, 222–224
　formation of, 213–214
　ground rules for, 217–218
　issues facing, 219–220
　mission of, 214–215
　obstacles faced by, 215–218
　unions and, 216–217, 224, 225
just-in-time materials delivery, 11

Kami, Michael, 266
Kanter, Rosabeth Moss, 96
Kiefer, Lou, 213
Kieffer, Don, 142, 240
Kirchner, Keith, 213, 227
Knackert, Gerald, 64
Kolbe, Rich, 234
Kourpias, George, 213
Kurt Salmon Associates (KSA), 23

labor contracts, 44–46
Landies, Bob, 60, 61
Lawler, Edward, 20–21, 23, 24, 72, 77,
　146–147
leadership
　in circle organization, 132–133
　indirect, 263–264

learning of, 178–182
traditional view of, 15–16
Leadership and Strategy Council (LSC),
　133, 138, 139
Leadership Business Process Module,
　118
learning
　from experience, 238–240
　first Awareness Expansion session,
　　69–82
　fourth Awareness Expansion ses-
　　sion, 174–178, 242
　goals of, 170–171
　at Harley, 167–169, 178–182
　of leadership, 178–182
　Lifelong Learning Centers,
　　184–185
　OLC and, 176–178
　Port-a-pit session, 172–173
　second Awareness Expansion ses-
　　sion, 169–176
　skill building, 189–190
Learning Lab, 245–246
Learning Maps, 185–187
Lewandowski, Ron, 184
Lifelong Learning Centers, 184–185
Likert scale, 111
Local Site Committees (LSCs), 53, 56,
　57
Lucas, Jim, 126

*Management in Crisis, or Why the
　Mighty Fail*, 266, 267
Marquette University, collaboration
　with Harley-Davidson, 182
Maslow, Abraham, 22, 25, 146
Mason, Cory, 235
Materials as Needed (MAN), 11
May Big One, 49–55
Miehle-Goss-Dexter, 13
Miller, Herman, 27, 31

Milwaukee Area Technical College, collaboration with Harley-Davidson, 184
model, for change, 36–37
motivation
　challenge and, 147
　money and, 261
　rewards and recognition and, 149–150

Nelson, Rollie, 266

Operations Committee, 58–61
organization
　alternative types of, 122–135
　circle, 131–144
　role of, 121–122
　team-based, 124–125
Organizational Learning Center (OLC), 176–178, 239, 242, 245–247

partnering
　defined, 209
　unions and, 211–213
Paterson, Jim, 16–17, 49, 58, 59, 63, 68, 84, 93, 98, 104–105, 122, 127, 133, 179, 196, 197, 198, 200
Peer Network, 184–185
Performance Effectiveness Process (PEP), 84
　and career development, 116–118
　and compensation, 151–153
　evolution of, 114–116
　obstacles to, 119–120
　origins of, 107–114
　as part of Business Process, 102
　purposes of, 152
Pinto, Jim, 213, 227

process, aspects of, 37
Produce Product Group (PPG), 142
product development, 242
　customers and, 249
　difficulties with, 243–245
　factors in, 249–250
　PDL2T and, 250–253
　Product Development Center, 253
　shared vision of, 247–250
Product Development Leadership and Learning Team (PDL2T), 250–253
　assessment of, 254
profits, as part of vision, 98

Quinn, James Brian, 72, 74

Reagan, Ronald, 14
Reilly, Ray, 179
Responsive Organizations, Inc. (ROI), 3, 21
rewards and recognition, 149–150
　at Harley-Davidson, 151
Rindo, Darlene, 186
Root Learning, Inc., collaboration with Harley-Davidson, 185–187

Salaried Rewards Study Group, 158
Salmon, Kurt, 23
Savino, Tim, 86, 109, 114, 142, 171, 177, 238
Schon, Don, 246
Schumpeter, Joseph, 259
Senge, Peter, 242, 245, 258, 266, 267
Seven Habits of Highly Successful People, 175
Short-Term Incentive Plan (STIP), 150, 158
Sloan, Alfred, 259

Softail, 10
Statistical Operator Control (SOC), 11
Stead, Jerre, 72
Storm, Dave, 234–235, 238, 254
SWOT analysis, 35

team-based organization, 124–125
    natural work groups and, 127–130
Tinker Toy exercise, 73–74
Toffler, Alvin, 182
Town Hall meetings, 58–59
Training Best Practices Circle, 186
Tschurwald, Laurel, 234, 235
Tuttle, Mark, 247
Twain, Mark, 270

Ulrich, David, 179
unions, 45, 211
    and Joint Vision, 48, 51
    and JPIC, 216–217, 224, 225
    labor contracts and, 44–46
    membership size of, 67
    negotiations with, 62
    and partnering, 211–213

relationships with, 43, 45, 57–58, 256
and suspension of Joint Vision, 63

Vallely, Hugh, 248, 251, 253
values
    determining, 153–154
    importance of, 257
    learning about, 182–183
    organizational, 31
    shared, 257–258
variable compensation, 157–160
vision, setting, 30–35

warranty costs, 198–199
Washington, George, 261
Weber, Filippa ("Flip"), 39, 44, 45, 62,
    63, 66, 68, 153
Werner, Earl K., 247–248, 250, 251,
    252, 254
Witzak, Bernie, 70, 93
work groups
    characteristics of, 129
    defined, 128
work unit plans, 101–102

About the Authors

RICH TEERLINK retired as Chairman and CEO of Harley-Davidson in 1999. During his eighteen years with Harley, he served as Chief Financial Officer, President, Chief Executive Officer, and Chairman of the Board. He was appointed to the board of directors in 1982 and was part of the leadership team that led the revitalization of the company. In 1986, he helped to guide Harley back to public ownership. Prior to joining Harley, he had the benefit of working at large and small, public and private companies at both the corporate and divisional levels in line and staff assignments. During that time he held key executive positions at Herman Miller, RTE Corporation, Union Special Corporation, and MGD Graphic Systems. Teerlink received an undergraduate degree in accounting from Bradley University and an M.B.A. from the University of Chicago. He currently serves on the boards of directors of Harley-Davidson, Johnson Controls, Snap-on Incorporated, and Bering Truck Corporation. He is a frequent speaker to business organizations internationally and an active participant in many business and community organizations.

LEE OZLEY has been an organizational consultant, coach, and adviser to more than eighty organizations in North America and Europe for the past thirty years. His clients, who have included Harley-Davidson, Cummins Engine Company, National Steel, Air Canada, and Lockheed Martin, have ranged broadly from small, family-owned companies to large, unionized manufacturing organizations. Prior to becoming a consultant, Ozley spent time as an operating official in both union and management organizations. He received his undergraduate degree from Auburn University and his graduate degree from the University of Wisconsin, where he focused on the work of Abraham Maslow. He is the author of numerous articles. Currently semi-retired, he devotes his time to a small number of select clients and frequently presents and lectures to trade associations, universities, and other organizations.

Teerlink and Ozley are both Corporate Fellows at Auburn University's Graduate School of Business.